ALSO BY C. EDWARD GOOD

Mightier than the Sword—Powerful Writing
    in the Legal Profession

Who's (oops) Whose Grammar Book Is This Anyway?

All the Grammar You Need to Succeed in Life

C. Edward Good

MJF BOOKS
NEW YORK

Published by MJF Books
Fine Communications
322 Eighth Avenue
New York, NY 10001

Who's (...Oops!) Whose Grammar Book Is This, Anyway?
LCCN 2003103205
ISBN-13: 978-1-56731-576-9
ISBN-10: 1-56731-576-3

This edition is published by MJF Books in arrangement with Capital Books.
Originally published by Capital Books as *A Grammar Book for You and I
(Oops! Me)*.

Printed in the United States of America.

MJF Books and the MJF colophon are trademarks of Fine Creative Media, Inc.

WCM   20   19   18   17   16   15   14   13   12

For **Miss Helen V. Hamrick**,
my English teacher in junior high school,
who helped me fall in love
with the language.

In memory of my best childhood friend,
William Hugh Womble III,
who knew no fear.

CONTENTS

AUTHOR'S NOTE

This book is not heavily footnoted. I rely on just a few favorite sources. Instead of having to cite them in full throughout the book, I'll provide their citations here and then refer to them in the short forms indicated.

Garner Oxford: Bryan A. Garner, *The Oxford Dictionary of American Usage and Style,* published by Oxford University Press, Oxford, England, 2000.

Garner Legal: Bryan A. Garner, *A Dictionary of Modern Legal Usage,* second edition, published by Oxford University Press, Oxford, England, 1995.

Follett: Wilson Follett, *Modern American Usage: A Guide,* revised by Erik Wensberg, published by Hill and Wang, New York, New York, 1998.

Fowler: Henry W. Fowler, *A Dictionary of Modern English Usage,* second edition, revised by Sir Ernest Gowers, published by Oxford University Press, Oxford, England, 1965.

New Fowler: Henry W. Fowler, *The New Fowler's Modern English Usage,* third edition, edited by R. W. Burchfield, published by Clarendon Press, Oxford, England, 1996.

Kane: Thomas S. Kane, *The Oxford Guide to Writing,* published by Oxford University Press, Oxford, England, 1983.

Strunk & White: William Strunk Jr., and E. B. White, *The Elements of Style,* fourth edition, published by Allyn and Bacon, Needham Heights, Massachusetts, 2000.

Random House: *The Random House Dictionary of the English Language,* unabridged second edition, published by Random House, New York, New York, 1987.

PREFACE

On some other planet . . . far, far away . . . .

Junior-high students sit in those old wooden school desks, the ones with chewing gum wads stuck underneath and *Lumpy Loves Babs* carved on top. Up front, under the watchful eye of Miss Hamrick—our no-nonsense English teacher—Billy Womble tries to diagram a sentence on the chalkboard. Momentarily uncertain where to put the prepositional phrase, he regains his composure and finishes with a flourish, smirking at Damron, the troublemaker in back taking aim with spit wad in cafeteria straw.

Miss Hamrick spots him. "Up front with you, Damron. On your feet. In front of the class." Reluctantly he assumes the position up front, checking his fly, just to make sure—to the great glee of everyone else. We relish the coming justice. We know the punishment will fit the crime. For we too have been there before.

"All right, Damron. Now perhaps you can help the class with verb conjugation."

"Yes, ma'am," Damron dutifully responds.

"Good. Now conjugate the verb *to ride* in the third person."

"*Third* person?" Damron groans. He knows what will come. The class perks up, waiting for the shoe to fall.

"Third person. That's right, Damron. Third person. Now go ahead."

"He rides, he rode, he will ride . . . ."

"Damron, be fair. Include *all* third persons." The class falls silent. Waiting. Eager for the *denouement.*

"He/she rides . . . ."

"No, Damron. Don't forget to include *it.*"

Beads of sweat forming on his troubled brow, Damron begins, "He/she/it rides, he/she/it rode . . . ."

The class erupts, delighting in Damron's pronunciational discomfort. Dear Miss Hamrick has no clue.

"Settle down, class. Now go ahead, Damron. We're listening."

"He/she/it rides, he/she/it rode, he/she/it will ride, he/she/it has ridden, he/she/it had ridden, he/she/it will have ridden."

"Very good, Damron. Now the progressive tenses."

"He/she/it is riding, he/she/it was riding, he/she/it will be riding, he/she/it has been riding, he/she/it had been riding, he/she/it will have been riding."

"Excellent. Now sit down, Damron. And put your spit wads away."

That was yesterday.

Today, sad to say, spit wads have given way to automatic weapons; grammar, to trendy theories that just don't seem to work.

In too many English classes across America, grammar is passé; verb conjugation, a forgotten relic of the past. Indeed, if students learn about verbs at all, they learn to conjugate them in Spanish, French, or German. Today, under modern educational theory, the study of grammar is viewed by people daring to call themselves experts as a nuisance, as unnecessary dogma, as only slightly related to the skills of the writer. Students will "get it" by reading. They will absorb grammar through "osmosis."

Since 1980, I have conducted training programs in effective writing for lawyers, managers, scientists, engineers, government officials, and other smart people. Working with thousands of professionals across the country, I have seen and heard it all. During a training program for a federal agency, a graduate of Harvard Law School (I am not making this up, as Dave Barry would say) looked at me and said, "Ed, I'll be frank. I really don't know what a prepositional phrase is."

In a writing seminar for a corporation, a participant with a British accent asked me to recommend a grammar book because, she said, "I don't know the difference between a noun and a verb. They didn't teach me these things in England."

In *England?* It's *their* language, for heaven's sake. They don't teach grammar? And she wants *me* to recommend a grammar book? Little ole *southern* me recommending a grammar book to a *Brit?* Wow! Dear Miss Hamrick would be so proud.

Well, instead of recommending one, what the heck, I'll write one. I'll call it *A Grammar Book.*

Why the title? Easy. When a bookstore browser goes into the local bookstore and asks for "a grammar book," the clerk will then direct the customer to *A Grammar Book for You and I, Oops, Me!* Clever, huh? It's dry stuff, folks, but vital to your success in life. I'll need every possible edge to get you to fork over your hard-earned money to buy and then read this soon-to-be-a-major-motion-picture runaway best-seller.

To keep you interested, I'll do my best to make the subject come alive and relate directly to the everyday choices you make when you put pen to paper or fingers to keyboard to say what you have to say. Thus, you can expect lots of salacious scenes replete with parsing, dangling participles, conjugation, and other kinky-sounding practices.

I'll do what I can to make this the course in grammar you never had in high school and now need to succeed in life.

So welcome, class. Take your feet off the desk. And Damron, sit up and pay attention. Today we will learn about the subjunctive mood . . . .

Sheesh. I sound just like Miss Hamrick.

INTRODUCTION

GRAMMAR? LIKE, WHO CARES?

Some years ago Miss Hamrick carried around a ruler (I *am* making this up), poised to rap the knuckles of students only slightly offending the English language. She would pounce on subject-verb disagreements. She would cringe at violations of the rules on the case of pronouns. She could ferret out any misuse of simple linking verbs. These days, of course, my dear English teacher would run out of rulers; her students, out of knuckles.

She would attack without mercy the talking head who said with an accent fortunately taught only in schools of broadcasting:

> "Join Bernie **and I** as we bring you up-to-the-minute issues of the day . . . ."

He should have said, "Join Bernie **and *me*** . . . ."

She would whack the knuckles of a reporter who wrote in a column for millions to see:

> "The agency **could of decided** to postpone the new program . . . ."

He should have written, "The agency **could** *have* **decided** to postpone . . ."

She would be swatting knuckles left and right as major networks display on the screen toward the end of basketball games "Who to foul," or as people on the news or just in everyday conversation say "just between you and I" or "I feel badly about that," or as today's youth stumble through entire conversations, grunting and groaning at one another, apparently all the while actually transferring some sort of information—known only to themselves—from one brain to another:

> "Like, she waslike whoa, so I'mlike how'dja know that? and she's like what's the big deal? And like I'mlike-who-like-cares? Know-I'm-sayin'?"

So, I'mlike, who cares? Indeed. Who does care?

Newsweek doesn't. In an article entitled "So I'm Like, 'Who Needs This Grammar Stuff?'"[1] the authors report that grammar really makes no difference. Easy for them to say as they boot up their computers, write correctly, and knock down six figures in the process.

It gets worse. According to *Newsweek*:

> "Most of the grammar rules are already dead or dying," says Joseph Williams, a professor of English and linguistics at the University of Chicago. Students' language skills in general seem to be on the downswing, he says. "I used to say that every year, but I never really meant it until the last few years."

So I'm like, who cares.

Why should *you* care? Well, quite obviously you do, for you have spent your hard-earned money for *Who's (Oops) Whose Grammar Book Is This Anyway*? You care because you feel a distinct void in you education. You care because you feel uncomfortable when asked to write a report or business letter or college theme. And you feel uncomfortable for the simple reason that language is something that either sounds good or doesn't. If it sounds good to you, it passes grammatical muster. If it doesn't, something is wrong. Better rewrite it. But how?

You care because way down deep you think that some sort of comprehensible theory of style should enable you to determine why some writing is good and some downright awful. You receive the typical feedback from your boss or professor: "Awkward," she writes in the margin; "wordy," she advises with a red pencil. Great. Don't be awkward. And don't use so many words. That way, you'll write better.

No, that kind of advice rarely helps. That's where grammar comes in. By learning the grammar of the language—its structure—the way it fits together—you'll begin to see the words, phrases, and clauses you habitually use and those you tend to avoid. Then, when you see the rather limited constructions you turn to time and time again in your style, you'll be able to broaden and strengthen it by choosing structures missing before you had the foresight to purchase this two-thumbs-up masterpiece on the entirety of the English language.

> **By learning the grammar of the language—its structure—the way it fits together—you'll begin to see the words, phrases, and clauses you habitually use and those you tend to avoid.**

So sit back, read, and learn the way our English language works. When certain grammatical principles become a part of you, you'll be able to watch the good writers and see exactly what they do to make their words race across the page, commanding you, the reader, to pay attention from beginning to end. When you watch what the good writers do, you'll then be able to adjust your style and become one of them—a person in command of the English language, able to construct award-winning sentences at will, without breaking a sweat. You'll become a member of The Writers Club.

Then you can relax and wait for your *A*.

Or a raise in pay.

NOTE
1. "So I'm Like, Who Needs This Grammar Stuff?" *Newsweek*, October 20, 1997, p. 15.

PART ONE

Your Word Bag:

The Eight Parts of Speech

Whenever you write a report to your boss, a thesis for your professor, or a letter to your lover, you reach down in your bag of words, pull out the appropriate one, and plop it down on paper or computer screen. Then another, and another, and another. Slowly but surely your sentences take shape, your meaning shines through, your paper assumes a coherent form.

You hope.

As an aspiring grammarian, you must realize that your bag of words is divided into just eight pouches. Every time you reach in, grab a word, and use it in a particular way in your sentence, that word comes from *just one* of these eight compartments—the eight parts of speech: (1) nouns, (2) verbs, (3) adjectives, (4) adverbs, (5) pronouns, (6) prepositions, (7) conjunctions, and (8) interjections.

Repeat the names ten times and commit them to memory. You're going to need them.

THE SIMPLE SENTENCE: SUBJECT AND PREDICATE

Each of those sentences you write breaks down into two distinct parts: the subject and the predicate. The subject consists of a *noun* or *pronoun* (or a group of words acting as a noun) and other words modifying, or associated with, the noun or pronoun. The predicate includes the *verb* and other words modifying, or associated with, the verb.

In the quintessential American sentence, John hit the ball, the subject is *John* and the predicate is *hit the ball.* Indeed, as you write with action verbs like *hit,* your mind should search for a three-part idea:

1. who or what (the subject)	1. John
2. does what (the verb)	2. hit
3. to what (the direct object)	3. the ball

Or, if you've decided to use the verb *to be,* your mind should search for a three-part idea as well:

1. who or what (the subject)	1. John
2. *is* (the verb)	2. is
3. what (the subject complement)	3. the catcher
or like what (the predicate adjective)	3. strong
or where (an adverbial phrase)	3. in the batter's box

The best writers put the key thing they want to say in these three parts of the sentence.

Don't panic. I know I'm throwing some grammatical terms at you: *direct object, subject complement, predicate adjective, adverbial phrase.* You'll learn all about them soon. To stop and explain them here would distract us from this overview.

> **The best writers put the key thing they want to say at the subject-verb-object position in the sentence.**

We'll return for a more careful look at basic sentence structure a bit later. But first I must introduce another key concept you'll need as we begin our journey through the wonderland of grammar. You need to know the difference between a *phrase* and a *clause.*

A KEY CONCEPT: PHRASES VS. CLAUSES

When you reach into your bag of words and plunk words down on paper, you organize them into chunks. This group of words does one thing; that other group does another. Rarely do you pull out just one word and end the writing project right there.

All groups of words break down into two types: phrases and clauses. The sole distinguishing feature of a clause is the presence of a *conjugated verb*. The sole distinguishing feature of a phrase is the absence of a conjugated verb. Here's a phrase: **over the rainbow** (no conjugated verb). And here's a clause: **when I fall in love** (the conjugated verb is *fall*).

What's a conjugated verb? We'll find detailed answers in chapters 2 and 10, which thoroughly explain what verbs do. Suffice it to say right now that a conjugated verb shows three things: *tense, person,* and *number.*

Three Things Shown by Conjugated Verbs

1. tense: *when* the verbal activity took place
2. person: *who* engaged in that activity, did *I* do it (first person), did *you* do it (second person), or did, well uh, *he/she/it* do it (third person)
3. number: *how many* people or things did it (singular or plural)

So look at the following phrases. (I will use some grammatical terms, but don't worry if you don't know what they mean right now.) They are phrases because a conjugated verb does not appear:

Phrases: No Conjugated Verb

1. **under the table** (prepositional phrase)
2. **available to him** (adjectival phrase)
3. **when in doubt** (a phrase with a strange name, a *truncated clause*)

Now look at these phrases. You'll see that they have verbs in them. But notice that those verbs are not conjugated. You do not know *when* (tense), *who* (person), or *how many* (number):

Verbal Phrases: But No Conjugated Verb

1. **to win the race** (infinitive phrase)
2. **managing the operation** (present participial phrase)
3. **arranged by size** (past participial phrase)

Compare the above phrases with the following clauses. Notice the conjugated verb in each clause. Notice that some of the clauses do not complete a thought (they're called *dependent clauses* or *subordinate clauses*). Notice that others qualify as a complete sentence (they're called *independent clauses*):

Clauses: Note the Conjugated Verb
1. when you **finish** work (dependent or subordinate clause)
2. before you **leave** (dependent or subordinate clause)
3. John **hit** the ball. (independent clause)
4. so that you **can express** yourself better (dependent or subordinate clause)
5. Before you **leave,** you **must complete** the assignment. (one dependent clause and one independent clause)

Got it? A phrase is a bunch of words *without* a conjugated verb in it. A clause is a bunch of words *with* a conjugated verb in it. If the clause can stand by itself as a complete sentence, it's called an independent clause. If it can't, it's called a dependent or subordinate clause.

When you pull the eight types of words from your word bag, you typically arrange them in two kinds of chunks. You form either phrases or clauses.

EIGHT PARTS OF SPEECH
Amazing, huh? You can compartmentalize the entire English language into just eight categories. Each one—each part of speech—then performs specially assigned functions. Who, you might legitimately ask, assigns these special functions? Who dreams up all this stuff? Who makes up the rules?

No one knows, really. I personally believe that my eighth-grade English teacher—Miss Hamrick—was there at the dawn of linguistic time and remains firmly in command. She surely carried a lot of clout way back at Kaiser Junior High School, back when Lumpy, Billy, Miles, Mason, Damron, Donny, CB, Rhet, Fred, Harris, and I didn't care much for English. We paid far more attention to English Leather shaving lotion and visible bra straps than dangling participles.

Perhaps the tentacles of Miss Hamrick extend throughout the English-speaking world. Maybe she sits as Chair English Teacher in total control of all rules of grammar and all eight parts of speech. In the 1950s, she probably headed up some sinister, underground English Teacher SWAT Team charged with enforcing all the rules they imposed on us quivering, fearful, ignorant writers in our Elvis-centered world who paid no attention whatsoever to *conjugating, parsing,* and who knows what other unmentionable activities.

Whoever makes them up, the rules do (believe it or not) make eminently good sense. And people in power—bosses, teachers, lovers—know the rules by heart. Or pretend they do. They expect you to follow the rules. To learn them and make them one with your writing style, you start, naturally enough, at the beginning, with, you guessed it, the . . . eight parts of speech.

Now I know you're dying to take a more careful look at the word bag, but I believe just a bit more of an overview will help you survive your first grammar lesson.

You can further divide all English words, that is, the eight parts of speech, into two subcategories: (1) working words and (2) glue words.

Working Words

The workhorses of our language include the four major parts of speech: (1) nouns, (2) verbs, (3) adjectives, and (4) adverbs. To this list, we should add some of the pronouns, primarily those denoting people (e.g., *he, she, you, they*) and some others. These words carry the vast bulk of your message. Though some of the others—conjunctions, prepositions, other pronouns, and interjections—do contain some meaning, the gist of what you say ordinarily rides on the backs of the working words.

Consider, for example, the 77 words appearing in the preceding paragraph. When I list just the 56 working words, you can see most of the message unfold. Read them in order, and you'll see what I mean:

56 Working Words

workhorses our language include four major parts speech nouns verbs adjectives adverbs this list we should add some pronouns primarily those denoting people *he, she, you, they* some others these words carry vast bulk your message some others conjunctions prepositions other pronouns interjections do contain some meaning gist what you say ordinarily rides backs working words

Now look at a list of the 21 words that don't qualify as working words. These are the glue words. Let's see what they have to say:

21 Glue Words
the of the of and to of the and the of though of the and the of on the of the

Not much there. It goes without saying which list does the job of informing us.

Does a rule of style emerge from this feature of our language—that working words carry the bulk of our message? Yes. Improve your writing by using more working words and fewer glue words.

Of course, I'd like to take credit for conceiving this idea, but, alas, I can't. Dean Richard Wydick, the former dean of the University of California at Davis School of Law, wrote a wonderful little book called *Plain English for Lawyers* (Carolina Academic Press, 2d ed., 1985). In it, he urges us to use more working words and fewer glue words. (All lawyers out there should read Wydick's book. You may obtain a copy by calling 919-489-7486. Have your credit card handy. And keep the receipt. It's deductible.)

> **Improve your writing by using more working words and fewer glue words.**

Look at what happens when you follow the rule. I borrow an exercise from Dean Wydick's book. Look at, and try to read, this lawyerly gobbledegook, with the **working words** appearing in bold type:

> The **testimony** that **was given** by **Reeves went** to the **heart** of the **defense** that **he asserted,** which **was his lack** of the **specific intent to escape.** (15 working, 12 glue.)

Now look at Dean Wydick's revision. By favoring working words, he chops out more than half the glue words:

> **Reeves's testimony went** to the **heart** of **his defense,** that **he had no specific intent** to **escape.** (12 working, 5 glue.)

Better, don't you think?

Glue Words

The other parts of speech—those that are not nouns, certain pronouns, verbs, adjectives, adverbs—glue parts of the language together. Conjunctions and prepositions and some kinds of pronouns (words like *that* and *which*) serve the main purpose of gluing words to other words. I don't mean to imply their insignificance in writing. They are vastly important. But unsophisticated writers often use way too many prepositions and other glue words.

> **Unsophisticated writers often use too many prepositions and other glue words.**

The final part of speech, the interjection, doesn't appear very much in formal writing, for it announces elements of surprise. *"I'm like wow!"* is an interjection, and while it shows up way too often in speech these days, it rarely sees the light of day in writing, primarily because those who utter lots of *I'mlikewow*s don't write very much.

So with that brief introduction and subcategorization of the entire English language from eight parts of speech down to two basic types of words, we must still turn to the eight categories themselves and learn all about the eight parts of speech.

Let's study them one at a time.

Nouns: Words That Name

et's begin our detailed look at the eight parts of speech with the noun. I guess we all remember our school teacher's definition, that is, if you went to school when teachers taught grammar: A noun is a person, place, thing, or idea.[1] Good definition. Here's another from *The Random House Dictionary of the English Language:*

> Any member of a class of words that are formally distinguished . . . typically by the plural and possessive endings and that can function as the main or only elements of subjects or objects, as *cat, belief, writing, Ohio, darkness.* Nouns are often thought of as referring to persons, places, things, states, or qualities.[2]

That's an interesting definition, and one you might use when trying to identify how a particular word is acting in your sentence. Can you make it plural? Can you add a possessive ending to it? If so (and the word isn't a pronoun), you've got yourself a noun. Try it out on *darkness.* Plural: *darknesses?* I guess one could experience several *darknesses.* Possessive: *darkness's?* What might *darkness* possess? The *darkness's secrets?* That, too, seems to work, even if it's a bit of a stretch from everyday usage.

Another question will help you identify a word as a noun: Is the word capable of *being possessed?* Just put the word *my* or *his* or *her* before the word and see if the two make sense. Thus: my cat, my belief, my writing. So a noun not only can possess something else but can be possessed.

You might think of nouns as *naming words.* It's not hard to see why our primitive ancestors dreamed them up, at roughly the same time Miss Hamrick came on the scene. When we used to grunt at one another in caves, mama cave dweller (her name was *Amber*) and papa cave dweller (his name was *Igor*) undoubtedly pointed at things, made some guttural sounds, and grunted some sort of word that stuck and became the name of that thing.

> First, a warning. To the uninitiated, grammar is boring. But you must learn some concepts before tackling the chapters on writing style. So grit your teeth, clench your fists, curse the author, but keep your eyes wide open. This stuff is mind numbing—but very, very important.

Amber and Igor must have grunted a word for those horned animals over there grazing in the field, the ones that cooked up nice as the primitive forerunners to a Big Mac. Grunt, grunt, grunt, and we got *cow.* Grunt, grunt, uh, groan, and we got *bucket* for milking the cow. These words that name all tangible things—living or not—are nouns.

Indeed, our cave dwellers no doubt gave each other names, so they grunted out *Wilma, Fred, Derik, Stephanie, Heather, Amber, and Igor.* They went places and formed countries and cities, so they came up with *France* and sometime later *Peoria.* And when they traveled to *France* and ate too many *escargot,* they grunted *upset tummy* and ultimately *Pepto-Bismol.* So nouns could name not only the person *Igor,* the place *France,* or the thing *escargot,* but a feeling, even a bad one, like *stomachache.*

FORMING PLURALS

Notice that words are characterized as nouns by their ability to form plurals. (Some pronouns have this ability as well, e.g., *other* and *others.*) You will form the plural for most nouns by adding *-s* or *-es.*

The "Just Add -s" Rule

Consider these plurals formed by the "just add *-s*" rule:

Singular	Plural
book	books
car	cars
Igor	Igors
N	Ns
Titanic	*Titanics*
1960	1960s
IRA	IRAs

Many people violate the "just add -*s*" rule, often by using an "apostrophe -*s*" to form the plural. You should use the apostrophe only when you must avoid an ambiguity. Here are some examples of the "just add -*s* rule" in action:

- **proper names—just add** -*s:*

    The tribe had three **Igors** and two **Ambers.**

- **capital letters—just add** -*s*, **unless the result would be ambiguous:**

    She writes her **Ns** in a strange way.

    but:

    She writes her **I's** in a strange way.

- **lowercase letters—use the apostrophe:**

    Mind your **p's** and **q's.**

- **italicized videotape or book—just add** -*s* **and don't italicize the** -*s:*

    The video store ordered six ***Titanics.***

- **decades or other numbers—just add** -*s:*

    She was stuck in the **1960s.**

- **acronyms or abbreviations—just add** -*s* **(if periods do not appear):**

    The young couple set up two **IRAs.**

    but:

    He roomed with two **M.D.'s.**

- **words referred to as words—italicize the word and add a nonitalicized** -*s:*

    He used too many ***howevers*** in his style.

If you violate the "just add -*s*" rule and use the apostrophe, please study chapter 41 on the apostrophe.

The "Just Add -*es*" Rule

If you don't add an -*s* to form the plural of a noun, chances are you'll add -*es*. Consider the "just add -*es*" rule:

- **nouns ending in a consonant and a** -*y*—**change** -*y* **to** -*i* **and add** -*es:*

variety	varieties
sentry	sentries

    but **proper names ending in** -*y,* **just add** -*s:*

Mary	Marys
Penney	Penneys
Harry	Harrys

    but **nouns ending in a vowel and a** -*y,* **just add** -*s:*

boy	boys
key	keys

- **nouns ending in** -*s,* -*ss,* -*ce,* -*sh,* -*ch,* -*tch,* -*ge,* -*dge,* -*x,* **and** -*ze*—**just add** -*es:*

gas	gases
witch	witches
box	boxes

Note: These endings are called *sibilants.*

- **some nouns ending in a consonant and an** -*o*—**just add** -*es:*

tomato	tomatoes
mosquito	mosquitoes
potato[3]	potatoes

but **for some, add either** -*es* **or** -*s:*

banjo	banjoes or banjos
cargo	cargoes or cargos

and **for some, add only** -*s:*

piano	pianos

and **for those ending in a vowel and an** -*o,* **just add** -*s:*

cameo	cameos

The "Add or Do Something Else" Rule

Then we have a fairly long list of words that form their plurals in varying ways. Everyone knows that the plural of *child* is *children,* the plural of *foot* is *feet,* the plural of *woman* is *women,* and *man* is *men,* and *louse* is *lice.* And so on. Some people get all agitated when they see the plural of *memorandum* formed by adding -*s: memorandums.* But a quick check of a reputable dictionary reveals that *memorandums* is perfectly acceptable.[4]

So for words like *fungus, passer-by, man-of-war, vertex,* and others, I'll simply punt and suggest that you (1) check the dictionary and (2) be aware of your audience and adhere to its preferred style.

Group Nouns

Finally, some nouns that look singular might be treated as plural. Words such as *group, team, majority,* and many others are called *collective nouns* or *group nouns.* If the members of the group are acting individually, then the noun is plural and requires a plural verb: The **majority** of courts **have**

followed Roe v. Wade. But if the group acts as a unit, then the noun is singular and requires a singular verb: The **majority** of Senators **has now voted** for the bill. We'll return to this issue in chapter 19 when we study the rules on *subject-verb agreement in number* (singular or plural).

FORMING POSSESSIVES

Words are also characterized as nouns by their ability to form possessives. Again, some pronouns have this ability as well *(other, other's)*. So before we explore the main functions of nouns, let's pause to address an issue that sparks considerable controversy in offices, classrooms, faculty lounges, and Bubba's Bar & Grill. How do you make a noun possessive? For singular nouns, just add "apostrophe *-s*"; for plural nouns ending in an *-s,* just add an apostrophe. The rule is easy to follow but trips up a lot of people.

What happens if the singular noun ends in an *-s*? How do you make the word *boss* possessive? Simple. Follow the rule: Add "apostrophe *-s*" to make a singular noun possessive. Thus:

> The **boss's** rules governed our acts.
> **Congress's** policy showed up in the statute.
> Bridget **Jones's** Diary

This is Rule 1, page 1 of *Strunk & White.* It is also the rule of the *Chicago Manual of Style* and other leading style books.

The singular-noun rule does have a few exceptions. Form the possessives of biblical persons ending in *-s* by adding an apostrophe: Jesus' disciples; Moses' followers. Also, by tradition we write: for appearance' (righteousness', etc.) sake.

If two or more possessors possess the same entity, then add "apostrophe *-s*" to the last possessor: Sam and Linda's children (Sam and Linda are mom and dad). But if each possessor separately possesses, then add "apostrophe *-s*" to each possessor: Sam's and Linda's children (Sam and Linda each have their own children).

One final note. Many businesses use plural words to form their names. Even though the name of the business is itself a singular noun, you would just add an apostrophe to the plural word to form the possessive: General Motors' annual report. I have no clue on how to form the possessive of

McDonald's. McDonald's's annual report? McDonald's' annual report? Maybe just McDonald's annual report.

WHAT NOUNS DO

What do nouns do in our language? It's crucial that you know, for you cannot begin to engage in any kind of grammatical analysis without knowing the roles of all eight parts of speech. Nouns do about 10 things in the English language, and we will study them more deeply in chapter 9, appropriately titled "Nouns: What They Do."

The main roles of nouns break down into three types: (1) subject, (2) object, and (3) complement. To discuss these three broad functions, I will necessarily have to mention verbs, so if you're not too sure about verbs, you might want to jump ahead and skim the chapter on verbs and then return to this discussion on nouns. Problem is, when you read chapter 2 on verbs, you'll need some knowledge of nouns. Sorry about this organizational disjointedness, but the language is very interrelated, and it's just not possible to talk intelligently about nouns without mentioning verbs. And vice versa. So you've got to start somewhere.

1. GRAMMATICAL SUBJECT

Every complete sentence has a word (sometimes a group of words) that serves as the grammatical subject of the sentence. The grammatical subject is always a noun or a group of words acting as a noun. The subject might also be a pronoun, which is a word taking the place of a noun.

> **The grammatical subject is always a noun (or pronoun) or a group of words acting as a noun.**

The subject stands as the main beacon in the sentence. Your reader's attention should focus on that subject. That grammatical subject should reveal the main thing you're talking about in your sentence. That subject will then naturally gravitate to its verb. Together the subject and the verb should form the main message of your sentence.

Let's look at the previous paragraph and write down the subject-verb pairs in the main clauses in the sentences. (We'll leave out the that serves and we're talking about clauses, and postpone discussing these structures, known as *dependent* or *subordinate clauses.* We're just interested in the *main* subject-verb pairs.) By reading these pairs of words, you can see the crucial function of the noun (and the equally crucial function of the verb):

Subject-Verb Pairs
sentence has
subject stands
attention should focus
subject should reveal
subject will gravitate
subject and verb will form

Exercise

Now you try it. Take a pen and circle the subject-verb pairs in the following passage, written by Sir Winston Churchill. Just focus on the main clauses, that is, the main sentences. You may ignore any subject-verb pairs that appear in dependent clauses (such as *that had been seen*). Also, writers and speakers often use two or more subjects in a sentence, as I just did in this sentence with my *writers and speakers*. And don't overlook or ignore those sentences having two or more verbs, such as my *don't overlook or ignore* in the sentence you are now reading. Finally, be aware that a pronoun might serve as the subject of a sentence.

> With 1588 the crisis of the reign was past. England had emerged from the Armada year as a first-class power. She had resisted the weight of the mightiest empire that had been seen since Roman times. Her people awoke to a consciousness of their greatness, and the last years of Elizabeth's reign saw a welling up of national energy and enthusiasm focusing upon the person of the Queen. In the year following the Armada the first three books were published of Spenser's *Faerie Queene*, in which Elizabeth is hymned as Gloriana. Poets and courtiers alike paid their homage to the sovereign who symbolised the great achievement. Elizabeth had schooled a generation of Englishmen.[5]

Answer to Exercise

Here are the subject-verb pairs in the main clauses. The **<u>subject</u>** appears in bold underline, the **verb** in bold:

> With 1588 the **<u>crisis</u>** of the reign **was** past. **<u>England</u> had emerged** from the Armada year as a first-class power. **<u>She</u> had resisted** the weight of the mightiest empire that had been seen since Roman times. Her **<u>people</u> awoke** to a consciousness of their greatness, and the last **<u>years</u>** of Elizabeth's reign **saw** a welling up of national energy and enthusiasm focusing upon the person of the Queen. In the year following the Armada the first three **<u>books</u> were published** of Spenser's *Faerie Queene*, in which Elizabeth is hymned as Gloriana. **<u>Poets and courtiers</u>** alike **paid** their homage to the sovereign who symbolised the great achievement. **<u>Elizabeth</u> had schooled** a generation of Englishmen.

We might pause and take some notes about Mr. Churchill's style. First, the word *symbolised* is not misspelled. That's the way our British cousins do it: They misspell a lot of words. Just kidding. Mr. Churchill, naturally, is spelling words the British way. Second, notice that Mr. Churchill ordinarily begins sentences with the grammatical subjects. In the seven sentences, only the first *(With 1588)* and the fifth *(In the year following)* begin with words other than the grammatical subject of the sentence. A rule of style does emerge: Ordinarily, start most sentences with the grammatical subject. Or put another way: Don't wait too long to get your sentence going with the grammatical subject.

Now don't misinterpret what I say. Do not think for a minute that you should begin every sentence with the subject. I've had some students in my writing classes report that other teachers had instructed them to avoid starting sentences with words other than the grammatical subjects. That's just flat-out wrong. All good writers use a variety of phrases and clauses to begin sentences before they get to the grammatical subjects. They just take care not to do it too often.

> **Together the subject and the verb should form the main message of your sentence.**

TUCK AWAY THIS THOUGHT

Before we leave this overview of the grammatical subject, you might want to tuck away a thought for future reference. When we study pronouns, we'll have to hang out the dirty laundry of too many smart people in this world, for we'll have to discuss the *case* of pronouns. Messing up *who/whom, I/me, she/her, he/him,* and *we/us* ranks as one of the most frequent grammatical mistakes people make.

So here's the thought: We've seen that nouns act as subjects. We'll learn that pronouns can take the place of a noun. When a pronoun elbows aside a noun that is acting as a subject, then guess what? That pronoun must appear in the *subjective case.* Get it? *Subjects? Subjective case?* Pretty clever, don't you think? I'll return to the problem, drill it into you, and ultimately make you cringe when you hear people say, "*Me* and Susan are going to the movie." Of course, they should say, "Susan and *I* are going to the movie."

In the above exercise, you were to identify the subject-verb pairs in the main clauses. Here, for your interest, are the subject-verb pairs in the three dependent clauses:

With 1588 the crisis of the reign was past. England had emerged from the Armada year as a first-class power. She had resisted the weight of the mightiest empire **that had been seen** since Roman times. Her people awoke to a consciousness of their greatness, and the last years of Elizabeth's reign saw a welling up of national energy and enthusiasm focusing upon the person of the Queen. In the year following the Armada the first three books were published of Spenser's *Faerie Queene,* in which **Elizabeth is hymned** as Gloriana. Poets and courtiers alike paid their homage to the sovereign **who symbolised** the great achievement. Elizabeth had schooled a generation of Englishmen.

2. TWO BASIC KINDS OF OBJECTS
Object of a Verb

As their next major function, nouns serve as *objects*. Just as we saw that a noun subject joins the verb to state the main message of the sentence, we now see that a noun *object* joins a special kind of verb to form what's called a *direct object*. Again, we have to borrow from the upcoming discussion on verbs.

> **A noun can serve as the *direct object* of a transitive verb.**

Most verbs in the English language are action verbs; that is, they describe some sort of activity taking place. And most action verbs fall into a class we call *transitive verbs*. I know, I know, here come more grammatical terms, but we can blame it on that cave dweller who first grunted *transitive verb*. (Miss Hamrick? That you?)

In Latin, *trans* means *across*. A transitive verb takes the action expressed by the verb from the grammatical subject and carries it *across* to the recipient of that action, which is called the direct object. Let's go back to John hit the ball.

John is a noun. *John* is the subject of the sentence. The verb *hit* is a transitive verb. It carries the idea of *hitting* from the word *John,* who causes the hitting, to the word *ball,* which receives the hitting. Now, *ball* is a noun, too. *Ball* is the direct object of *hit.* We can expand on these ideas a bit by pointing out that the subject *John* is the *agent* of the action and the direct object *ball* is the *recipient* of the action.

In my profession—OK, I admit it, I'm a lawyer—we have lots of *'ors* and *'ees.* We have *employers* and *employees,* we have *offerors* and *offerees,* we have *trustors* and *trustees, mortgagors* and *mortgagees,* and the list goes on and on. Basically, the *'or* person does or gives something, and the *'ee* person receives something. So I'll borrow from my own profession and coin a couple of terms: *do-ors* and *do-ees.* In my John-hit-the-ball sentence, *John* is the do-or, and *ball* is the do-ee. *John* is the *hit-or;* the *ball* is the *hit-ee.*

Quite simply, a transitive verb is an action verb that is capable of having both a do-or and a do-ee. You can make yourself the do-or and just say *I* .... Then say the verb. Thus: I hit. Now see if there's a possible do-ee. Can you *hit* something or somebody? The answer is yes. You can hit a ball. The verb, therefore, is transitive.

Try it out with a couple of more verbs. Use *write*. I write .... Can I *write* something? Yes. I can **write** a best-selling, hard-to-put-down **grammar book.** The verb *write* is capable of having the noun *grammar book* stuck directly on it. Therefore, it's a transitive verb. And the noun that sticks is the direct object. Try it with *delve*. I delve .... Can I *delve* something? No, I cannot. I cannot **delve the matter.** I must **delve into** the matter. Because I cannot stick a noun directly onto *delve,* it is not a transitive verb and cannot have a direct object. (We'll learn in chapter 2 that *delve* is an *intransitive verb.*)

We'll return to a deeper discussion of verbs in the next chapter. For now, just remember a very important role of the noun: It can serve as a direct object. Remember that a direct object receives the action from a transitive verb. In legal lingo, a direct object is the do-ee.

Object of a Preposition

That's one kind of object, the object of a transitive verb. But the noun serves another important role as an object. This next kind of object is called the *object of a preposition.* Once again, because of the inter-relationship of these ideas, we have to borrow from an upcoming discussion on another part of speech, the *preposition.*

For now, let's ponder an important fact about nouns: They have a hard time jumping onto the back of a sentence and sitting there all by themselves. Only a few roles of the noun enable it to hop up on a sentence without some help, and we'll discuss them in chapter 9. For most functions, the noun must rely on a dab of glue to get onto a sentence and stay there. Voilà! A glue word. The preposition will help the noun.

> **A noun can serve as the object of a preposition.**

Consider this beginning of a sentence: He put .... Now let's try to stick two nouns onto the sentence: *cup* and *table*. We can take either one, and it'll stick nicely to the verb *put*. Why does it readily stick? Because *put* is transitive and therefore capable of having a direct object. So *he* can *put* the *cup* ....

Here's our sentence, beginning to form:

He put the cup ....

But now we want to stick the noun *table* onto the sentence. But we can't, not as long as *cup* is sitting there occupying the position of direct object. Watch:

He put the cup **the table.**
Or: He put **the table** the cup.

It just won't go anywhere:

The table he put the cup.
He **the table** put the cup.

The noun *table* needs help getting onto the back of the sentence. A preposition saves the day:

He put the cup **on** the table.
He put the cup **under** the table.
He put the cup **above** the table.

TUCK AWAY ANOTHER THOUGHT

Thus we see the two main types of objects: objects of verbs (which must be transitive verbs) and objects of prepositions. And just as we tucked away a little thought when we explored the function of nouns as grammatical subjects, we can tuck away an equally important thought about the pronoun problem I mentioned above. Remember the problem that trips up smart people when they stammer over *who/whom, he/him, she/her, I/me, we/us?* Well, back there I said that when pronouns take the place of nouns acting as grammatical subjects, they must appear in the subjective case.

So now here's another thought to tuck away: When a pronoun takes the place of a noun that is acting as the object of a verb or as the object of a preposition, it must appear in the *objective case.* Neat, huh? *Objects ... objective case.* What a clever language Miss Hamrick dreamed up.

In these sentences the words *on the table, under the table,* and *above the table* are called *prepositional phrases.* The noun *table* serves as the object of those prepositions.

Complement

We saw that a noun acts as the subject of the sentence. When the verb in the sentence is transitive, then another noun can attach to that verb and act as the direct object of the sentence.

But suppose the verb in the sentence is not an action verb but is . . . well, suppose it's the verb *is.* That is, suppose the verb in the sentence is some form of the verb *to be.* Later, in chapter 12, we'll discuss the verb *to be* at some

> The noun following the verb *to be* is called the *complement;* it's also called the *predicate noun* or the *predicate nominative.*

length. (We might even figure out what the meaning of the word *is* is.) For right now, file away in your brain the eight forms of the verb *to be:*

> *am, is, are, was, were, been, being, be*

So if we start out a sentence with that good old noun *John* and follow it with the verb *is,* then we get:

> John is . . . .

In the English language we will usually follow this expression with either an adjective or a noun (an adjective is a word modifying a noun). If we use an adjective, we might get:

> John is **big.** (The adjective *big* modifies the noun *John.*)

For future reference, this adjective is called a *predicate adjective.*

We might also follow the expression with a noun. If we use a noun, we might get:

> John is my **friend.**

The noun *friend,* which follows the verb *to be,* is called the *complement;* it's also called the *predicate noun* or the *predicate nominative.*

TUCK AWAY YET ANOTHER THOUGHT

Let's end this overview of the noun with yet another thought to tuck away in that brain of yours, which is probably becoming a bit crowded right now. We learned that pronouns substituting for subjects must appear in the subjective case; pronouns substituting for objects, in the objective case. This final broad function of nouns—the complement or predicate noun—also requires the subjective case when pronouns take the place of a predicate noun. We'll return to the problem of pronoun case in chapters 5 and 22.

By now, you're likely a bit tired of listening to me jabber away about old cave dwellers grunting at one another, so I'll pass the podium to you and perhaps your family as you gather around the dinner table to ponder a bit of grammar. It's exercise time. Here's a pop test.

Pop Test: Identify Nouns
Here's a well-known piece. Take your pen and circle those words you think are nouns:

> Oh say can you see by the dawn's early light
> What so proudly we hailed at the twilight's last gleaming?
> Whose broad stripes and bright stars through the perilous fight,
> O'er the ramparts we watched were so gallantly streaming?
> And the rockets' red glare, the bombs bursting in air,
> Gave proof through the night that our flag was still there.
> Oh say does that star-spangled banner yet wave
> O'er the land of the free and the home of the brave?

Answer to Pop Test
Now here's the answer, with the **nouns** appearing in bold type. Some were a bit tricky, so I've provided a bit of commentary.

> Oh say can you see by the **dawn's [1]** early **light**
> What so proudly we hailed at the **twilight's [1]** last **gleaming [2]**?

Whose broad **stripes** and bright **stars** through the perilous **fight,**
O'er the **ramparts** we watched were so gallantly streaming?
And the **rockets' [1]** red **glare,** the **bombs** bursting in **air,**
Gave **proof** through the **night** that our **flag** was still there.
Oh say does that **star [3]** -spangled **banner** yet wave
O'er the **land** of the **free** and the **home** of the **brave?**

1. *dawn's, twilight's,* and *rockets'*

Remember the dictionary definition of the noun? It's a word characterized by plurals and possessive endings. In our good old national anthem, we have three nouns appearing in the possessive: *dawn's, twilight's, rockets'.* The possessive endings, "apostrophe *-s*" or "*-s* apostrophe," should have tipped you off that these words are nouns.

Notice also that the word *dawn's* does not really serve a traditional function as a noun. It's really acting as an adjective. You can see this feature of our language by recognizing that *dawn's* is not the object of the preposition *by.* The word *light* serves as the object of *by:* **by** the dawn's early **light.**

Neither is the word *rockets'* the subject of *gave proof.* The word *glare* serves that role. Thus you can see that the possessive noun usually leaves something unsaid. It needs the word that it possesses, and that word will serve the noun role: **rockets'** red **glare** ... **gave proof** ....

2. *gleaming*

You might not have gotten this one, because *gleaming* looks like a verb. Indeed the word it rhymes with, *streaming,* does serve as a verb. But the possessive noun *twilight's* should have tipped you off that the thing possessed will typically be a noun. Also, you can see the preposition *at.* You can see that the prepositional phrase is not completed by the words *at the twilight's last* . . . . No, we need a noun to hang onto the preposition *at.* And the word *gleaming* fills the bill: **at** the twilight's last **gleaming.**

Later we'll learn that *gleaming* is an *-ing* verb that acts as a noun. It's called a *gerund.* Don't fret about it now, and don't worry if you failed to circle *gleaming.* Many other people probably missed it, too.

3. *star*

The word *star* is a bit tricky as well. The word is very much a noun. In this sentence it is joining forces with *spangled* to serve as an adjective. The word *spangled,* we'll learn a bit later, is a verb form called a *past participle.* In English we often join nouns with past participles to form an array of structures called *compound adjectives,* i.e., multiword adjectives. Look at these compound adjectives formed with nouns and past participles: **government**-controlled economy, **computer**-generated image, and **shark**-infested waters. Thus: **star**-spangled banner.

ACTING LIKE NOUNS: PHRASES AND CLAUSES

I realize that you are glued to these pages, riveted by the compelling material and scintillating presentation. But just in case your attention is wandering a bit, LET ME SHOUT AT YOU AND WAKE YOU UP BECAUSE I'M ABOUT TO SAY SOMETHING VERY IMPORTANT.

There. Pay attention, Damron.

To understand the English language, you must grasp some key concepts. One is this: Other words or chunks of words, words that are not nouns, can act as nouns in your sentences; that is, they can perform the functions of a noun. I will introduce the primary words and chunks of words here, even though we have yet to discuss some of the terms in much detail. Just remember, the eight parts of speech are highly interrelated, so talking about nouns, for example, often requires talking about verbs and other parts of speech.

> **A variety of words and chunks of words in our language can serve the role of noun. Let's call them *noun substitutes.***

Also, keep this in mind: There are two main types of word chunks, clauses and phrases. A clause is a bunch of words with a conjugated verb in it. A phrase is a bunch of words without a conjugated verb in it.

A variety of words and chunks of words in our language can serve the role of noun. Let's call them *noun substitutes.* We'll return to noun substitutes in chapter 17. If you diagramed sentences in your youth, you will no doubt recall putting entire phrases and clauses in the space where a noun would ordinarily go. Here's a list of the most prevalent noun substitutes, along with examples. In the examples, the **word** or **chunk of**

words substituting for a noun appears in bold. I'll also indicate what noun function the noun substitute is serving.

Phrase Acting As a Noun	Example
1. Prepositional phrase acting as the subject of the sentence.	**Under the table** is the place to look.
2. Present participial phrase (*-ing* phrase) acting as the direct object of the verb *enjoyed.* (An *-ing* phrase acting as a noun is called a *gerund.*)	The man enjoyed **sitting on the park bench.**
3. Infinitive phrase (*to* phrase) acting as the subject of the sentence.	**To write with power** was his ultimate goal.

Notice that numbers 2 and 3 are verbal phrases. Notice also that those verbs (*sitting* and *to write*) are *not* conjugated. They do not reveal time, person, or number. Thus, the word chunks they form are phrases, not clauses.

We can conjugate a verb, form a clause, and then use the entire clause as a noun. Fact is, we do this all the time: He wished **that he could be like Mike.** When you look up *wish* in the dictionary, you find that it has transitive definitions. Thus, *wish* can take a direct object. You've learned in this chapter that direct objects are nouns. What's the direct object of *wish?* The entire clause—that he could be like Mike—enters the sentence, acts as a noun, and serves the role of direct object.

Let's dream up some clauses and make them serve the noun functions we've studied in this chapter: (1) grammatical subject of the sentence, (2) object of a verb, (3) object of a preposition, and (4) subject complement or predicate noun. Here's one of the clauses we'll use below: who **did** the homework. Notice that we have a bunch of words with a conjugated verb (*did*) in it. That's a clause.

Clause Acting As a Noun	Example
1. Clause acting as the subject of the sentence.	**That he succeeded** surprised the panel of judges.

2. Clause acting as direct object of the transitive verb *knew.*

The teacher knew **who did the homework.**

3. Clause acting as the object of the preposition *to.*

The teacher gave a prize to **whoever did the homework.**

4. Clause acting as a predicate noun.

The problem was **whether he could fulfill our expectations.**

One final observation. Notice that we create most of these fake nouns with verb forms. Later we'll see that the reverse is not true: We cannot properly take virtually any noun form and turn it into a verb form. We can manipulate and change a noun and turn it into a verb. We can—most unfortunately—take the noun *priority* and turn it into a verb and then *prioritize our agenda.*

You'll begin to learn in this book that the verb form provides enormous power, for it can enter the language as a noun. We'll learn later that the verb can also enter the language as an adjective. It can even enter the language as an adverb. (Remember adverbs? They are words that modify verbs.) That's right; a verb can modify a verb: **To improve** her swing, the professional golfer **practiced** every day. See how the verb *to improve* describes the verb *practiced?* It shows *why* she practiced.

That's versatility. That's power. For that reason, verbs are the secret of the powerful writer.

Another Pop Test: Identify the Three Main Functions of Nouns

Here's the same passage by Mr. Churchill, the one where you identified subject-verb pairs. You've already identified the subjects. Now identify any verbal objects or objects of prepositions. (Notice, please, that there are no subject complements in the passage.) Watch for transitive verbs followed by nouns—these are verbal objects. Watch for nouns that follow prepositions—these are objects of prepositions. The **subjects,** which you've already identified, appear in bold underlined type. Find the verbal objects and objects of prepositions. The answer appears below.

With 1588 the **crisis** of the reign was past. **England** had emerged from the Armada year as a first-class power. **She** had resisted the weight of the mightiest empire that had been seen since Roman times. Her **people** awoke to a consciousness of their greatness, and the last **years** of Elizabeth's reign saw a welling up of national energy and enthusiasm focusing upon the person of the Queen. In the year following the Armada the first three **books** were published of Spenser's *Faerie Queene*, in which Elizabeth is hymned as Gloriana. **Poets and courtiers** alike paid their homage to the sovereign who symbolised the great achievement. **Elizabeth** had schooled a generation of Englishmen.

Answer to Second Pop Test

Here's the Churchill passage, with **subjects** in bold underlined type, *objects of prepositions* in bold italic type, and **_verbal objects_** in bold underlined italic type:

With *1588* the **crisis** of the *reign* was past. **England** had emerged from the Armada *year* **[1]** as a first-class *power*. **She** had resisted the **_weight_** of the mightiest *empire* that had been seen since Roman *times*. Her **people** awoke to a *consciousness* of their *greatness,* and the last **years** of Elizabeth's reign saw a **_welling up_** **[2]** of national *energy* and *enthusiasm* **[3]** focusing upon the *person* of the *Queen*. In the *year* following the **Armada** **[4]** the first three **books** were published of Spenser's *Faerie Queene,* in which Elizabeth is hymned as *Gloriana*. **Poets and courtiers** alike paid their **_homage_** to the *sovereign* who symbolised the great **_achievement_**. **Elizabeth** had schooled a **_generation_** of *Englishmen*.

A few comments:

1. The proper noun *Armada* here is serving as a noun modifier. We'll learn more about how nouns can modify nouns in chapter 9, "Nouns: What They Do."

2. Notice how the *-ing* verb *welling up* serves as the object of the transitive verb *saw.* As such, the *-ing* verb is a gerund, that is, an *-ing* verb acting as a noun.

3. Notice that the preposition *of* has two objects: *energy* and *enthusiasm.*

4. Here's the one noun acting as the object of a verbal phrase: *following the Armada*. All other objects of verbs are direct objects, that is, they attach to conjugated verbs:

> **Verbs and Direct Objects**
> resisted weight
> saw welling up
> paid homage
> symbolised achievement
> schooled generation

NOUNS: A SUMMARY

At this stage, we are still just exploring the eight parts of speech. The first is the noun. In this chapter we've learned that nouns serve to name things, people, places, ideas, feelings, and other abstractions. One way to test a word to see if it's acting as a noun is to make it plural or add a possessive ending. If those changes work (and the word is not a pronoun), then the word is a noun.

We've also looked at the three main functions of nouns: (1) grammatical subjects, (2) objects, and (3) complements or predicate nouns.

Every sentence has a subject, which joins with a verb to form the two basic parts of the sentence: the subject and the predicate.

Nouns also serve as objects. If the subject joins with a transitive verb, then we can have yet another noun stick directly onto that verb. That noun will receive the action of the verb, and we call it the direct object. Nouns are also helped up onto the backs of sentences with the little word known as the preposition. The noun sticking to the preposition is called the object of the preposition.

Thus we get three main functions of nouns: subjects, objects, and complements.

If the subject joins with the verb *to be*, then another noun can hook directly to the verb *to be*. That noun will restate the subject of the sentence, and we call it the complement or the predicate noun.

Thus we get three main functions of nouns: subjects, objects, and complements. There are others, and we will explore them in chapter 9.

Finally, we tucked away some thoughts in this chapter. We saw that nouns act as subjects and, when they follow the verb *to be*, as complements or predicate nouns. These subjective uses of nouns give rise to another rule we'll encounter when we study pronouns: A pronoun taking the place of a noun that acts as a subject or a complement (or predicate noun) must appear in the subjective case. We also saw that nouns act as objects, and when pronouns take the place of nouns acting as objects, those pronouns must appear in the objective case. We'll look more carefully at the case of pronouns in chapters 5 and 22.

Now let's move on to the most important word in the English language, the verb.

NOTES

1. In *Oops, Me!*, and in all my writing, I use uppercase to begin a full sentence following a colon. This is the traditional and most prevalent style. The uppercase alerts your readers that a complete sentence is coming. Lowercase will tell them that a list or something less than a complete sentence follows the colon. *Garner Oxford* acknowledges that most writers use the uppercase to begin a complete sentence following the colon but suggests that lowercase "more closely ties the two clauses together." *Garner Oxford*, p. 69. (See author's note before the preface for full citations of frequently cited sources.) I opt for uppercase. In my view, alerting the readers to an upcoming complete sentence will aid and hasten their reading. See chapter 35, which discusses the colon.

2. *Random House*, p. 1327.

3. Would someone please buy an extra copy of *Oops, Me!* and send it to former vice-president Dan Quayle? He needs practice with *potato*.

4. *Random House*, p. 1199.

5. Winston S. Churchill, *A History of the English Speaking Peoples*, vol. 2, p. 133 (Dodd, Mead & Co. 1960)

2

Verbs: Words That Do or Are

The most important word in the English language is the verb.

Without it, we cannot construct a complete sentence. As a matter of fact, if you want to write a one-word complete sentence, that one word must be a verb. Watch. See? There, I used two words and wrote two grammatically correct and complete sentences. (The subjects in these one-word sentences are implied. I'm using one-word commands, called *imperatives,* where the subject is the implied *you.* Thus, You watch and Do you see?)

We'll learn in this chapter that verbs perform this crucial, sentence-forming role when they appear in their conjugated form. But we'll also learn of their incredible power in their unconjugated forms. Because of this versatility, the verb becomes the word of choice among savvy writers. F. Scott Fitzgerald is quoted as saying, "All fine prose is based on the verbs carrying the sentence."[1] So when you finish this chapter, you should start right now developing your style around one of the key ideas in this book: verb-based prose.

Achtung!
Grammar does not excite the senses of most normal people. So do not seek thrills in these pages. *Conjugation* **is not what you think. Pay attention. This stuff is very, very important. And mind numbing.**

Let's begin our study of verbs by dividing them into four groups. When we finish, I'll add a fifth.

FOUR KINDS OF MAIN VERBS

We can first divide all main verbs into two broad categories: action verbs and no-action verbs. Thousands reside in the action-verb group, only a handful in the no-action group. Each of these groups further subdivides into two additional groups:

Action Verbs
1. Transitive Action Verbs
2. Intransitive Action Verbs

> **The most important word in the English language is the verb.**

No-Action Verbs
3. The Verb *To Be*
4. Linking Verbs

Before you can ever claim membership in The Writers Club, you must become adept at identifying these four types of verbs. Your profiting from much of the remainder of this book, especially the sections on developing a powerful style, will depend on your mastering the grammatical concepts associated with the verb form. So, Damron, put away your spit wads and pay attention. Oh my goodness, I *am* Miss Hamrick!

THE ACTION VERBS

When our forebears were grunting all those nouns that named people, animals, and things, they also noticed that people did things; animals moved around, made noises, and ate stuff; and tangible things could move and affect other things. They noticed activity. They perceived action. So they grunted some words to describe all the activity around them: The baby **crawled**, the cow **mooed**, the wheel **rolled**, the fire **blazed**, the spear **snagged** the fish, and, of course, John **hit** the ball.

The action verb was born.

The Transitive Verb

As Amber and Igor became grammatically aware, Amber noticed that action verbs came in two models. One described someone (the subject) doing something (the verb) to someone or something (the direct object). Thus, the spear (subject) snagged (verb) the fish (direct object). Or John (subject) hit (verb) the ball (direct object). These short, simple, three-part sentences seem limitless:

Three-Part Sentences with Action Verbs
Mary wrote the novel.
The court decides the case.
The doctor removed the tumor.
The criminal broke the law.
The politician will dodge the question.

So way back at the dawn of grammatical time, Amber and Igor noticed that, among all the action verbs they had created, most had the capability of sticking directly to a noun. These action verbs could seemingly *pick up* a noun all by themselves. *Write* could pick up *book*. *Hit* could pick up *ball*. *Snag* could pick up *fish*. To name these kinds of action verbs, Amber and Igor first grunted: *noun-picker-upper*.

> **The transitive verb is an action verb that is capable of having a direct object.**

For they knew that this most prevalent of the action verbs had the unique ability to pick up a noun and complete the action of the verb: John (the do-or) hit (the action) the ball (the do-ee). But because the term *noun-picker-upper* would never survive in the faculty lounge, our ancient grammarians went back to the drawing board and then grunted: *transitive verb*.

Much better.

To be admitted to The Writers Club, you must know what a transitive verb is. You must know that it's an action verb. You must know that it's an action verb that can pick up a noun all by itself. You must know that you can stick a noun directly on the transitive verb.

To test an action verb to see if it has a transitive definition, you can ask yourself this question about the verb:

Can I [verb] somebody or can I [verb] something?

Just plug in the verb and ask the question. If the answer is yes, then the verb has a transitive definition. Your mind works like this: *Hmmmm, "write," can I "write" something? Yes, I can write a book. "Write," therefore, is transitive. Hmmmm, "debug," can I "debug" something? Yes, I can debug the computer. "Debug," therefore, is transitive. Hmmmm, "proceed," can I "proceed" something? Nope. I can't "proceed" the investigation. "Proceed," therefore, is not transitive.*

Why is it important to know what a transitive verb is? Two reasons. First, when we study the active and passive voices, you'll learn that only transitive verbs can appear in the passive voice. Second, if you go around grunting *noun-picker-upper* all the time, you'll never make it in the faculty lounge.

Your understanding of the transitive verb will grow when you fully comprehend its opposite, the intransitive verb.

Exercise

But first, try your hand at identifying the transitive verbs in the following passage. Look not only for the main verbs of the main clauses but also for the verbs that form dependent clauses. Look, too, for verbal phrases (hints: *winning, searching,* and *compassing*). When you spot a transitive verb, circle it. Watch for the nouns (or noun clause) serving as objects of these verbs; when you find them, you've identified a transitive verb. The answer appears at the end of the discussion on intransitive verbs:

> The success of the seamen pointed the way to wide opportunities of winning wealth and fame in daring expeditions. In 1589 Richard Hakluyt first published his magnificent book, *The Principal Navigations, Traffics and Discoveries of the English Nation.* Here in their own words the audacious navigators tell their story. Hakluyt speaks for the thrusting spirit of the age when he proclaims that the English nation, "in searching the most opposite corners and quarters of the world, and, to speak plainly, in compassing the vast globe of the earth more than once, have excelled all the nations and peoples of the earth."[2]

The Intransitive Verb

Our forebears noticed something else about their growing list of action verbs. Some lacked the ability to pick up a noun all by themselves. They could not earn that coveted label, *noun-picker-upper.* Thus, when they saw Amber moving rapidly across a field, they grunted *run.* And when they tried to connect the action verb *run* with the noun *field,* they just couldn't do it. All the grunting in the world just wouldn't make it work:

> Amber runs **field.**
> Amber **field** runs.
> **Field** Amber runs.

They noticed that a group of action verbs needed a go-between in forming a relationship with a noun. So they turned to the little glue word, the preposition, and discovered how to complete their thoughts. These three-part sentences would consist of the subject, the verb, and a word or phrase ordinarily showing *where, when, how,* or *why* the action took place:

> ***Three-Part Sentences with Action Verbs***
> Amber runs across the field.
> Amber ran next to the field.
> Amber will run around the field.
> Amber runs fast.

When they tried out a few grunts to name this kind of action verb, they stopped short of *no-noun-picker-upper* and *can't-pick-up-no-noun* and decided on: *intransitive verb.*

As they contemplated these intransitive verbs, they realized that many of them comprised the verbs describing the movement or location of a person or thing. Since the movement of a body constitutes action having to do with that body, then in the nature of things there is no third object to receive any of that action. That third object—if it could exist—would be a direct object. It would be a noun *picked up* by the verb. Thus, the reason an intransitive verb cannot pick up another noun lies in the meaning of the verb itself. The verb often is describing a movement or location of the grammatical subject. A direct object just can't enter the picture.

Thus, each of the body-motion or body-location verbs has an intransitive definition:

> Amber **runs** across the field.
> Amber **walked** through the woods.

Amber **skips** along the creek.

Amber **moseyed** up to the bar.

Amber **will stand** still.

Amber **froze**.

Amber **stopped**.

The basic structure of our language provides the big tip-off to help us determine whether an action verb is transitive or intransitive: The transitive verb needs no preposition to attach to a noun, whereas the intransitive verb must have a preposition to attach to a noun. Further, the trick question will always nail a verb as transitive or intransitive: *Can I [verb] somebody or something?* If yes, the verb is transitive. If no, the verb is intransitive.

Naturally enough, sometimes the answer to that trick question is yes *and* no. Many action verbs have both transitive and intransitive meanings. Many of these you know off the top of your head. Others require quick, furtive trips to the dictionary. In many dictionaries, you'll find a *"v.t."* or *"v.i."* preceding the definitions of a verb. They mean: "verb transitive" or "verb intransitive."

> **The transitive verb needs no preposition to attach to a noun, whereas the intransitive verb must have a preposition to attach to a noun.**

Let's look at a few verbs that are always intransitive. Try out the trick question. Notice that the pure intransitive verb has an urge for a preposition, which it needs to form a relationship with a noun. Often the verb has a permanent deal with a particular preposition.

Verb	Trick Question	Answer	Type	Preposition Urge
delve[3]	Can I *delve* something?	No	Intransitive	*into*
comply	Can I *comply* something?	No	Intransitive	*with*
sashay	Can I *sashay* something?	No	Intransitive	*into, over, in* (others)
proceed	Can I *proceed* something?	No	Intransitive	*with, to* (others)

Now let's look at some verbs that have both meanings—intransitive and transitive. For example, the intransitive body-motion verb *walk* needs the preposition *to* in order to get:

> Igor **walked to** the store.

But if *Igor* takes along his dog, the verb takes on a transitive meaning and we get:

> Igor **walked his dog** to the store.

The verb *run* is similar. As a verb form, it has 122 definitions. The first 52 are intransitive; the next 70, transitive.[4] Here are some verbs that have both transitive and intransitive meanings:

Verb	Question and Example	Answer	Type	Preposition Urge
walk	Can I *walk* something? Igor walked to the store.	No	Intransitive	*to, away from* (others)
walk	Can I *walk* something? Igor walked his dog. Igor walked the refrigerator up the stairs.	Yes	Transitive	
run	Can I *run* something? Igor ran away from the dog.	No	Intransitive	*to, away from* (others)
run	Can I *run* something? Igor ran guns across the border.	Yes	Transitive	
provide	Can I *provide* something? Igor provided for his children. Congress has the power "to provide for the common defense."	No	Intransitive	*for*

Verb	Question and Example	Answer	Type	Preposition Urge
provide	Can I *provide* something? Igor provided food for his children.	Yes	Transitive	

The key test for transitiveness remains the same: Can you stick a noun directly onto the verb? If so, the resulting statement shows a transitive definition of that verb. By the same token, if the verb will not accommodate a noun and yearns for a preposition, then your statement is showing an intransitive definition of the verb.

> **The test for transitiveness remains the same: Can you stick a noun directly onto the verb?**

Got it? Good, for it's very important that you understand the difference between transitive verbs and intransitive verbs. Why? Because you can't get into The Writers Club unless you do.

Exercise

Let's see how good you are. Here's the same passage you used earlier when identifying transitive verbs. You circled them. Now underline the intransitive verbs. The answer appears below:

> The success of the seamen pointed the way to wide opportunities of winning wealth and fame in daring expeditions. In 1589 Richard Hakluyt first published his magnificent book, *The Principal Navigations, Traffics and Discoveries of the English Nation.* Here in their own words the audacious navigators tell their story. Hakluyt speaks for the thrusting spirit of the age when he proclaims that the English nation, "in searching the most opposite corners and quarters of the world, and, to speak plainly, in compassing the vast globe of the earth more than once, have excelled all the nations and peoples of the earth."

Answers to Exercises on Transitive and Intransitive Verbs

The **transitive verbs** appear in bold type, their ***direct objects*** in bold italic type; the <u>**intransitive verbs**</u> appear in bold and underlined type.

The success of the seamen **pointed** the *way* to wide opportunities of **winning *wealth and fame*** in daring expeditions. In 1589 Richard Hakluyt first **published** his magnificent ***book,*** *The Principal Navigations, Traffics and Discoveries of the English Nation.* Here in their own words the audacious navigators **tell** their *story.* Hakluyt **speaks** for the thrusting spirit of the age when he **proclaims [1]** that the English nation, "in **searching** the most opposite *corners and quarters* of the world, and, to **speak** plainly, in **compassing** the vast *globe* of the earth more than once, **have excelled** all the *nations and peoples* of the earth."

1. *proclaims*

   The verb *proclaims* is transitive; its direct object is too bulky to reveal in *bold italic type,* for the direct object is the entire clause: *that the English nation ... have excelled all the nations and peoples of the earth.* (Notice the British rule of treating a group noun— *nation*—as plural: nation ... have excelled.)

Here are the verb-noun pairs showing transitive verbs and their objects:

Transitive Verb	Direct Object
pointed	way
winning	wealth and fame
published	book
tell	story
proclaims	that the English nation, "in searching the most opposite corners and quarters of the world, and, to speak plainly, in compassing the vast globe of the earth more than once, have excelled all the nations and peoples of the earth."
searching	corners and quarters
compassing	globe
have excelled	nations and peoples

Let's now explore the other broad group of verbs, the no-action verbs.

NO-ACTION VERBS

Recall that we've divided all verbs into two groups, *action* and *no-action*. The action verbs consist of two kinds: transitive and intransitive. Transitive verbs have direct objects. Intransitive verbs don't.

The no-action category also breaks down into two subgroups. The first consists of only one verb, the verb *to be,* which is unique among all verbs, perhaps among all words. The second consists of a group of verbs called *linking verbs.* Let's study the verb *to be* first and then the linking verbs.

The Verb *To Be*

The verb *to be* shows existence or, as the case may be, nonexistence. This existential feature of the *be* word prompted Shakespeare's Hamlet to ask, "To be or not to be, that is the question." The verb *to be* also shows that something takes place, happens, or will occur in the future, as in The meeting is next week. It shows that something occupies a particular place, as in The book is on the shelf. It shows that things can remain as before, as in Let it be.

> **The verb to be is unique among all verbs, perhaps among all words.**

The verb *to be* serves to join the grammatical subject of the sentence with either an adjective or a noun to describe or identify the subject. When it connects an adjective, that adjective is called the *predicate adjective.* Thus: John is **big.** When it connects a noun, that noun is called the *subject complement* or *predicate noun* or *predicate nominative.* The subject complement restates what the subject *is.* Thus: Mary is **president.** And sometimes it connects a phrase showing *where* or *when* something *is.* Thus: John is **in the batter's box.**

Like the other verbs we've visited, the verb *to be* serves to form three-part sentences. Recall that the transitive verb typically joins the subject and the direct object to form a three-part sentence, as in (1) John (2) hit (3) the ball. The intransitive verb, while it has no object, typically has a third part that helps complete the thought, as in (1) Amber (2) ran (3) across the field.

Some typical three-part sentences with the verb *to be* serving as the main verb include:

Three-Part Sentences with the Verb To Be

Amber was angry.
Jane is the leader.
I am from the South.
The book is on the table.

In chapter 12, we will learn that the verb *to be,* when overused, tends to weaken your writing style. So right now, if you can tear yourself away from this gripping page-turner, you should review some of your own writing and see how often the verb *to be* shows up. Better yet, try to listen to yourself and see how much you rely on *be*'s when you talk. Look and listen for these eight words:

am, is, are, was, were, be, being, been

Also listen for *be*'s that show up as contractions, as in:

there's, here's, it's, he's, she's, and others

Exercise

Take a look at the following passage. Put circles around each construction of the verb *to be.* Also, underline the third part of each main message in each sentence. That is, try to identify the noun (predicate noun), adjective (predicate adjective), or phrase that follows the verb *to be* and constitutes the third part of the main clause. (You'll also find that the verb *to be* helps form the passive voice [The case *was* decided by the court] and the progressive tense [We *are* studying effective writing].)

Victory over Spain was the most shining achievement of Elizabeth's reign, but by no means the only one. The repulse of the Armada had subdued religious dissension at home. Events which had swung England towards Puritanism while the Catholic danger was impending swung her back to the Anglican settlement when the peril vanished in the smoke of the burning Armada at Gravelines. A few months later, in a sermon at St Paul's Cross, Richard Bancroft, who was later to be Archbishop of Canterbury, attacked the Puritan theme with the confidence of a man who was convinced that the Anglican Church was not a political contrivance, but a divine institution.[5]

Answer to Exercise

The Verb *To Be:* Constructions of the **verb to be** appear in bold type. The third part of each sentence appears in bold underlined type and shows the **predicate noun, predicate adjective,** or **phrase** that completes the main thought. Passive-voice constructions and progressive tenses, which require the verb *to be,* are parenthetically revealed.

> Victory over Spain **was** the most shining **achievement** of Elizabeth's reign, but by no means the only **one** **[1]**. The repulse of the Armada had subdued religious dissension at home. Events which had swung England towards Puritanism while the Catholic danger **was** impending *(progressive tense)* swung her back to the Anglican settlement when the peril vanished in the smoke of the burning Armada at Gravelines. A few months later, in a sermon at St Paul's Cross, Richard Bancroft, who **was** later **to be Archbishop of Canterbury, [2]** attacked the Puritan theme with the confidence of a man who **was** convinced *(passive voice or adjective* **[3]***)* that the Anglican Church **was** not a political **contrivance,** but a **divine institution.**

1. **was . . . achievement . . . but . . . one**
You might have underlined *achievement* but failed to underline *one.* I missed it in my first draft but caught it in one of my umpteen proofs. Mr. Churchill has joined two predicate nouns, the second being the pronoun *one.* Note the conjunction *but,* the word that does the joining. We'll learn all about conjunctions in chapter 6 and parallel structure in chapter 18.

2. **was . . . to be Archbishop of Canterbury**
This one gets a bit tricky. The verb *was* is followed by an infinitive *to be* phrase, perhaps acting as the predicate noun of *was.* Within that phrase, the *to be* in turn is followed by its own noun complement, *Archbishop of Canterbury.*

   Alternatively, we could analyze the phrase *to be Archbishop of Canterbury* as an adverbial phrase modifying *was.* Again, within that phrase the *to be* has its own noun complement, *Archbishop of Canterbury.*

3. was convinced

We can view the word *convinced* as either the past participle in the passive-voice construction *was convinced* or as an adjective, in which case you would underline *convinced*. Since there is not really an actor, that is, a *convincer,* the word *convinced* probably acts more like an adjective. This will become clearer when we study the passive voice in chapter 13.

Linking Verbs

In point of fact, the verb *to be* is also a linking verb. But I prefer to put *be* in a category all by itself and then treat linking verbs separately. We learned above that the verb *to be* can connect a grammatical subject to a noun (predicate noun) (Mary is **president**), to an adjective (predicate adjective) (John is **big**), or to a phrase (Nancy is **in financial trouble**). The linking verbs do the same thing: They link a subject to a predicate adjective, a predicate noun, or a phrase. Broadly, the *be*'s and the linking verbs are called *copulative verbs*. (See? I told you these pages would sizzle! Should be worth a few back-cover reviews about two thumbs being up, way up!)

In addition to the eight forms of *be (am, is, are, was, were, be, being, been)*, the linking verbs include:

Some Linking Verbs	Sentence
appear	He **appears** awkward.
become	She **became** nervous.
grow	He **has grown** weary.
remain	She **remains** fatigued.
feel	He **feels** <u>**bad**</u> about that.
prove	This procedure **proved** difficult.
sound	He **sounded** very sick.
look	She **looks** smashing.
smell	The stale milk **smells** foul.
taste	The steak **tasted** delicious.

One problem that often arises with linking verbs is the tendency some people have of following a linking verb with an adverb, not an adjective. In the table above, you'll find the correct use of *feel* as a linking verb.

Some people insist on saying, I feel **badly** about that. Note that *badly* is an adverb, not an adjective (though there is a colloquial definition of *badly* as an adjective to mean *sick* or *unwell*). If the person really does feel badly (the adverb), it means he has deficient tactile abilities or perhaps a calloused soul incapable of doing a very good job of feeling. The linking verb *feel* must link noun to adjective, not adverb. The person feels *sorry* or *regretful.* Thus: He feels **bad** about that.

> **The linking verbs link a subject to a predicate adjective, to a predicate noun, or to a phrase.**

Actually, many verbs that are otherwise action verbs can, in certain sentences, serve more as a linking verb than as a transitive or intransitive verb. And when they do, you should be careful to link them to adjectives, not to adverbs.

Consider the action intransitive verb *stands* in this sentence: The men stood silent. Isn't *silent* meant to describe the standers, not the act of standing? If so, then *stood* serves as a linking verb, or in grammatical lingo, as a *copula.* As such, it should link to adjective *(silent)*, not adverb *(silently)*. Does an army *travel light?* Or *lightly?* The *light* modifies the army, not the action of traveling. Thus: The army **travels light.**[6]

When faced with these dilemmas, insert the verb *to be* into the sentence and see if that is your intended meaning. If so, the verb is a linking verb that should link to an adjective, not an adverb.

A FIFTH TYPE OF VERB: HELPING VERBS

The main verbs we use in the English language break down into the four major verb types: (1) action transitive verbs, (2) action intransitive verbs, (3) the verb *to be,* and (4) linking verbs. When we conjugate these verbs into the various tenses, we'll need some help from the fifth category of verb: (5) *helping verbs,* also called *auxiliary verbs.*

Every verb (that is, every one-word verb) has a one-word present tense and a one-word past tense. Thus: He runs (present tense); he ran (past tense). But try out any other tense, and you'll have to use helping verbs. Try future tense: He **will** run. Try present perfect tense: He **has** run. Try past progressive tense: He **was** running. Thus, in basic verb conjugation, we see the need for this fifth type of verb, the helping verb.

Helping verbs also enable us to express various conditions: If he **could** type, he **would** write the next great American novel. Helping verbs help us express permission: You **may go** to the movie. Helping verbs help us express one's ability to do something: She **can play** golf extremely well. Helping verbs enable us to ask questions: **Do** you think he cares? **Will** he win the race?

In the English language, we have 16 auxiliary verbs. The three *primary auxiliaries* are *be, do,* and *have,* which we use to accomplish various things:

1. *Be* forms the progressive tense (I **am writing**)
   and the passive voice (This issue **was decided** last week).
2. *Do* asks questions (**Do** you care?)
   and negates actions (He **does not** run very well).
3. *Have* forms the perfect tenses (I **have seen** the movie).

Thirteen *modal auxiliaries* enable us to show various conditions, abilities, and obligations: *can, could, dare, may, might, must, need, ought (to), shall, should, used (to), will,* and *would.*

And then we have other words that sneak in and act as auxiliary verbs. How else to classify the word *better* in that famous song:

You **better** watch out, you **better** not cry, you **better** not shout,
I'm telling you why. Santa Claus is coming to town.

Or what does *had better* do here: We **had better** leave early to avoid the rush.

Seems to me that *better* and *had better* act as auxiliary verbs.

Here's a partial list of the roles auxiliaries play:

Helping Verb	Function
can	shows ability
	He **can score** at will.
may	grants permission
	You **may go** to the movie.
	also shows a condition
	He **may want** a new career.
might	shows a condition
	He **might want** a new career.

Helping Verb	Function

Helping Verb

must

have, has, had,
   will have

be

be

should

would

could

will

do

Function

shows obligation
You **must** file the document on time.

forms perfect tenses
We **have** seen this movie before.
We **had** finished dinner when they
   arrived.
The court **will have** decided this
   issue by the time Congress acts.

forms progressive tenses
We **are** studying grammar.

forms passive voice
The ball **was** hit by John.

shows compulsion
You **should** read this book.

expresses a condition
They **would** come if they had a car.

expresses a possibility
You **could** do it if you tried.

forms future tense
He **will** profit from this relationship.

forms questions, lends emphasis,
   negates
Do you care?
Please **do** come for coffee.
He **does not** write very well.

    Please note that these verbs have various meanings, so all possibilities do not appear above. Also note that some of these verbs serve not only as auxiliary verbs but as main verbs. Thus: He **has** over one million dollars; he **willed** his fortune to charity; she **does** good work.

    Incidentally, when you use an auxiliary verb to produce one of these two-word (or more) verb forms, your creation is called a *compound verb.*

In the English language, we have 16 auxiliary verbs. The three *primary auxiliaries* are *be, do,* and *have.* The 13 *modal auxiliaries* are *can, could, dare, may, might, must, need, ought (to), shall, should, used (to), will,* and *would.*

An issue that will arise when we study adverbs in chapter 4 is the proper placement of adverbs when they modify a two-word (or more) verb form. Thus, which is it? I **definitely** <u>have</u> <u>decided</u> to buy the book. I <u>have</u> <u>decided</u> **definitely** to buy the book. I <u>have</u> **definitely** <u>decided</u> to buy the book. Which one is correct? Stay tuned.

FIVE KINDS OF VERBS: A SUMMARY

Let's look back and make certain we all understand the five kinds of verbs. Broadly, we have two groups of main verbs, action and no-action, which further break down into four types of main verbs:

Action Verbs

1. *Transitive verbs* are those action verbs that can have a noun attached directly to them, as in **write book, hit ball,** or **answer questions.**

2. *Intransitive verbs* are those action verbs that cannot attach directly to a noun; they need the help of a preposition, as in **walk to** the store, comply **with** the regulations, proceed **with** the inquiry.

No-Action Verbs

3. *The verb* to be can serve either as a main verb or as an auxiliary verb. When it acts as a main verb, it typically couples a grammatical subject with an adjective (predicate adjective), as in **John is big** or The sunset is **beautiful.** Or it couples a grammatical subject with another noun (predicate noun), as in **Mary is president** or War is **hell.** Or it might couple a grammatical subject with a phrase, as in **The book is on the table** or He is **from the South.** When it acts as an auxiliary verb, the verb *to be* forms the progressive tense, as in We **are studying** grammar, or the passive voice, as in The ball **was hit** by John.

4. *Linking verbs* are non-*be* verbs that link a grammatical subject to an adjective (Watermelon tastes **good**), to a noun (She seems an honest **woman**), or to a phrase (He looks **out of sorts**).

Those are the four types of main verbs: (1) action transitive, (2) action intransitive, (3) no-action *to be,* and (4) no-action linking.

The fifth kind of verb is not a main verb, but (5) an auxiliary verb, also called a helping verb. It does not form a sentence all by itself. Instead, it hooks up with a main verb and helps it show vari-

> **F. Scott Fitzgerald is quoted as saying, "All fine prose is based on the verbs carrying the sentence."**

ous tenses or conditions or states, as in **By the time I arrived, he had** com-pleted the assignment.

Now it's time to take a look at the various forms of a verb, particularly its *infinitive, finite,* and two *participial* forms.

VERBS IN FOUR DIFFERENT FORMS

Main verbs appear in four different forms: (1) infinitive, (2) finite, (3) present participle, and (4) past participle. In Miss Hamrick's class, we learned the "principal parts" of verbs, which are similar to my "four forms": (1) infinitive, (2) past tense, (3) present participle, and (4) past participle.

When teaching people about verbs, I prefer to distinguish between *infinitive* and *finite* verbs and then introduce the two participles, the *present participle* and the *past participle.* Note that the second "form" *(finite verb)* encompasses the second "principal part" *(past tense).*

Let me briefly introduce the four forms and then discuss them more fully below:

1. *Infinitive Verb.* In the raw, base-verb state, each verb has an *infinitive* form. Ordinarily, we think of the infinitive as the base verb preceded by the preposition *to,* as in **to win** the game or **to run** around the bases.

2. *Finite Verb.* When you use a verb to form a sentence, you use it in its *finite* form, that is, its *conjugated* form. Verb conjugation

will show *tense, person, and number,* as in She **won** the game (past tense, third person, singular) or They **will run** around the bases (future tense, third person, plural).

3. *Present Participle.* To serve a variety of functions, every verb has a form called the *present participle,* which you create the same way for all verbs: Just add *-ing,* as in She was **winning** the game or He will be **running** around the bases.

4. *Past Participle.* Finally, also to serve a variety of functions, every verb has a form called the *past participle,* which for many verbs you form by adding *-ed,* as in The court has **decided** this issue or The issue was **decided** by the court.

Unfortunately for small children and others trying to learn English, you also form many past participles in other ways, such as by adding an *–n,* as in *shown* or *seen,* or by adding other endings like *-elt* for *felt* or *-ilt* for *built.* Verbs that do not form their past participles through the addition of *-ed* are called *irregular verbs.* This feature of our language stumps children and visitors from other lands. You'll often hear small children following ordinary rules of adding *-ed* to form a past participle and saying, "I have builded it."[7]

> **Main verbs appear in four different forms: (1) infinitive, (2) finite, (3) present participle, and (4) past participle.**

Let's look separately at each of the four forms: (1) infinitive, (2) finite, (3) present participle, and (4) past participle.

1. The Infinitive Verb

Academic tomes might go on for pages defining the meaning of the infinitive form of a verb. I, on the other hand, have developed a definition requiring only a single sentence:

> The infinitive form of a verb is the one you would ordinarily look up in the dictionary.

Ordinarily, you wouldn't look up *seen* in the dictionary. Instead, you'd look up *see.* That's the infinitive. You wouldn't look up *written* in the dictionary. You'd look up *write.* That's the infinitive. You wouldn't look up *making,* you'd look up *make.* That's the infinitive. See? It works. Thus, for any verb, you know the infinitive form: It's the word you would ordinarily look up in the dictionary.

Now what's an infinitive?

This always stumped me back in Miss Hamrick's class. I kept getting hung up on notions of *infinity.* Under this cosmic view, verbs led to nowhere, or at least to some other planet

> **Thus, for any verb, you know the infinitive form: It's the word you would ordinarily look up in the dictionary.**

far, far away. Certainly beyond our solar system. The word *infinitive* just didn't seem to help.

Then came the term *finite verb.* It took me quite some time to realize that a *finite* verb is the opposite of an *infinitive* verb. Seems to me, they should make the terms more symmetrical. Either *infinitive* should be *infinite* or *finite* should be, uh, *finitive.*

Many, many years after those glorious days in Miss Hamrick's English class, it all began to come together. The true notion of infinitive and finite verbs finally jelled.

The infinitive has no reference in time (tense), reveals nothing about the agent of the verb-like activity (person), and says not a word about how many people are engaging in that verb-like activity (number). Thus, when I write the infinitive phrase **to win the game,** you have no idea about whether this game took place in the past, is going on right now, or will take place in the future. You don't know who's winning the game. You don't know how many people are playing the game. It could be a football game with 22 people playing, or it could be a game of solitaire. Thus, an infinitive verb has no finite state of time, people, or number of people.

In chapter 10, we will discuss verbs again and find out that infinitives perform a very important role in our language: They allow us to write *infinitive phrases,* as in, **to have, to hold, to love, to honor, to cherish** . . . to cite the wedding vows. And we'll see that these infinitive phrases can act as nouns (He wanted **to win the game**), as adjectives (The best way **to go** avoids the traffic jam), or as adverbs (The homeowner brandished his gun **to frighten the intruder**). In chapter 10, you'll learn that infinitive phrases always show up in the styles of powerful writers. You'll also learn that, yes, you can split infinitives. Even Miss Hamrick would approve.

2. The Finite Verb

A finite verb is just that: finite. It's finite in time, as in present, past, future, and other time dimensions. And when we talk about time in relation to verbs, in grammarian parlance we are talking about *tense.* As we'll see later in this chapter, we have six major tenses in the English language:

> present (she **decides**)
> past (she **decided**)
> future (she will **decide**)
> present perfect (she has **decided**)
> past perfect (she had **decided**)
> future perfect (she will have **decided**)

Six additional tenses enable us to express an ongoing action:

> present progressive (she is **deciding**)
> past progressive (she was **deciding**)
> future progressive (she will be **deciding**)
> present perfect progressive (she has been **deciding**)
> past perfect progressive (she had been **deciding**)
> future perfect progressive (she will have been **deciding**)

Notice that the verb *decide* forms its past tense by adding *-ed.* Notice also that its *past participle,* which shows up in the perfect tenses, also has the *-ed* ending. A verb that forms its past tense and past participle by adding *-ed* is called a *regular verb.* Regular verbs also include those that form their past tense and past participle by adding *-d* or *-t,* as in *heard* and *dealt.*

Other verbs aren't so friendly, for they form their past tense and past participle in an irregular way, usually by changing a vowel in the verb: *begin* (present tense in the first person, second person, and third person plural), *began* (past tense), and *begun* (past participle). Naturally, we call this kind of verb an *irregular verb.* Below we'll learn more about the past participle and past tense of irregular verbs.

A finite verb is also finite in identifying *who* is accomplishing the action it expresses. In grammarian-speak, we call this feature of verbs *person*. In its finite state, the finite verb reveals if *I* am doing it, *you* are doing it, or *somebody else* is doing it. If **I am doing** the action of the verb, then the finite verb appears in the *first person*. If **you are doing** it, then the finite verb appears in the *second* person. And if **she is doing** it or **he is doing** it, then the finite verb appears in the *third* person. Note the *am doing* (first person), *are doing* (second person), and *is doing* (third person) in the previous sentence.

Finally, a finite verb is finite in identifying how many people or things are
accomplishing the verb-like activity. In
grammarian lingo, we call this feature
of verbs *number*. If just one person or
thing is doing it, then the finite verb

> **A finite verb is a conjugated verb. And, on the other side of that coin, an infinitive verb is one that is not conjugated.**

appears in the *singular*. If more than one person or thing is doing it, then the finite verb appears in the *plural*. (Smart people usually don't make many mistakes in tense and person, but they do make some colossal blunders when it comes to number. We'll review this problem of *subject-verb disagreement* in chapter 10, when we study verbs in more detail, and in chapter 19, which is devoted exclusively to this common grammatical mistake.)

How do we get these finite states? Simple. We produce them by *conjugating* the infinitive verb. Thus, a finite verb is a conjugated verb. And, on the other side of that coin, an infinitive verb is one that is not conjugated. The infinitive form does not reveal *who* (person), *when* (tense), or *how many* (number).[8]

Below, after discussing the present and past participles, we'll return to finite verbs and run everybody through the process of *verb conjugation*. That should be fun.

3. The Present Participle

Every verb in the English language has a present participle, and you form it the same way for every verb: Just add *-ing*. Sometimes you'll have to drop an ending "silent *-e*," as in *write* and *writing*. Sometimes you'll have to double up an ending consonant, as in *begin* and *beginning* or *occur* and *occurring*. But all present participles end in *-ing*, and for that reason, I have dubbed them the "*-ing* verbs."

What do *-ing* verbs do in our language? They serve some very important roles.

First of all, when we join them with the verb *to be,* we form what's called the *progressive tenses,* which are illustrated above. This tense shows an ongoing action, as in We **are studying** grammar or We **will be reviewing** this matter tomorrow.

> **Every verb in the English language has a present participle, and you form it the same way for every verb: Just add *-ing.***

Second of all, the *-ing* verb can form a phrase that acts as an adjective, as in the player **sitting next to the coach** or the song **climbing to number one on the charts.**

Third, one-word *-ing* verbs form powerful adjectives, as in the **smoking gun** or the **controlling** issue.

Fourth, the *-ing* verb can act as a noun. When it does, it's called a *gerund,* as in **Winning the game** was his ultimate objective or **Practicing her swing each day** improved her golf game. These *-ing* verbs always show up in a powerful writing style, and we'll return to study them further in chapter 10.

4. The Past Participle

Every verb also has a past participial form, which, for most verbs, you create by adding *-ed, -d,* or *-t.* As with present participles, you'll sometimes have to double up an ending consonant: The past participle of *occur* is *occurred.* Check the dictionary.

> **Every verb has a past participial form, which, for most verbs, you create by adding *-ed.* But many verbs form their past participles in an irregular way: They won't add *-ed;* instead, they add something else or dream up an entirely new word to perform their past participial duties.**

Naturally, I have named these verbs after me: They're called the "*-ed* verbs." Unfortunately, many verbs form their past participles in an irregular way. They won't add *-ed;* instead, they add something else or dream up an entirely new word to perform their past participial duties. There's no rhyme or reason that tips you off to this irregularity. People brought up in grammatical households know the past participles of most verbs, because their moms and dads corrected them when they said, "I have builded it."

One of the functions of past participles helps you identify their correct form. Past participles serve two roles in verb conjugation: They help you form (1) the perfect tenses (illustrated above) and (2) the passive voice. You form the perfect tenses by coupling a form of the auxiliary verb *to have* with the past participle and the passive voice by coupling a form of the verb *to be* with the past participle.

> **You can identify the past participle of any verb just by completing this trick sentence in the present perfect tense: *I have [insert correct verb form here].***

You can identify the past participle of any verb just by completing this trick sentence in the present perfect tense:

    I have [insert correct verb form here].

Thus, here are some regular verbs, whose past participles are formed by adding *-ed.* You identify the past participle by completing the trick sentence:

Verb	Trick *I have* Sentence	Past Participle
form	I have *formed* the sentence.	formed
decide	I have *decided* this issue.	decided
provide	I have *provided* these examples.	provided
remember	I have *remembered* these clues.	remembered

Here are some irregular verbs. You can identify their past participles by completing the *I have* trick sentence:

Verb	Trick *I have* Sentence	Past Participle
see	I have *seen* the movie.	seen
ride	I have *ridden* the horse.	ridden
feel	I have *felt* your pain.	felt
build	I have *built* the deck.	built
keep	I have *kept* the secret.	kept

As mentioned above, the past participle also serves to form the passive voice. Just join any form of the verb *to be* with the past participle, and you get the passive-voice form of the verb. We'll study active and passive voice in detail in chapter 13. For now, take a look at these passive-voice constructions (all appear in the past tense):

Verb	Passive-Voice Sentence	Past Participle
decide	The case *was decided* by the court.	decided
build	The stadium *was built* by Acme, Inc.	built
ride	The horse *was ridden* by Susan.	ridden
provide	The test *was provided* by the coach.	provided

When we discussed present participles above, we saw that they show up in a conjugated form: the progressive tense. Now we see that the past participle shows up in two conjugated forms: the perfect tense and the passive voice. Above we saw that the present participle can also act as an adjective and as a noun (i.e., a gerund). Here, too, the past participle can act as an adjective. It cannot, however, act as a noun. As an adjective, it can show up as an adjectival phrase, as in The bill **passed by the House** cut taxes, or it can act as a one-word adjective, as in the **torn** pocket or the **conjugated** verb.

Botching the Past Tense and Past Participle

Some people confuse the past tense with the past participle. Usually, they will use the past participle instead of the correct past tense. You will hear some people say, I **seen** it, when they should say, I **saw** it. Or they will use the past tense instead of the correct past participle: We could have **went** to the movie. Cold chills run up the spines of listeners who are grammatically aware.

Naturally, people can't make this mistake with regular verbs, because the past tense and the past participles are the same. So they botch the past tense and past participles of irregular verbs. In the English language, we have fewer than 200 of these verbs.[9] Here are some causing the most trouble. Remember, use the past tense for statements showing that something happened in the past. Use the past participle to form the perfect tenses (with *have*) or the passive voice (with *to be*). I have included some regular verbs (*sneak* and *dive*) that either have developed some acceptable irregular forms (*snuck* and *dove*) or cause all sorts of arguments (*loan* as a verb):

Verb	Past Tense	Past Participle
arise	arose	arisen
awake	awoke	awoken[10]
awaken	awakened	awakened
(wake)	woke	woken
(waken)	wakened	wakened
beat	beat	beaten
become	became	become
begin	began	begun
bend	bent	bent
bet	bet	bet
bite	bit	bitten
bleed	bled	bled
blow	blew	blown
break	broke	broken
bring	brought	brought
burst	burst	burst
cast	cast	cast
come	came	come
dive (regular)	dived	dived
dive (irregular)	dove (OK in America)[11]	dived
do	did	done
drink	drank	drunk
drive	drove	driven
fall	fell	fallen
forget	forgot	forgotten
forgive	forgave	forgiven
freeze	froze	frozen
get	got	gotten
give	gave	given
go	went	gone
hang (a picture)	hung	hung
hang (a criminal)	hanged	hanged
kneel	knelt	knelt
lay (to place)	laid	laid
(lie) (to recline)	lay	lain
lead	led	led
lend	lent	lent

Verb	Past Tense	Past Participle
(loan)	loaned	loaned[12]
light	lit	lit
ride	rode	ridden
ring	rang	rung
rise	rose	risen
see	saw	seen
shine	shone	shone
shrink	shrank	shrunk
sing	sang	sung
sneak (regular)	sneaked	sneaked
sneak (irregular)	snuck (OK in America)[13]	snuck
speak	spoke	spoken
speed	sped	sped
spend	spent	spent
spring	sprang	sprung
steal	stole	stolen
sting	stung	stung
stride	strode	stridden
string	strung	strung
swear	swore	sworn
sweat	sweat	sweat
swim	swam	swum
take	took	taken
tear	tore	torn
throw	threw	thrown
thrust	thrust	thrust
wear	wore	worn
weave	wove	woven
wind	wound	wound
write	wrote	written

DEVELOPING YOUR LOVE AFFAIR WITH VERBS

Pretty neat, these verbs. They aren't content to serve just the verb function in the language, that is, the finite verb function of creating sentences. In their infinitive, present participial, and past participial forms they can elbow out other parts of speech and act as nouns, adjectives, and adverbs.

Some of the *-ing* verbs have even morphed into prepositions, as in *barring, concerning, regarding,* and others.

Let's move onward, and one hopes forever upward, and learn all about verb conjugation.

> **Powerful words, these verbs. Maybe that's why Victor Hugo once said, "The word is the verb, and the verb is God."**

WHAT DO FINITE VERBS DO IN OUR LANGUAGE?

Every verb in the English language has two states or dimensions, two realms, if you will. In the infinitive state, the verb only reveals the activity described: to hit or to run. From either of these, we do not know who is hitting or running (person), when the hitting or running is taking place (tense), or how many people or things are doing the hitting or running (number). To learn this *who-when-how many* information about the activity, we must convert the infinitive verb into the finite verb. To pull that off, we must *conjugate* the verb.

Frankly (and sadly) most of us learned basic conjugation in foreign-language class. We learned to conjugate verbs in Spanish, French, or Latin. Unfortunately, many people did not learn basic conjugation in English class. Some did not learn correct conjugation. For example, in a course I taught at a corporation, one of my students—a graduate from a top law school—told me that her English teacher had said way back in high school that you should never put the word *had* in front of a verb . . . as I just did when I wrote teacher had said.

Oh my goodness, we have a problem here. An English teacher has decided to abolish the past perfect tense, also known as the *pluperfect* tense. I gently informed the student that her teacher was a dolt.

CONJUGATING VERBS

Regardless of where you learned to conjugate verbs or whether you ever learned to conjugate verbs, I would be remiss in my duties as your English teacher if I didn't do as Miss Hamrick did to poor old Damron way back in the 1950s in Greensboro, North Carolina. So put your spit wads away, get up in front of the class, and conjugate the verb *to skip* in the six major tenses.

In your mind, you should form a chart like the one Miss Hamrick made Damron write on the chalkboard. Like this:

Tense: _____

Person	Singular	Plural
First Person	I _____	We _____
Second Person	You _____	You _____
Third Person	He/she/it _____	They _____

(You would use third-person singular when conjugating a verb with a given person's name, like Amber or Igor. You would even use third "person" when your subject is not really a person, but an object or thing or abstract idea—*it*. You would use third-person plural with two or more people's names or multiple names of objects, things, or ideas as the subject of the sentence. More about "subject-verb agreement in number" in chapters 10 and 19.)

> **When you conjugate a verb, you have to cover all three aspects of *finiteness*: time (that's *tense*), people (that's *person*, as in *first person, second person,* and *third person*), and quantity (that's *number*, as in *singular* or *plural*).**

To conjugate the verb *to skip,* we simply insert the correct form of the verb in the blank lines above to yield the correct finite form for each of the six major tenses. Before we do that, however, we need to clue everybody in about the six major tenses: present, past, future, present perfect, past perfect, and future perfect.

PRESENT TENSE: TODAY

Some authors write novels in the present tense, and it drives me bats. Whenever I browse in a bookstore, seeking the latest in top beach literature, I always sneak a few peaks to make certain the author does not use the present tense in the narrative: John **looks** longingly at Mary, who **looks** back with total disinterest as she **removes** the olive from her Waterford crystal martini glass, **pops** it in her mouth, **turns** on a dime, and **stalks** out of the room. Those books I always put back on the shelf. Each of the authors is telling a story, the story necessarily happened in the past, and they won't get a nickel of my beach-literature budget if they pretend that the story is happening *right now* as I soak up the rays with a cooler full of strawberry daq . . ., uh, Kool-Aid.

That's what the present tense does: It ordinarily tells the reader of an activity that is occurring right now. The present tense speaks of *today.*

(Please note, however, that the present tense can also refer to the future: The game is tomorrow. See the discussion of the future tense below.)

Now we do have a technique in writing called the *historical present tense,* used most often in describing what authors do in their books. (I use the historical present tense above when criticizing beach novelists.)

Even though Fitzgerald has long since departed this world, we might analyze *The Great Gatsby* with the historical present tense: In Gatsby, Fitzgerald **uses** color to paint the mood on East Egg. He **captures** the mood with his pulsing lights ....

We might even use the same technique when describing a document. Though a document

> **Every one-word verb in the English language has a one-word present tense. And that one word is the same as the infinitive form for all persons and all numbers except third-person singular. (The verb to be is the sole exception; its present tense is not the same as the infinitive form.)**

might have been written in the past, we would describe what it *does* in the present tense: Acme's annual report **shows** the continued growth of the widget business. On page 7, the report **describes** promotional efforts ....

Forming the Present Tense

Every one-word verb in the English language has a one-word present tense. And that one word is the same as the infinitive for all persons and all numbers *except third-person singular:*

> to write (infinitive)
> I write (first-person singular)
> you write (second-person singular)
> we write (first-person plural)
> you write (second-person plural)
> they write (third-person plural)

For the third-person singular, you will ordinarily add *-s* to form the present tense:

> he/she/it writes

We form third-person singular of verbs ending in *-y* by changing the *-y* to *-ies:*

> he/she/it verifies

We form third-person singular of verbs ending in *-ss* by adding *-es:*

> he/she/it confesses

Also, verbs like *go* and *do* form their third-person singular form by adding *-es:*

> he/she/it goes
> he/she/it does

Finally, some verbs, like *have,* do break the "add *-s* or *-es* rule" to form third-person singular:

> he/she/it has

Thus, to summarize, we use the base infinitive form of the verb to form the present tense of all persons and all numbers except third-person singular. For the third-person singular, we change the infinitive form, typically by adding *-s, -es,* or *-ies.*

An exception to this rule is the verb *to be,* which has three words (am, are, is) for the present tense:

> I am (first-person singular)
> we are (first-person plural)
> you are (second-person singular)
> you are (second-person plural)
> he/she/it is (third-person singular)
> they are (third-person plural)

THE PAST TENSE: YESTERDAY

Here's the tense the novelist should use, for the past tense describes what took place yesterday and not right now on the beach. Thus, from our novel of purple beach prose above: John **looked** longingly at Mary, who **looked** back with total disinterest as she **removed** the olive from her Waterford crystal martini glass, **popped** it in her mouth, **turned** on a dime, and **stalked** out of the room. Poor John. Regardless of tense, he always gets shot down.

Forming the Past Tense

Every one-word verb in the English language has a one-word past tense. For most verbs (for all persons) you form it by adding -ed. Thus, their past tenses and their past participles are the same: I **decided** the issue yesterday (past tense); I have **decided** to take a leave of absence (present perfect tense using the past participle).

Other verbs are not so friendly and form their past tense in an irregular way. Thus, the past tense of *drink* is *drank,* and its past participle is *drunk:* I **drank** the orange juice last night (past tense *drank*); I have **drunk** too many mugs of strawberry Kool-Aid today (present perfect tense using the past participle *drunk*). When in doubt about the correct form for past tense and past participle, just look up the verb in the dictionary. You'll find the past tense listed first, then the past participle, and then the present participle.

> Every one-word verb in the English language has a one-word past tense. For most verbs (for all persons) you form it by adding -ed. Other verbs are not so friendly and form their past tense in an irregular way.

THE FUTURE TENSE: TOMORROW

When the activity you describe isn't happening right now (present tense) and didn't happen yesterday (past tense), perhaps it'll take place tomorrow (future tense). In English, we have several ways of expressing futurity. We can use the present tense and write,

> Tip-off **is** tonight at 7:00 on ESPN.
> The game **begins** tomorrow night.

Or we can use what's called the present progressive tense and write,

> The game **is being televised** tonight at 7:00 on ESPN.

Or we can turn to a variety of verb combinations and write,

> The game **is about to be** broadcast.
> The game **is going to be** broadcast.

Or in the South, where I come from,

> The game**'s fixin' to be** broadcast.

All these, and more, can show the future.

Forming the Future Tense

The future tense we remember from grade school, however, is the one formed with the words *shall* and *will*. For most writing in American English, we simply insert the verb *will* before the base infinitive verb and produce the future tense in *all* persons—singular and plural. If you want to form the future tense of *write* for the *first person* in most

> **In most American writing, use *will* to form all future tenses for all persons (first, second, and third).**

writing that uses American English, then say, I **will write** the book (singular) or We **will write** the book (plural).

At least that's the American rule.

If you live in England or other British Commonwealth country, if you wish to speak or write British English, or if you routinely want to produce a highly formal tone, then you should use *shall* to form the future tense in the first person. Thus: I **shall write** the book (singular) or We **shall write** the book (plural). If you count yourself in this group, you are no doubt quite ready to organize a massive book burning with my book providing the kindling, for you would not allow *will* to show the future tense in the first person.

In the words of *Garner Oxford:*

> But with only minor exceptions, *will* has become the universal word to express futurity, regardless of whether the subject is in the first, second, or third person. *Shall* is now mostly restricted to two situations: (1) interrogative sentences requesting permission or agreement [*shall we dance?*] and (2) legal documents, in which *shall* purportedly imposes a duty.[14]

Entire essays could be, and have been, written about the differences between *shall* and *will*. [15] These go beyond the question of forming the future tense and delve into the use of *shall* and *will* to show determination and compulsion.

Here, in this discussion of verbs, I need to present only this rule: In most American writing, use *will* to form all future tenses for all persons (first, second, and third). If you're writing something that is quite formal or intended for an audience likely to get its collective nose out of joint over the American approach, then follow standard British English: Use *shall* to form the future tenses in the first person and *will* for second and third persons.

Actually, in formal expository writing, the issue won't arise very often for one simple reason: The first person doesn't show up too much in formal writing. You will face the problem in letter writing, however, for it's the rare letter that doesn't say something like this: I will call you with our answer sometime next week. In America: I will call you .... In England: I shall call you .... Or perhaps I should say, I shall **ring** you ....

THE PERFECT TENSES

In addition to the three main tenses of present, past, and future, the English language allows us to make three statements about accomplished facts. We use one of the three perfect tenses to show a perfected action that *has taken place* as of the present time (present perfect tense), that *had taken place* as of a past time (past perfect tense), or that *will have taken place* as of a future time (future perfect tense).

Forming the Perfect Tenses

As I noted above in the discussion of past participles, you form the perfect tenses by conjugating the verb *to have* and adding the past participle of the verb.

Thus, the three perfect tenses (in first-person singular) look like this:

Present Perfect Tense	I **have decided** to retire.
Past Perfect Tense	I **had decided** to retire.
(also called Pluperfect)	
Future Perfect Tense	I **will (shall) have decided** to retire.

CONTROVERSY

In my writing courses, students sometimes contend that the perfect tenses don't say anything different. For example, they'll argue that *I have decided* doesn't say anything different from *I decided.* Or they'll say that *I had decided* differs not one bit from *I decided.* They're wrong, of course, else they'd be teaching the course.

The perfect tenses show an accomplished fact in relation to a particular point in time in the present, the past, or the future. Take this sentence and you'll see that you cannot express the thought in any other way:

When I arrived, he <u>had finished</u> his dinner.

Substitute the straight past tense for the past perfect tense and see what you get:

When I arrived, he <u>finished</u> his dinner.

This latter statement suggests, or could suggest, that *<u>after</u> I arrived, he finished his dinner,* whereas the past perfect tense makes it plain that *by the time I got there he had already finished his dinner.*

So the teacher who advised one of my students never to put the word *had* in front of a verb just didn't know what she was talking about. With a single utterance, she abolished the past perfect tense.

CONJUGATING VERBS IN THE SIX MAJOR TENSES

Now you're ready to conjugate the verb *to skip.*

To do it, you must include all tenses: present, past, future, present perfect, past perfect, and future perfect. You must account for all persons: first, second, and third. And you must indicate number: singular or plural. Back in Miss Hamrick's class, she made us take out a piece of notebook paper and write down the chart:

Verb: _____
Tense: _____

Person	Singular	Plural
First Person	I _____	We _____
Second Person	You _____	You _____
Third Person	He/she/it _____	They _____

Then we had to fill in each tense, meaning that we had to copy the blooming chart six times, a real chore with notebook paper and no copy-and-paste technology. Then we'd insert the assigned verb and conjugate to our little hearts' content.

Naturally, with regular verbs, conjugation was a piece of cake. All we had to do was add an -s, -ies, or -es for the third-person singular, add -ed for all past tenses, singular and plural, and put *will* down for all the future tenses (although Miss Hamrick insisted on *shall* for first-person future tenses). Then we had to be sure we could conjugate *have,* because we needed it for the perfect tenses, where we'd just add the -ed verb. Again, those were the regular verbs.

> To conjugate a verb, show all tenses: present, past, future, present perfect, past perfect, and future perfect. Account for all persons: first, second, and third. And indicate number: singular or plural.

So let's take a regular verb (one that forms its past tense and past participle through the simple addition of -ed) and fill in the six charts. Let's use the intransitive regular verb *skip:*

Conjugating a Regular Verb

Verb: skip
Tense: *Present*

Person	Singular	Plural
First Person	I skip	We skip
Second Person	You skip	You skip
Third Person	He/she/it skips	They skip

Verb: skip
Tense: *Past*

Person	Singular	Plural
First Person	I skipped	We skipped
Second Person	You skipped	You skipped
Third Person	He/she/it skipped	They skipped

Verb: skip
Tense: *Future*

Person	Singular	Plural
First Person	I will (or shall) skip	We will (or shall) skip
Second Person	You will skip	You will skip
Third Person	He/she/it will skip	They will skip

Verb: skip
Tense: *Present Perfect*

Person	Singular	Plural
First Person	I have skipped	We have skipped
Second Person	You have skipped	You have skipped
Third Person	He/she/it has skipped	They have skipped

Verb: skip
Tense: *Past Perfect*

Person	Singular	Plural
First Person	I had skipped	We had skipped
Second Person	You had skipped	You had skipped
Third Person	He/she/it had skipped	They had skipped

Verb: skip
Tense: *Future Perfect*

Person	Singular	Plural
First Person	I will (or shall) have skipped	We will (or shall) have skipped
Second Person	You will have skipped	You will have skipped
Third Person	He/she/it will have skipped	They will have skipped

Conjugating an Irregular Verb

Our grades plummeted when we had to conjugate irregular verbs in Miss Hamrick's class. There was no way to figure out a scheme or system that would explain the necessary forms of irregular verbs, that is, the past tense and the past participle. For regular verbs, no problem, just add -*ed* to form both the past tense and the past participle.

But for irregular verbs, we had to engage in that most dreaded of all academic exercises: *memorization*. We had to memorize the forms of irregular verbs. So Miss Hamrick would set up all sorts of weird chants we'd have to engage in. I can hear her now:

Miss Hamrick:	Repeat after me, class.
Damron:	Repeat after me, class. (That always brought down the house!)
Miss Hamrick:	Up front with me, Damron. We shall lead.
Miss Hamrick/Damron:	*Drink. Drink, drank, drunk.*
Class:	*Drink. Drink, drank, drunk.*

And Miss Hamrick and Damron would chant us through the most frequently used irregular verbs. The formula was always the same: State the infinitive form of the verb *(drink)*; then repeat the first-person present tense *(drink)*, then the past tense *(drank)*, and then the past participle *(drunk)*:

Miss Hamrick/Damron:	*Ride. Ride, rode, ridden.*
	Write. Write, wrote, written.
	Know. Know, knew, known.
	Throw. Throw, threw, thrown.
	Lie. Lie, lay, lain. (To lie down for a nap.)
	(Damron smirks.)
	Lay. Lay, laid, laid. (To place something.)
	(Damron smirks again.)
	Lie. Lie, lied, lied. (To tell a falsehood.)

If we chanted the chant over and over again, we found we could make it through the conjugation of an irregular verb. Let's fill in the charts for the irregular verb *to see*. First, we must hear that chant coming from the past millennium:

See. See, saw, seen.

Verb: see
Tense: *Present*

Person	Singular	Plural
First Person	I see	We see
Second Person	You see	You see
Third Person	He/she/it sees	They see

Verb: see
Tense: *Past*

Person	Singular	Plural
First Person	I saw	We saw
Second Person	You saw	You saw
Third Person	He/she/it saw	They saw

Verb: see
Tense: *Future*

Person	Singular	Plural
First Person	I will (or shall) see	We will (or shall) see
Second Person	You will see	You will see
Third Person	He/she/it will see	They will see

Verb: see
Tense: *Present Perfect*

Person	Singular	Plural
First Person	I have seen	We have seen
Second Person	You have seen	You have seen
Third Person	He/she/it has seen	They have seen

Verb: see
Tense: *Past Perfect*

Person	Singular	Plural
First Person	I had seen	We had seen
Second Person	You had seen	You had seen
Third Person	He/she/it had seen	They had seen

Verb: see
Tense: *Future Perfect*

Person	Singular	Plural
First Person	I will (or shall) have seen	We will (or shall) have seen
Second Person	You will have seen	You will have seen
Third Person	He/she/it will have seen	They will have seen

The Most Irregular of the Irregular Verbs: The Verb *To Be*
In the entire English language, one verb stands out: the verb *to be*. It serves more roles than most verbs, for it can be a main verb and a primary auxiliary verb. As an auxiliary, it serves the vital roles of forming the passive voice (The ball **was** hit by John) and the progressive tense (John **was** hitting the ball over the fence).

Miss Hamrick could never make up a chant about the irregular forms of the verb *to be* because it doesn't have just one past-tense form like the other irregular verbs do. It does have the standard one-word present participle, *being*, and the standard one-word past participle, *been*. But there's not a chant like *drink-drank-drunk* available for the verb *to be*. Instead of using the infinitive form for the present tense and one word for each of the standard four forms (infinitive, past tense, past participle, present participle), the verb *to be* uses three words to express present tense and two words to express past tense. Thus, the verb *to be* uses eight words to express the standard forms:

Eight Words Showing the Various Forms of the Verb *to be*

Form	*To Be*
Infinitive	1. to be
Present tense	2. am
	3. are
	4. is
Past tense	5. was
	6. were
Past participle	7. been
Present participle	8. being

In contrast, only four words are needed to show the forms of the irregular verb *see:*

Four Words Showing the Various Forms of an Irregular Verb

Form	*To See*
Infinitive	1. to see
Present tense	1. see (same as infinitive)
Past tense	2. saw
Past participle	3. seen
Present participle	4. seeing

It's vital, of course, that you be able to conjugate the verb *to be* throughout all tenses, for you'll need all these forms when you create the progressive tenses and the passive voice. Study, please, a conjugation of the verb *to be:*

Verb: to be
Tense: *Present*

Person	Singular	Plural
First Person	I am	We are
Second Person	You are	You are
Third Person	He/she/it is	They are

Verb: to be
Tense: *Past*

Person	Singular	Plural
First Person	I was	We were
Second Person	You were	You were
Third Person	He/she/it was	They were

Verb: to be
Tense: *Future*

Person	Singular	Plural
First Person	I will (or shall) be	We will (or shall) be
Second Person	You will be	You will be
Third Person	He/she/it will be	They will be

Verb: to be
Tense: *Present Perfect*

Person	Singular	Plural
First Person	I have been	We have been
Second Person	You have been	You have been
Third Person	He/she/it has been	They have been

Verb: to be
Tense: *Past Perfect*

Person	Singular	Plural
First Person	I had been	We had been
Second Person	You had been	You had been
Third Person	He/she/it had been	They had been

Verb: to be
Tense: *Future Perfect*

Person	Singular	Plural
First Person	I will (or shall) have been	We will (or shall) have been
Second Person	You will have been	You will have been
Third Person	He/she/it will have been	They will have been

SIX MORE TENSES: THE PROGRESSIVE TENSES

Once Amber and Igor had learned all about the verb *to be* and present participles, they grunted the two together and developed a way to show a continuity of action. It was one thing to grunt, Igor eats and quite another to grunt, Igor is eating. By melding the verb *to be* with the present participle, they were then able to conjugate any verb in the six *progressive tenses*. All they had to do was conjugate the verb *to be* and then add the present participle.

> **The progressive tenses show an ongoing action.**

Verb: to write
Tense: *Present Progressive*

Person	Singular	Plural
First Person	I am writing	We are writing
Second Person	You are writing	You are writing
Third Person	He/she/it is writing	They are writing

Verb: to write
Tense: *Past Progressive*

Person	Singular	Plural
First Person	I was writing	We were writing
Second Person	You were writing	You were writing
Third Person	He/she/it was writing	They were writing

Verb: to write
Tense: *Future Progressive*

Person	Singular	Plural
First Person	I will (shall) be writing	We will (shall) be writing
Second Person	You will be writing	You will be writing
Third Person	He/she/it will be writing	They will be writing

Verb: to write
Tense: *Present Perfect Progressive*

Person	Singular	Plural
First Person	I have been writing	We have been writing
Second Person	You have been writing	You have been writing
Third Person	He/she/it has been writing	They have been writing

Verb: to write
Tense: *Past Perfect Progressive*

Person	Singular	Plural
First Person	I had been writing	We had been writing
Second Person	You had been writing	You had been writing
Third Person	He/she/it had been writing	They had been writing

Verb: to write
Tense: *Future Perfect Progressive*

Person	Singular	Plural
First Person	I will (shall) have been writing	We will (shall) have been writing
Second Person	You will have been writing	You will have been writing
Third Person	He/she/it will have been writing	They will have been writing

Finally, we do have another set of possible conjugations: the passive voice of a transitive verb. We'll postpone a conjugation in the passive voice to chapter 13 when we discuss the passive voice in detail.

VERBS: A SUMMARY

We're going to return to verbs in chapters 10 and 11, when we explore Word War I, the battle between nouns and verbs. For right now, you need to remember that all verbs break down into five groups.

The main verbs subdivide into (1) action transitive verbs, which can form a direct relationship with a noun, called a direct object, (2) action intransitive verbs, which cannot stick directly to a noun and need the help of a preposition, (3) the verb *to be,* which as a main verb links a grammatical subject to an adjective, another noun, or a phrase, and as an auxiliary verb forms the progressive tense and the passive voice, and (4) linking verbs, which link a grammatical subject to an adjective, another noun, or a phrase. The fifth group is the (5) auxiliary verbs, which join with main verbs to form tenses, ask questions, create negatives, and show various conditions, abilities, and obligations.

We also explored four forms of the verb:

1. *Infinitive Verb.* The infinitive form of the verb is the word you'd ordinarily look up in the dictionary (write). We use the base infinitive, without the word *to,* to form many of the tenses. The one-word present tense (I **write,** you **write**) uses the infinitive, the sole exception being third-person singular, which adds an -*s,* -*ies,* or -*es* (he or she **writes**). The past tense has its own form (**wrote**). Then we form the future tense by joining the base infinitive with *shall* or *will* (you will **write,** she will **write**).

   The base infinitive also joins with auxiliary verbs to show various conditions, orders, grants of permission, negations, and many other states of verbs (you should **write,** you used to **write,** she ought to **write**).

   Put the word *to* in front of the infinitive, and you have what we think of as the infinitive form of the verb. The infinitive does not specify any finite time dimension or any specific person performing the action of the verb or any particular number of people performing the action. The infinitive can join with other words and form what's called an infinitive phrase, which can act as a noun (He wanted **to write a grammar book**), an adjective (The hardest book **to write** is a grammar book), or an adverb (**To write a grammar book,** you must practice your skills as a writer and be a little bit crazy).

2. *Finite Verb*. The finite form of the verb is the verb appearing in its conjugated states. The finite verb reveals *when* something happens (tense), *who's* doing it (person), and *how many* are doing it (number). We saw that our language provides six major tenses (present, past, future, present perfect, past perfect, and future perfect) and six additional progressive tenses to show an ongoing action (present progressive, past progressive, future progressive, present perfect progressive, past perfect progressive, and future perfect progressive). We also saw how to conjugate those verbs that are regular (they add *-ed* to form the past tense and the past participle) and those that are irregular (they do not add *-ed* to form the past tense and the past participle).

3. *Present Participle*. Every verb has a present participle. To form it, add *-ing*. You might have to drop an ending silent *-e* (writing) or double up an ending consonant (**occurring**) (check the dictionary). The *-ing* verb shows up in verb conjugation when it joins with the verb *to be* to form the six progressive tenses (We **are writing** a grammar book). But the *-ing* verb does far more when it forms a phrase. It acts as a noun *(gerund)* (**Writing a grammar book** was fun), as an adjective (The guy **writing the grammar book** is nuts), or sometimes as an adverb (He went nuts **writing a grammar book**). It also serves as a one-word adjective (The grammar book won the **writing** award).

4. *Past Participle*. Every verb also has a past participle. For the regular verbs, add *-ed* (or sometimes *-d* or *-t*). Sometimes you must double up an ending consonant (**occurred**) (check the dictionary). For irregular verbs, complete this sentence and you'll discover the past participle: I have [insert verb] **(written).** If you do not know the past participle, check the dictionary, which will list the past tense first, the past participle second, and the present participle third. The past participle also shows up in verb conjugation, but it serves not one role like the present participle, but two roles. It joins the verb *to have* and forms the perfect

tenses (He **has written** the grammar book). It joins the verb *to be* to form the passive voice (The grammar book **was written** by me). Further, as we saw with the infinitive and the present participle, the past participle forms the past participial phrase, which can act only as an adjective (**Written in 2001,** the grammar book sold millions of copies). The past participle also serves as a one-word adjective (the **written** agreement).

This chapter was no cakewalk. I realize that. So if you remain confused about verbs, I have a suggestion: Read the chapter again. To become a member of The Writers Club, you *must* understand verbs.

Now let's continue our look at the eight parts of speech and study the words that modify nouns: adjectives.

NOTES

1. Steven D. Stark, *Writing to Win,* p. 22 (Doubleday 1999).
2. Winston S. Churchill, *A History of the English Speaking Peoples,* vol. 2, p. 133 (Dodd, Mead & Co. 1960).
3. The verb *delve* does have an archaic definition as a transitive verb: *to dig, excavate. Random House,* p. 529.
4. *Random House,* pp. 1681–82.
5. Churchill, *A History,* vol. 2, p. 137.
6. These examples appear in the earlier edition of Wilson Follett's *Modern American Usage,* pp. 50–53 (1966).
7. The word *builded* is an archaic past participle of the verb *build.* Recall the second verse of *The Battle Hymn of the Republic:* "I have seen him in the watch-fires of a hundred circling camps; they have **builded** him an altar in the evening dews and damps."
8. Later we'll see constructions allowing infinitives to reveal tense and voice. They do not reveal number or person, however.
9. A fairly complete list appears in *Garner Oxford,* pp. 195–97.
10. *New Fowler* refers to the network of forms for these words—*awake, awaken, wake, waken*—as a "philological nightmare." *New Fowler,* p. 82.
11. The word *dove* can serve as the past tense of *dive.* Longfellow used it in 1855; F. Scott Fitzgerald used it in 1940; and the *New Yorker* used it in 1988 and 1989. *New Fowler,* p. 222. In your master's thesis, you should used the older form of the past tense—*dived.* Please note, however, that the past participle of *dive* is always *dived.* Thus, you would not say, I have **dove** into the pond. Instead: I have **dived** into the pond.
12. The word *loan* has been a verb in the English language for more than 800 years. Though some say its use should be restricted to financial settings, it

means the same as *lend*. So you may loan money or loan clothing to the flood victims. In formal settings, you should use *lend* as a verb and *loan* as a noun. *Random House,* pp. 1126–27.

13. Acknowledging that *snuck* does not often appear in highly formal writing, *Random House* notes that it does appear in fiction and in journalism. *Random House,* p. 1807. Use *sneaked* in your master's thesis.

14. *Garner Oxford,* p. 304.

15. See *New Fowler,* pp. 706–707; see *Follett,* pp. 275–77.

3

Adjectives: Words That Describe

ONE-WORD ADJECTIVES
Adjectives describe or modify nouns or pronouns. They come in many varieties. Many consist of a single word, in which case they usually precede the noun they modify. Thus: the **high** mountain, the **low** valley, and the **red** wagon. Sometimes, however, even these single-word adjectives can come after the noun they modify. Consider the song with the lyrics about the mountains **high** and the valleys so **low.** Or think about the statement: He painted his wagon **red.**

When adjectives do come before the noun they modify, they appear in what's called the *attributive position.*

Single-word adjectives can come after the words they modify. The verb *to be* and the other linking verbs enable us to position an adjective, not in the attributive position, but in what's called the *predicative position,* that is, the adjective appears in the predicate. Thus: The wagon is **red,** the mountain is **high,** and the valley is **low.** Even without the verb *to be,* some adjectives follow the words they modify: the body **politic,** the heir **apparent,** the village **proper.**

THREE STATES OF ADJECTIVES: *GOOD, BETTER, BEST*
Recall how we defined nouns as words capable of having plurals and possessive endings. Adjectives (and their first cousin, the adverb) also

have a feature that distinguishes them. They come in three states. First, the raw adjective—in its *positive* state—merely describes the noun modified; it doesn't care about how this particular person or thing stacks up against other members of the same noun class.

If I hand you *a **hot** plate,* the adjective *hot* describes the positive state of the plate and cares not one whit about how the plate compares in temperature with other hot plates. In its second state, however, the adjective wants to show that this thing or person has more of the trait it expresses than other things or people in the same noun class. The adjective has a *comparative* form to express this condition. Thus, if I hand you *a **hotter** plate,* you start to worry about taking hold without a hot pad or glove. And in its third state, the adjective sticks its neck out and boasts that this particular thing or person has the

> Forming the comparative and superlatives of adjectives gets a bit tricky. You have two options. Either you can add the ending -*er* to form the comparative and -*est* to form the superlative, or you can put *more* before the adjective to form the comparative and *most* to form the superlative.

most of the trait it expresses. The adjective uses its *superlative* state for this ultimate in brags. So you would probably refuse to pick up *the **hottest** plate.*

Forming the comparative and superlatives of adjectives gets a bit tricky. You have two options. Either you can add the ending -*er* to form the comparative and -*est* to form the superlative, or you can put *more* before the adjective to form the comparative and *most* to form the superlative.

Thus, take the adjective *fast.* He is a **fast** runner. To show that he's a better runner than the next guy, we say, He is a **faster** runner. And if he always wins the race, we say, He is the **fastest** runner of all.

But consider the adjective *difficult.* We would say, This was a **difficult** test. But we would not say, This was a **difficulter** test. Instead, we'd say, This was a **more** difficult test. We wouldn't say, This was the **difficultest** test. Instead, we'd say, This was the **most** difficult test of all.

You ask, therefore, how to tell when to use the -*er* and -*est* endings and when to use the helping words *more* and *most?* There's no hard-and-fast rule, but four rules of thumb will help:

Thumb Rule 1: The Syllable Rule

One-syllable adjectives: in almost all cases, use *-er* and *-est*.

> big, bigger, biggest
> small, smaller, smallest
> thin, thinner, thinnest

In some expressions, however, even one-syllable adjectives use *more* to form the comparative: more sweet than sour.

Two-syllable adjectives: in many cases, use *-er* and *-est*.

> happy, happier, happiest
> narrow, narrower, narrowest
> silly, sillier, silliest

Two-syllable adjectives: some always require *more* and *most*

> bizarre, more bizarre, most bizarre
> steadfast, more steadfast, most steadfast

Two-syllable adjectives: some can use either the suffixes or the *more-most* technique

> clever, cleverer, cleverest *or* clever, more clever, most clever
> cruel, crueler, cruelest *or* cruel, more cruel, most cruel

Three-syllable adjectives: use *more* and *most*

> difficult, more difficult, most difficult
> memorable, more memorable, most memorable

Thumb Rule 2: The Participle Rule

Remember that present participles (*-ing* verbs) and past participles (*-ed* verbs) can act as adjectives: **thrilling** movie, **tired** golfer. When you show these participial adjectives in comparative or superlative states, you always use *more* and *most*. Thus, the **more thrilling** movie and the **more tired** golfer.

Thumb Rule 3: The Sounds-Weird Rule

Sometimes the *-er* and *-est* endings just sound strange. For example, the correct comparative and superlative forms of *common* are *commoner* and *commonest*. But these words sound strange, the first like some Cockney character pushing a barrow in the East End of London, the second like some sort of dangerous subversive.

Thus: *common, more common,* and *most common* would be regarded as "correct" by most people (simply because they're used to hearing these forms). In formal settings, however, you should choose the correct forms, *commoner* and *commonest.*

Thumb Rule 4: The Look-It-Up Rule

You can always find the answer in the dictionary. Look up *common,* and immediately following the word you'll find the endings *-er, -est.* These entries show how to form the comparative and superlative forms of the adjective.

Now look up the word *different.* Notice that following the entry you do not find the endings *-er, -est.* The absence of these endings means that you use *more* for the comparative and *most* for the superlative.

As with all rules, we find exceptions. It would be correct to use a present participle as an adjective and say in the superlative, **Dean Smith is the winningest** coach of all time. The same would not hold true for the comparative form. The expression **more winning** coach works fine; but **winninger** coach doesn't cut it.

Finally, please note that some adjectives have only one state, the positive state. Put another way, some adjectives cannot display the degrees shown by the comparative and the superlative states or through further modification by adverbs like *very, largely, quite,* and others. People often fail to recognize, for example, that *unique* is just that, *unique.* There are no degrees of uniqueness. Either something is unique, or it's not. Thus, it makes no

> Some adjectives have only one state, the positive state, and cannot display the degrees shown by the comparative and the superlative states or through further modification by adverbs like *very, largely, quite,* and others. *Unique* is just that, *unique.* It makes no sense to say, *This was a very unique movie.*

sense at all to say, This was a **very unique** movie. Other adjectives not capable of being broken down into degrees include *absolute, complete, equal, excellent, impossible, perfect, possible, supreme, total, utter,* and others. But rules were made to be broken, so you'll often hear, This task was **absolutely** impossible.

ARTICLES: *A, AN,* AND *THE*

At this point in our study of the eight parts of speech, it's a good idea to discuss three little words we have a hard time classifying in the English language—the articles, *a, an,* and *the.*

They don't constitute a separate part of speech. Because they are associated with, and come before, nouns, they look and act a lot like adjectives. But they don't describe nouns, they don't

> **We have two kinds of articles, the definite article *the* and the indefinite articles *a* and *an*.**

attribute qualities to the thing or person named by the noun, and they don't have any comparative or superlative forms as other adjectives do. Instead, they identify nouns as nouns, defining the thing or person named as a general class or as a specific member of a larger class.

We have two kinds of articles, the definite article *the* and the indefinite articles *a* and *an*. The words *a* and *an* actually descended from the number *one*. Igor got tired of grunting, Pass me **one** tankard of bitters, and started grunting, Gimme **a beer**. The indefinite article *a* was born. And when he wanted a particular beer, Igor learned to grunt, Gimme **the** beer. The definite article *the* was born.

The indefinite article—the words *a* or *an*—always comes before a singular noun, never a plural noun. You might want to refer to a general group of things named by the particular noun. Thus, you refer indefinitely to **a beer, an** apple, or **a** political party in general without specifying which beer, which apple, or which political party. If you're thinking about a particular beer, apple, or political party, then you will refer instead to **the** beer, **the** apple, or **the** political party.

Often you will generalize about plural nouns. When you do, the indefinite articles *a* and *an* are not available to show that you're generalizing. So to show generality with plural nouns, you omit the definite article *the*. Thus, you'll say that you enjoy **books** or that you prefer **raisins, not apricots.**

Omitting articles or including them often stumps those learning English as a second language. In my writing courses for lawyers, those who learned English as a second language will frequently put in unneeded articles and omit needed ones. Often, it is impossible to explain why sometimes the articles should not appear and sometimes they should. It takes an "ear" for the language, which can only be developed over time.

But to help out as best I can, I share the following discussion with these international lawyers:

A Brief Discussion on Omitting Articles

Read this sentence:

John hung pictures on his office walls.

Now read this sentence:

John hung **the** pictures on his office walls.

Both are correct usage. But what is the difference in meaning? If you said, "John hung pictures on his office walls" to a friend, the friend would likely respond, "I bet his office looks better now." But if you said, "John hung **the** pictures on his office walls," then either your friend would ask, "Which pictures?" or you know that your friend already knows which pictures you're talking about.

> **Omitting articles or including them often stumps those learning English as a second language.**

When you say *the pictures,* you're specifying a particular set of pictures, singling them out, and distinguishing them from all other pictures. But if you just say *pictures,* certainly it means John hung specific pictures, but you don't care, or don't know, which ones they are. You're much more interested in showing that John did something about his ugly office.

This difference is very slight and often hard to understand. Remember, the word *the* singles out and points to a specific one or specific ones.

Leaving the article out produces a meaning of generalization, even if specific items had to satisfy that general situation (specific pictures).

Now notice that this "article dropping" usually applies only to plural nouns. You would not say, John hung picture. Either you would say, John hung **a** picture to show you don't care which one it was, or you would say, John hung **the** picture to show that you're referring to a specific picture. The first statement (with *a*) says that *John fixed up his office.* The second statement (with *the*) says that John hung a specific picture on the wall, you care about which one, and your listener or reader also cares or should care about this particular picture that you're singling out.

Sometimes, however, you can and should drop articles with singular nouns. Study these two statements:

> He filed the lawsuit against his competitor in court.
> He filed the lawsuit against his competitor in **the** court.

In the first statement, the writer is saying, *He sued the competitor.* In the second, the writer is singling out a particular court and the reader is likely to ask, *Which court?*

The British drop articles before singular nouns denoting places or times more than we Americans do. The British would say, He went to hospital. Or, In future, he will go to hospital. Or, In future, we will be at table in hospital.

Americans would say, He went to the hospital, or In the future, he will go to the hospital, or In the future, we will be at the table in the hospital. These are the same Americans, of course, who say, She went to school or He attends church. Go figure.

A vs. *An*

Writers sometimes confuse the use of the articles *a* and *an*. We were all taught that *a* precedes a word starting with a consonant and that *an* precedes a word starting with a vowel *(a, e, i, o, u).*

Here's the secret to making the rule work: The rule applies to the *sound* of the letter beginning the word, not just the letter itself. The way we *say* the word will determine whether or not we use *a* or *an*. If the word begins with a vowel sound, you must use *an*. If it begins with a consonant sound, you must use *a*.

For example, the word *hour* begins with the consonant *h*. But the *h* is silent, so the word has a vowel sound. Hence:

The rule on *a* vs. *an* applies to the sound of the letter beginning the word, not just the letter itself. The way we *speak* the word will determine whether or not we use *a* or *an*. If the word begins with a vowel sound, use *an*. If it begins with a consonant sound, use *a*.

an hour

The rule works the other way as well. Take the word *university*. It begins with the vowel *u*. But the *u* is pronounced as if it begins with the consonant *y*. Hence:

a university

But consider the word *umbrella,* also starting with *u*. It starts with the vowel sound *uh*. Hence:

an umbrella

Another vowel with a consonant sound is *o*. When spoken, the letter can sound as if it begins with the consonant *w*. Thus, we use the *a:*

a one-room apartment
a once-famous actor

The consonant giving us the most trouble is probably *h*. When the *h* begins a word and the first syllable is strongly pronounced, you should use *a*.

a history of Europe (accent falls on *hissss*)
a hero (accent falls on *heeee*)

But when the beginning *h* is weakly pronounced *(historic, habitual)*, you may use *an*, especially in British English.

an historic occasion (hisTORic)
an habitual offender (haBITual)

But these usages are becoming increasingly old-fashioned, so you may also use *a*.

> a historic occasion
> a habitual offender

Finally, the rule applies to acronyms as well. If you pronounce a letter as a letter and it begins with a vowel sound, you should precede it with *an*. The consonants with vowel sounds include *f, h, l, m, n, r, s*, and *x*.

> He flew in an SST.
> He fired an M-I.
> He attended an FDA hearing.

By the same token, if a vowel letter, with a consonant sound, is pronounced as a letter, you should use *a*.

> He made a U-turn.

Got it? So what is your grade?

> **An** A?
> **A** B?
> Surely not **an** F.

OTHER ONE-WORD ADJECTIVES

Adjectives became a recognized part of speech in the 1700s. They belong to a larger category, which grammarians sometimes use to describe words and groups of words: Adjectives (and adverbs) are *modifiers*. Above we saw those little words, the articles, that help describe the nouns we use in our sentences. Other words also form partial adjectival functions. They modify nouns but they don't have other attributes of adjectives, such as comparative and superlative forms. In addition to the articles, they include the demonstrative pronouns *this, that, these, those;* the possessive pronouns *my, your, his, her, its, our, their;* and quantifying words like *many, much, any, some, few,* and others. These words help modify nouns, but most of them do not have comparative and superlative states (*much* has no comparative or superlative form, but *few* does—*fewer, fewest*).

NOUN MODIFIERS

Ironically, another word often acts as a modifier of nouns. The noun itself often modifies another noun.

Our language overflows with noun modifiers: **football** game, **hot-dog bun**, **chair** legs, indeed the list seems endless. These words do an excellent job of saying just what we want to say: We will watch the **football game.** We do not have to say, We will watch the **game of football.**

These days, however, many writers overdo it and come up with long chains of nouns. In the military we might encounter a long chain of nouns: the Missile Reentry Control Surveillance Management System Team, or some such gibberish. We'll return to the problem of overusing *noun chains* in chapter 9, "Nouns: What They Do."

SOME TROUBLEMAKERS:
FEWER/LESS **AND** *DIFFERENT FROM/DIFFERENT THAN*

A couple of adjectives cause many writers a lot of trouble: (1) *less* vs. *fewer* and (2) *different from* vs. *different than.* Let's straighten out the problems.

1. Write with Fewer *Less*es.

Many writers confuse *fewer* and *less,* usually using *less* when they mean *fewer.* Let's review the differences between these words so that you can use each with precision.

Note that *fewer* and *less* are adjectives. Necessarily, they modify nouns. Right off the bat, we can identify a key difference between the two words: The word *less* modifies singular nouns, while *fewer* modifies plural nouns. Let's look at examples of each adjective when they modify tangible nouns, stuff you can pick up and see:

Less	Singular Noun	Sentence
less	salt	His doctor advised him to use **less salt.**
less	milk	Also, he should drink **less milk.**
less	food	Overall, he should eat **less food.**

Fewer	Plural Noun	Sentence
fewer	packets of salt	He should ask for **fewer packets** of salt.
fewer	glasses of milk	He should drink **fewer glasses** of milk.
fewer	items of food	He bought **fewer than nine items** of food.

Of course, the nouns modified by *fewer* and *less* can be abstractions or other intangibles, stuff you can't pick up and see. Again, follow the rule of modifying singular nouns with *less* and plural nouns with *fewer:*

Less	Singular Noun	Sentence
less	alcohol	These days, people consume **less alcohol.**
less	whispering	The teacher urged **less whispering.**
less	discovery	The defendant wanted **less discovery.**

Fewer	Plural Noun	Sentence
fewer	bottles of wine	People now order **fewer bottles** of wine.
fewer	whispers	The teacher asked for **fewer whispers.**
fewer	documents	The defendant wanted to produce **fewer documents.**

But the singular/plural distinction goes only so far. I could not, for example, say, I should eat less cookie. So the singular noun has some special trait prompting its need for *less*. As a rule, it will describe something that cannot be easily counted. Thus, the singular nouns *milk, medicine,* and *asphalt* are very tangible and capable of some sort of measurement, but the nouns themselves are not susceptible to any kind of tally. So you would want to drink less milk, take less medicine, and purchase less asphalt.

But if you take these nouns and identify those units of measurements, then you'll need to turn to *fewer* when you want to drink fewer ounces of milk, take fewer pills, and purchase fewer tons of asphalt.

Think of the noun modified as being one of two types: either (1) you can count 'em or (2) you can't, because the noun is naming an "amount" or "chunk" of something.

Think of a grocery cart (one of those with only three wheels working). When you look in other people's shopping carts, it looks as if they have a big blob of food in there. But actually they have separate items—items you can count . . . items you *do* count in the express checkout lane.

Most grocery stores botch it in their express-lane signs when they say, *Nine Items or Less.* In my experience, only Safeway gets it right: *Nine Items or Fewer.* You can—and do—count the 25 items the jerk in front of you has in his basket as he checks out in the express lane. He doesn't have *less* than nine items. He is supposed to have *fewer* than nine items.

Complain to your store manager and point out how the grocery store is further eroding the knowledge of grammar in America. And while you're at it, urge the manager first to edit and second to enforce the store's *nine-items-or-fewer* rule.

When the noun is uncountable, chances are it's an amount or chunk of something, or just a bunch of stuff you never think of counting and perhaps couldn't count if you tried: *less salt, less sand, less ambiguity.* But: *fewer grains of salt, fewer grains of sand, fewer ambiguities.*

So remember: Use *less* for singular nouns that are kind of chunky and *fewer* for plural nouns you can count.

Time and Money

You'll encounter a big exception to these *less-singular* and *fewer-plural* rules. Sometimes a *plural* noun is describing something that's chunky—a singular amount. Consider time and money. You will often describe an *amount* of time with a plural noun, e.g., *years.* Here, the use of *less* is correct:

He earned his degree in less than four years.

Here we are not counting years. We're measuring an amount or chunk of time. He might have earned his degree in three years and eleven months. The expression *fewer years* would fail to describe three years and eleven months. What would we mean if we used *fewer?*

> He earned his degree in **fewer than four years.**

This must mean that he earned his degree in either three years, or two years, or just one year. Those are the only measurements that could possibly be *fewer than four years*. Increments between those yearly milestones are not within the meaning of *fewer than four years*. Thus, we're not counting the years. Instead, we're using a plural noun to name a singular amount of time. Use of *less,* therefore, is correct.

Money, too, is rather chunky. Here, the use of *less* is correct as well:

> The court has jurisdiction of cases involving **less than 10,000 dollars.**

We're not counting dollars. Instead, we're pegging a single amount. So even though *dollars* is a plural noun, it actually states a chunk, an amount—a noun properly described by *less.*

If you are counting units of time, however, you should use *fewer*. In the following example, we are specifying exact numbers of days, not a chunk or set amount of time:

> The statute requires our response in not **fewer than ten** nor more than twenty days.

Thus, in a word, use *less* when you cannot count the noun modified. Use *fewer* when you can. Use *less* with singular nouns; *fewer,* with plural nouns. But if you're using a plural noun to measure a chunk or amount of money or time, then you should use *less* (less than five years, less than 2,500 dollars).

2. *Different from* or *Different than*?

The word *than* typically follows a comparative adjective, such as *closer* or *more bizarre*. You would thus say, K Street is **closer than** M Street. Or you would say, This movie was **more bizarre than** any movie she had ever seen. The word *than* suggests some sort of comparison. Hence we use the comparative adjective plus the word *than.* The expression is usually followed by a noun, pronoun, or other noun form.

The word *different* is an adjective, but it is not a comparative adjective. As a result, you'll find among some stylists a distinct preference for the expression *different from.* You would thus say, These shirts are **different from** the ones I bought last year. Or you would say, His car is **different from** mine. Here too the expression is followed by a noun or pronoun.

You'll need to use *different than,* however, when you want to follow the expression not with a noun but with a clause. The word *than* then serves as a conjunction that gets the clause going. Thus you would say, This experience was **different than** he thought it would be. Or you would say, My birthday this year was **different than** it was last year. In the latter example, if you used *different from,* you would have to provide a noun or pronoun to serve as the object of *from:* My birthday this year was **different from** <u>what</u> it was last year.

So a big distinction between the two expressions is this: *different from* typically requires a noun, noun form, or pronoun to complete the expression, while *different than* may be followed by a clause.

New Fowler says that both *different from* and *different than* have flourished in America.[1] I once thought that most professional writers would use the preferred *different from.* But on July 30, 2001, the following appeared on slate.com:

> Washington, D.C., is **different than** Hollywood, or Manhattan, or any other city in which young girls attach themselves to older, successful men.[2]

New Fowler notes that writers prefer *different from* in Britain. *Garner Oxford* urges the use of *different from* in America, because *than* implies a comparison and *different* is not a comparative adjective.[3]

But in Britain, as in America, we do find the two expressions *different from* and *different than* used interchangeably, though stylists favor *different from.* The OED traces the use of *different from* to 1590 and *different than* to 1644.[4] The British also use a structure sounding strange to American ears: *different to.* Consider this example:

> I found that a meadow seen against the light was an entirely **different** tone of green **to** the same meadow facing the light.[5]

Though it sounds strange, the structure *different to* is (how shall I say this?) similar to the structure *similar to*. If something can be *similar to* something else, why can't it be *different to* something else? We'll have to ask Igor, Amber, and Miss Hamrick.

So here's the best advice:

1. Ordinarily, favor *different from* over *different than*.
2. Use *different than* when you want a clause to follow the expression.
3. Be consistent within the paper.

MULTIWORD ADJECTIVES

The English language is remarkably versatile, for it allows us to make up words and expressions that don't otherwise appear in the dictionary. One type of expression we frequently invent is the *compound adjective,* which is an adjective consisting of more than one word. Examples include the **well-known** actor, the **widely used** procedure, the **decision-making** process, and on and on. Most writers do a good job of devising these words and a terrible job of spelling them correctly. If your supervisors or professors see the **widely-used** procedure on one page and the **recently acquired** software package on another, then they will rightly wonder about your attention to detail and your consistency in applying ordinary rules of spelling. Why include the hyphen in *widely-used* and omit it in *recently acquired?* Answer: The hyphen should appear in neither, and the problem of correct hyphenation never occurred to you.

> **If your boss or professor sees** *widely-used procedure* **on one page and** *recently acquired software package* **on another, then she will rightly wonder about your attention to detail and your consistency in applying ordinary rules of spelling. Does** *widely-used* **require a hyphen? What about** *recently acquired?* **Answer: Neither requires the hyphen.**

Some general observations can help you understand the principles behind the rules on hyphenating compound adjectives and therefore increase your chances of getting it right.

To begin, a *compound adjective* is a single expression made up of more than one word and acting as a single adjective. Look at the following compound adjectives: **publicly traded** stock, **well-known** actress, and

bookkeeping system. Notice that each is spelled in a different way: (1) open *(publicly traded)*, (2) hyphenated *(well-known)*, and (3) closed *(bookkeeping)*. And that's the issue you'll face: whether to spell the multiword expression as two or more words (open), as a hyphenated expression (hyphenated), or as a single word (closed).

Most hyphenation in compound adjectives occurs when the compound adjective comes before the noun, that is, in the attributive position. As a broad rule, when a compound adjective appears after the noun it modifies, that is, in the predicative position, it will not be hyphenated. Thus: the **well-known** actress. But: The actress is **well known.**

The broad and general rule, then, is this: When a multiword adjective comes before the word it modifies, hyphenate it; when it comes after the word it modifies, don't hyphenate it. But not all compound adjectives will have this ability to migrate from the attributive to the predicative position. You could not, for example, convert the **day-trip** trade to the trade is **day trip.** But you can convert the **ill-conceived** plan to the plan is **ill conceived.**

One of the most important exceptions to this general rule applies to the compound adjective formed with an *-ly* adverb *(widely)* and a participle *(used)* or other adjective. These expressions are never hyphenated. Thus:

> internationally **recognized** author (past participle)
> rapidly **increasing** revenues (present participle)
> newly **free** country (adjective)

Though it's difficult to classify all possible compound adjectives, you will find that many fall into one of various categories. These appear in chapter 40, "Hyphen."

Read the *Wall Street Journal*

If you want to see mostly consistent editorial work in the area of hyphenation, just read the *Wall Street Journal*. On any given day, on the front page, you will find scores of hyphenated words, all following the correct system of hyphenation. I personally like the system, for I believe it facilitates reading.

Here's a list of compound adjectives appearing on the front page of the April 19, 1994, edition of the *Wall Street Journal:*

11-year-old schoolboys	military-base conversion
American-style savagery	police charged a 13-year-old
banking and packaged-goods	with the fatal stabbing
companies	short-term interest rates
bone-numbing currents	so-called Brady bill
bungee-jump advocates	teeth-rattling fogs
cellular-phone services	Texas-based search firm
entry-level salaries	three-ring circus
executive-search firm	three-year profit streak
first-quarter profit	two-year-old boy
gun-control debate	U.S.-built artillery-targeting
Houston management-	systems
consulting firm	world-wide automotive
long-term contracts	operations
Look-on-the-Bright-Side	task-force member
Department	

On page B1 of the same issue, we find the following passage:

> The day-trip trade also is flourishing. Experts say people are staying closer to home on weekends and holidays, taking advantage of new daylong hot-spring packages and by-the-hour room rentals.

Note that *daylong* in the above passage is not hyphenated for the simple reason that it has achieved "word" status, which you can determine by checking an unabridged dictionary.

Now, in the *Washington Post,* in three headlines on the front page of the October 19, 1994, edition, one would find three compound adjectives consisting of nouns and *-ing* verbs. Note the inconsistent approach:

> base-closing test
> expense-paring efforts
> intelligence gathering methods (why no hyphen?)

MORE MULTIWORD ADJECTIVES: THE ADJECTIVAL PHRASE

Funny word, the adjective. When it appears as just one word, it must usually come before the word it modifies. Thus, we can write about the essential factor, and we must position *essential* before *factor*. But if we add some words to *essential*—typically a prepositional phrase—we get a group of words we can position after the word it modifies. Thus: The factors **essential to our success** include hard work and patience.

Put the adjectival phrase on your list of things to remember, for we'll come back to it in chapter 16 when we discuss ways to develop a powerful style.

ACTING LIKE ADJECTIVES: PHRASES AND CLAUSES

It's SHOUTING time again. Wake up. This stuff is important.

In chapter 1, you learned a key concept about chunks of words that act as nouns. Well, the same thing happens here with adjectives. Other chunks of words, words that are not adjectives in and of themselves, will act as adjectives in your sentences, that is, they will perform the function of an adjective, which is to describe a noun or pronoun. I will introduce the primary chunks of words here, using terms we have yet to discuss in much detail. Just remember, the eight parts of speech are highly interrelated, so talking about adjectives, for example, often requires talking about prepositions and other parts of speech.

> **There are two main types of word chunks, clauses and phrases. A clause is a bunch of words with a conjugated verb in it. A phrase is a bunch of words without a conjugated verb in it.**

Also, keep this in mind: There are two main types of word chunks, clauses and phrases. A clause is a bunch of words with a conjugated verb in it. A phrase is a bunch of words without a conjugated verb in it.

A variety of phrases in our language will serve the role of adjective. If you were among the fortunate few who diagramed sentences in your youth, you'll no doubt recall putting the phrases *under* the nouns they modified. Here's a list of the most prevalent phrases that act as adjectives, along with examples. In the examples, I'll bold the **adjectival phrase** and put the **<u>noun modified</u>** in bold underlined type:

Phrase Acting As an Adjective	Example
1. prepositional phrase	The **book** **on the table** featured beautiful photos.
2. present participial phrase (-*ing* phrase)	Look at the **man** **sitting on the park bench.**
3. past participial phrase (-*ed* phrase)	The money **deposited** **by the customer** paid off the loan.
4. infinitive phrase (*to* phrase)	The most popular **movie** **to hit the theaters in decades** was *Titanic*.
5. adjectival phrase (discussed above)	The **machines** **available to the weightlifters** required a complicated assembly.

Notice that numbers 2, 3, and 4 are verbal phrases. Notice also that those verbs are *not* conjugated. They do not reveal time, person, or number. Thus, these chunks of words are phrases, not clauses.

Now let's look at two typical adjectival clauses, the *restrictive (that)* clause and the *nonrestrictive* (comma *which*) clause. For good measure, I'll throw in some *who* and *whom* clauses as well. Don't panic if you don't know the differences between *restrictive* and *nonrestrictive* clauses. Right now we won't discuss these clauses, *that* vs. *which*, or *who* vs. *whom*. We'll postpone these juicy topics to chapter 5 on pronouns and chapter 14 on clauses vs. phrases. In the examples, I'll bold the **adjectival clause** and put the **noun modified** in bold underlined type:

Clause Acting as an Adjective	Example
1. restrictive *(that)* clause	This is the **song** **that hurts the most.**
2. nonrestrictive *(which)* clause	The **game,** **which attracted 100,000 people,** lasted more than five hours.
3. restrictive *(who)* clause	**He** **who laughs last** laughs best.
4. nonrestrictive *(who)* clause	**Senator Smith,** **who lost his notes,** gave the speech anyway.

5. restrictive *(whom)* clause | The **man whom she met at the club** would later become her husband.

6. nonrestrictive *(whom)* clause | This **author, whom we all admire,** finally succeeded after many years of obscurity.

7. restrictive *(whose)* clause | The **player whose enthusiasm carries the team** usually receives the MVP award.

8. nonrestrictive *(whose)* clause | The **songwriter, whose artistic work had stretched over decades,** acknowledged the standing ovation.

Don't fret. When you finish this book, you'll be an ace at distinguishing between *that, which, who, whom,* and *whose,* and at figuring out when you need a comma and when you don't.

And Now, an Exercise

Read the following review from the March 11, 2001, edition of the *New York Times,* p. B1. Underline all adjectives and circle the nouns they modify. Be sure to include single-word adjectives, articles, possessive pronouns, multiword adjectives, phrases, and clauses.

> Daniel Barenboim is a storyteller, not a poet. He's a storyteller because the pieces he conducts have a dramatic motion; they are always emphatically going somewhere. But he's not a poet because he doesn't stop to bring details into a sharper focus: a phrase, the nuance of a single tone, the kind of perfection that can make an audience hold its breath.

Answer to Exercise

The **adjectives (and articles)** appear in bold, the **modified nouns** in bold underline, *adjectival phrases* or *clauses* in italics.

Daniel Barenboim is **a <u>storyteller</u>,** not **a <u>poet</u>.** He's **a <u>storyteller</u>** because **the <u>pieces</u>** he conducts have **a dramatic <u>motion</u>;** they are always emphatically going somewhere. But he's not **a <u>poet</u>** because he doesn't stop to bring details into **a sharper <u>focus</u>: a <u>phrase</u>, the <u>nuance</u>** *of a single <u>tone</u>,* **the <u>kind</u>** *of <u>perfection</u>* that can make **an <u>audience</u>** hold **its <u>breath</u>**.

You might have misidentified certain prepositional or infinitive phrases as adjectives. Chances are those phrases serve instead as adverbs. So we'll use this same passage in the next chapter on adverbs.

Also, some of the adjectival phrases and clauses get a bit tricky. Perhaps the following table will help.

Adjective, Phrase, or Clause	Noun Modified
a	storyteller
a	poet
a	storyteller
the	pieces
a	motion
dramatic	motion
a	poet
a	focus
sharper	focus
a	phrase
the	nuance
of a single tone	nuance
a	tone
single	tone
the	kind
of perfection	kind
that can make an audience hold its breath	perfection
an	audience
its	breath

ADJECTIVES: A SUMMARY

In this chapter we've introduced ourselves to the adjective, which comes in a one-word form that either precedes or follows the noun it modifies.

When the adjective precedes the noun, it's in the attributive position. When it follows the noun, it's in the predicative position. Most one-word adjectives have positive, comparative, and superlative forms. As a rule, we add *-er* or *-est* to the positive form of adjectives of one or two syllables to form their comparative *(-er)* or superlative *(-est)* forms. For adjectives with three or more syllables, we ordinarily use *more* for the comparative and *most* for the superlative. These rules, like all rules in grammar, have their exceptions, so that we would not use the two-syllable adjective *careful* and say, **He was carefuler.** Instead, we'd say, **He was more careful.**

We also met those hard-to-classify words *a, an,* and *the.* We call them articles, but they don't constitute their own separate part of speech. Since we use articles to modify nouns, in much the same way we use adjectives, I included a discussion on problems associated with them in this chapter on adjectives. We also took a brief look at other words acting as adjectives: demonstrative pronouns *(this, that, these, those),* possessive pronouns *(my, his, her, their,* etc.), quantifying words like *many, much,* and *some,* and nouns that act as adjectives.

We introduced ourselves to expressions called compound adjectives. These multiword forms enable us to invent terms like the *how'd-ya-like-to-hyphenate-this-adjective exercise.* Other multiword adjectives include the adjectival phrase, which savvy writers use all the time.

Finally, we took a quick look at the adjectival role played by five phrases (prepositional, present participial, past participial, infinitive, and adjectival) and by two basic kinds of clauses (restrictive and nonrestrictive). The point is this: A chunk of words must always be serving some function in a sentence. If that chunk is not acting as a verb, a noun, or an adverb, then chances are good it's acting as an adjective.

Now we move on to another word that describes, the adverb.

NOTES

1. *New Fowler,* p. 212.
2. Dahlia Lithwick, "G-Girl Confidential," July 30, 2001, www.slate.com.
3. *Garner Oxford,* p. 101.
4. *New Fowler,* p. 212.
5. *New Fowler,* p. 212.

4

Adverbs: More Words That Describe

Just as adjectives modify nouns, adverbs modify verbs. But they can do more. Adverbs modify adjectives. Adverbs modify other adverbs. And adverbs can modify an entire sentence or clause.

When our forebears were getting together to form our early languages, they noticed that the noun *Igor* could engage in a verb-like activity and *run* across the field. Having already developed adjectives, the early grammarians were able to describe Igor as *quick*. "Look at Igor," they would grunt. "Igor is quick." Watching all the verb-like activity around them, they had some important questions they wanted answered about all these verbs. *Where was Igor running? Why was Igor running? How or in what way was Igor running? When was Igor running? Under what circumstances was Igor running?*

Then one day, Amber and Miss Hamrick decided not to describe Igor but to remark on his act of running. So, in a moment of brilliant inspiration, they grunted the world's first adverb: *Igor **quickly** runs across the field.*

MODIFYING ADJECTIVES AND OTHER ADVERBS

Amber and Miss Hamrick also wanted to further describe the adjectives they used to modify nouns. Not content with saying *the sunset is beautiful,* they became grandiose and said *the sunset is **unbelievably** beautiful.*

Thus, they developed the rule that adverbs can modify adjectives. Then it dawned on them that they might want to further describe the adverbs themselves. So instead of saying *Igor ran quickly,* they upped the ante and said *Igor ran **very** quickly.* Check out *very* in the dictionary, and you'll see that it's an adverb.

> **Adverbs modify verbs. They modify adjectives. They modify other adverbs. And they can modify an entire sentence or clause.**

MODIFYING AN ENTIRE SENTENCE OR CLAUSE

This section will undoubtedly get some readers' noses out of joint, because it points out that starting a sentence with the word *hopefully* is acceptable under modern theories of style. But watch out, many readers will think less of you if you start sentences with *hopefully.* So let's review the problem. Then you can decide whether to start a sentence with the term or not.

Consider what this expression means, if the adverb is taken to modify the verb in the sentence:

Quickly, Igor **will run** across the field.

The adverb describes the verb. When Igor runs across the field, he'll run *quickly.* Right? Now consider this sentence:

Hopefully, Igor **will run** across the field.

How can Igor *run hopefully?* Answer: He can't. Thus you can see why many grammarians fly into a tizzy when they see or hear sentences beginning with the adverb *hopefully.* Instead, the traditional grammarian would say:

One hopes that Igor will run across the field.
It is to be hoped that Igor will run across the field.
Igor, **one hopes,** will run across the field.

In the grammarians' view, one just cannot *run hopefully.* And they're right.

But what did Amber mean when she said, *Hopefully, Igor will run across the field?* She meant that she herself hoped that Igor will run across the field. The word *hopefully* describes the speaker or the writer or a generic *one* out there somewhere. It does not, in the speaker's view, describe the verb in the sentence. Instead, it sort of sums up the entire sentence.

Well, according to top authorities, adverbs do have this ability to modify entire sentences. When they do, they're appropriately called *sentence adverbs. New Fowler,* to name one, lists examples of sentences starting with an *-ly* adverb followed by a comma:

> Unhappily, there are times when violence is the only way in which
> justice can be secured.
> Agreeably, he asked me my name and where I lived.
> Frankly, I do not wish to stop them.[1]

The sources of these passages? T. S. Eliot's *Murder in the Cathedral* (1935), a 1987 issue of the *New Yorker,* and Brian Moore's *The Colour of Blood* (1987).

According to Mr. Burchfield, the editor of *New Fowler,* the *-ly* adverbs that modify entire sentences include, among others, *actually, basically, frankly,* **hopefully**, *regretfully, strictly,* and *thankfully.* He describes the "swift and immoderate increase in the currency of *-ly* adverbs used to qualify a predication or assertion as a whole." But he goes on to point out that the *Oxford English Dictionary* traces the use back to 1644.[2]

In *Garner Legal,* the author urges lawyers to avoid the use of *hopefully* as a sentence adverb: "The word received so much negative attention in the 1970s and 1980s that many writers have blacklisted it, so using it at all today is a precarious venture."[3] In *Garner Oxford,* however, the author writes: "The battle is now over. *Hopefully* is now a part of American English." But he cautions writers to consider their audiences: "Anyone using it in the new sense is likely to have a credibility problem with some readers."[4]

> **You should choose and use** *hopefully* **when you write for readers who don't care, or know very much, about stylistic debate. But if the audience tends to scowl at newfangled expressions, one hopes you will avoid** *hopefully* **like the plague.**

This war will continue to rage, no doubt. You should choose and use *hopefully* when you write for readers in many settings. After all, you have *New Fowler, Oxford English Dictionary,* and *Garner Oxford* on your side. But if your audience tends to scowl at newfangled expressions, one hopes you will avoid using *hopefully* as an adverb beginning a sentence.

THREE QUESTIONS ABOUT ADVERBS

Three questions typically arise about the correct use of adverbs: (1) Do all adverbs end in *-ly?* (2) Where do we put adverbs in the sentence? and (3) How do we form the comparative and superlative forms of adverbs?

1. Do All Adverbs End in *-ly?*

No.

We add the *-ly* ending to adjectives in order to convert them to adverbs. Thus, the adjective *easy* becomes the adverb *easily,* the adjective *rapid* becomes the adverb *rapidly,* and the adjective *careful* becomes the adverb *carefully.*

Not all adverbs end in -ly.

But many adverbs do not have the *-ly* ending. Some words have identical forms as adjectives and adverbs. Consider the word *fast.* It's an adjective, as in the **fast** runner or the **fast** car. But it's also an adverb. When describing Igor, our early grammarians grunted, *Igor runs **fast**.* They didn't say, *Igor runs fastly*.

Think about the word *straight.* It's an adjective, as in the **straight** line. But it can also act as an adverb when we say, We go **straight** to the point. We wouldn't say, We go **straightly** to the point.

Interestingly enough, when you modify verbs with adverbs, those ending in *-ly* have the capacity to come before the verb. But most of those not ending in *-ly* have a hard time preceding the verb they modify. We cannot say, for example, Igor **fast** runs or We **straight** go to the point.

A final point on the *-ly* ending. Many people (especially sportscasters) do not distinguish between adjectives and adverbs. They just use the adjective form to perform double duty and serve as adverbs. Basically, they've excised the *-ly* adverb from the language:

She swam that lap **easy,** don't you think, Mark?

In fact, just today, July 22, 2001, a commentator at the British Open observed:

> He hit that one **soft,** now didn't he?

If these announcers cared about the language, they would find out that *easy* indeed can serve as an adverb, but its adverbial use is a colloquial one, as in take it **easy.** The swimming announcer should have said, "She **easily** swam that lap, don't you think, Mark?" The golfing announcer should have said, "He hit that one **softly,** now didn't he?"

Unfortunately, sportscasters don't care about, or don't know, the language. As a result, they do a lot of damage.

2. Where Do We Put Adverbs in the Sentence?

As we learned in chapter 2 on verbs, every one-word verb has a one-word present tense and a one-word past tense. Thus: I write and I wrote. These one-word verbs are called *simple verbs.* Recall that all other tenses require more than one word. These multiword verbs are called *compound verbs.* They consist of one or more of the 16 auxiliary verbs (*be, do, have, can, could, dare, may, might, must, need, ought to, shall, should, used to, will, and would*) and the main verb. Thus: I will write, I have written, I was writing, I should have written, and so on.

When you modify a verb with an adverb, you must decide where to put it. In the previous chapter on adjectives, we learned of their rather rigid nature. They must usually appear in the attributive position, that is, before the noun they modify. But an adverb can move around in your sentence. Though all forms might not be preferred, you could say:

1. **Finally** we decided on the policy.
2. We **finally** decided on the policy.
3. We decided **finally** on the policy.
4. We decided on the policy **finally.**

Thus, whenever you use an adverb, you must decide where to put it. Some rules will guide your decision. First, for simple (one-word) verb forms, you should try to put the adverb before the verb, though sometimes you'll want to move it to the beginning or even to the end of the sentence. Thus: Igor **quickly** ran across the field. But: **Quickly,** Igor ran across the field. Or: Igor ran across the field **quickly.**

> **For compound verbs, don't be fooled into following a myth perpetrated by well-meaning but misinformed editors. Many would have you believe that you should keep the parts of a compound verb together and put an adverb either before or after it. Nothing could be further from the truth.**

Second, for compound (multi-word) verbs, don't be fooled into following a myth perpetrated by well-meaning but misinformed editors. Many would have you believe that you should keep the parts of a compound-verb form together and put an adverb either before or after the compound verb. Nothing could be further from the truth. In fact, just the opposite is true. When modifying a compound-verb form, you should usually put the adverb somewhere between the words. (Check that out: You <u>should</u> **usually** <u>put</u> ....)

So to put adverbs in their proper place, follow these seven conventions. The **adverbs** appear in bold type, the _compound verbs_ in underlined italic type:

1. **To stress the adverb, put it before the subject.**

   Emphatically, the parent <u>denied</u> the child's request to ride without a seatbelt.

2. **An adverb needing no emphasis comes after the subject and before the simple (one-word) verb.**

   The teacher **sometimes** <u>uses</u> the dictionary.

3. **Do not put an adverb between a verb and its object.**

   Avoid: I <u>understand</u> **entirely** the rule governing the placement of adverbs. (The word _understand_ is the verb and _rule_ is its object; no adverb should come in between.)

   Instead: I **entirely** <u>understand</u> the rule governing the placement of adverbs.

4. **An adverb modifying a two-word compound verb comes between the helping verb and the main verb.**

> The manager _will_ **probably** _review_ the salary scales next month.
> The president _has_ **often** _rejected_ similar arguments.
> The runner _was_ **consistently** _winning_ all her races.

5. **An adverb modifying a three-word compound verb comes after the first helping verb when the adverb modifies the entire thought communicated by the compound verb.**

> The students _have_ **certainly** _been forewarned_ about the risks of smoking.
> We _will_ **undoubtedly** _have received_ news from the school by that time.

6. **If an adverb strongly modifies the main verb, put it before the main verb, not after the first helping verb (in a compound verb with three or more words).**

> This argument _has been_ **repeatedly** _rejected_ by the personnel office.
> This policy _will have become_ **firmly** _entrenched_ in our tax law.

7. **An adverbial expression consisting of several words comes outside the compound verb, ordinarily after it.**

> The students _have been reminded_ **over and over again** to refrain from smoking.
> We _have been hearing_ this particular argument **off and on for several years.**

Wilson Follett devised the above principles.[5] He commented on them as follows:

These principles were practiced for many generations without anyone's having to think about them. Then strange things began to happen. Some influential source promulgated the doctrine that the compound verb is an indivisible unit, and that to wedge an adverb into it is a crime akin to the splitting of an infinitive. The results are uniformly bad.

Mr. Follett's "bad results" look like this, with repairs appearing parenthetically. The **adverbs** appear in bold type, the _compound verbs_ in underlined italic type:

1. It **long** _had been known_.
   (It _had_ **long** _been known_.)

2. It **officially** _was announced_ the other day.
   (It _was_ **officially** _announced_ the other day.)

3. They **unfailingly** _have been led_ by a brilliant passer.
   (They _have been_ **unfailingly** _led_ by a brilliant passer.)

4. This session of Congress **doubtless** _will see_ a lot of [bickering].
   (This session of Congress _will_ **doubtless** _see_ a lot of [bickering].)

5. Is "Doctor Zhivago" protected since it **first** _was published_ in Milan?
   (Is "Doctor Zhivago" protected since it _was_ **first** _published_ in Milan?)

6. The people upstairs **always** _are pounding_ [the walls].
   (The people upstairs _are_ **always** _pounding_ [the walls].)

7. [The council must decide] whether a 450-room skyscraper **accurately** _can be termed_ a motel.
   ([The council must decide] whether a 450-room skyscraper _can be_ **accurately** _termed_ a motel.)

All these adverbs should appear between the helping verb and the main verb.

Thus, in sum, in compound verb forms having two words, put the adverb between the two verb words. In compound verbs having three or more words, put the adverb after the first helping verb, but if the adverb seems to stress the main verb, then put it right before the main verb.

3. How Do We Form Comparative and Superlative Forms of Adverbs?

Recall in the last chapter that we can show various degrees of the descriptive qualities of adjectives:

hot plate (positive)   difficult task (positive)

hotter plate (comparative)   more difficult task (comparative)

hottest plate (superlative)   most difficult task (superlative)

Recall that to form the comparative, we either added the suffix *-er* to the adjective or preceded the adjective with the word *more*. For the superlative, we either added the suffix *-est* or preceded the adjective with the word *most*.

To decide which system to use for adjectives, we followed rules having to do with the number of syllables in the adjective. Very basically, one-syllable adjectives use *-er* and *-est;* some two-syllable adjectives use *-er* and *-est,* others use *more* and *most,* still others use either; three-syllable adjectives invariably use *more* and *most*.

> **How do we show various degrees of the descriptive qualities imparted by adverbs? Sometimes we add -er and -est, and sometimes we use *more* and *most*.**

Now, in our present study of adverbs, we confront the same issue: How do we show various degrees of the descriptive qualities imparted by adverbs? Answer? The same way. Sometimes we add *-er* and *-est,* and sometimes we use *more* and *most*.

The Syllable Rule

One-syllable adverbs use *-er* and *-est* to form comparatives and superlatives:

> Igor ran fast.
> Igor ran faster.
> Igor ran fastest.

The -*ly* Rule

Adverbs ending in *-ly* use *more* and *most* to form comparatives and superlatives:

> Igor spoke succinctly.
> Igor spoke more succinctly.
> Igor spoke most succinctly.

The Look-It-Up Rule

When in doubt, check the dictionary to find out, first, the proper form of the adverb and, second, its proper comparative and superlative forms.

The look-it-up rule requires some separate discussion. Before you try to form the correct comparative and superlative forms of an adverb, you must first figure out the correct form of the adverb. Which is it: You should write **clearer** or You should write **more clearly?**

At the North Grounds Exercise Center at the University of Virginia (where I used to go in a futile attempt to achieve some minimal level of physical fitness), one day I was checking the sign-up sheet for the exercise bikes. One student had written her name, but it was very hard to read. Another student had helpfully jotted down next to her name: *Write clearer.* So I helpfully jotted down next to the student's helpful advice: *"More clearly"* . . . *it's an adverb.* (We wordsmiths are real pains in the neck.) I later watched the helpful advisor when his turn on the exercise bike came. He went to scratch off his name, saw my helpful advice, and looked around and around, suspiciously.

Then I wondered whether I had given the correct "helpful advice." Having broken no sweat, I skipped the shower and hightailed it to the law library for a quick and stealthy glimpse at the dictionary. There I found that the word *clear* has both adjectival and adverbial definitions. Following the *adv.* designation, I found *"-er, -est,"* which shows the comparative and superlative forms of the adverb *clear.* Among the 74 definitions of *clear,* I found 3 for the adverbial version of *clear.* The first of these defines the adverb *clear* as *in a clear or distinct manner, clearly.*

Then, in the same dictionary, I found a separate entry for *clearly,* which labels the word as an adverb. The absence of *-er, -est* following this entry informed me that the comparative and superlative forms are *more clearly* and *most clearly.*

Thus, **write clearer** is correct, because *clear* is an adverb and adding *-er* will form the comparative form. And **write more clearly** is also correct, because *clearly* is an adverb and requires *more* to form the comparative. Personally, I would opt for **more clearly,** because those in the know would agree with me.

And the next time I hit the exercise bike, I'll try to remember to take along my unabridged.

ACTING LIKE ADVERBS: PHRASES AND CLAUSES

SHOUTING time. Wake up! Again, learning this concept about chunks of words that act as nouns, adjectives, and now adverbs is crucial to your future as a writer.

So here it is again, the key concept: Other chunks of words, words that are not adverbs in and of themselves, will act as adverbs in your sentences, that is, they will perform the function of an adverb, which is to describe a verb, adjective, or other adverb. I will introduce the primary chunks of words here, using terms we have yet to discuss in much detail. Just remember, the eight parts of speech are highly interrelated, so talking about adverbs, for example, often requires talking about prepositions and other parts of speech.

> **There are two main types of word chunks, clauses and phrases. A clause is a bunch of words with a conjugated verb in it. A phrase is a bunch of words without a conjugated verb in it.**

Also, keep this in mind: There are two main types of word chunks, clauses and phrases. A clause is a bunch of words with a conjugated verb in it. A phrase is a bunch of words without a conjugated verb in it.

A variety of phrases in our language can serve the role of adverbs. If you diagramed sentences in your youth, you'll no doubt recall putting the phrases *under* the words they modified. Here's a list of the most prevalent phrases that act as adverbs, along with examples. Note that the phrase can appear in a variety of places in the sentence. Note also that the adverb sometimes modifies the larger thought anchored by the verb. In the examples, the ***adverbial phrase*** appears in bold italics, the **verb or larger thought** in bold underline.

Phrase Acting As an Adverb	Example
1. prepositional phrase	John **ran** ***down the street***.
	In the morning, John **ran** a mile.
2. present participial phrase (*-ing* phrase)	A man **does weird things** ***facing death.***
3. infinitive phrase (*to* phrase)	He **was talking** ***to hear himself talk***. (Mark Twain)
	To achieve her goal, the student **studied daily**.

Clauses also act adverbially. A dependent clause might show *when, where, why, how,* or *under what circumstance* a verbal activity takes place. These dependent clauses begin with *subordinating conjunctions* such as *after, although, as, as if, as long as, as though, because, before, how, if, in order that, provided that, since, so (that), that, though, till, unless, until, what, whatever, when, whenever, where, wherever,* and *while.* Don't panic. If you don't know about subordinating conjunctions now, you will soon, for we discuss them in chapter 6, "Conjunctions: Words That Join."

Here are some examples. Note that the dependent adverbial clause can come before or after the main clause. Again, the **adverbial clause** appears in bold italics, the **verb or larger thought** in bold underline.

Clause Acting As Adverb	Example
1. dependent clause at the end	You **will not write** a good novel *unless you possess a sense of reality* . . . (Henry James)
2. dependent clause at the beginning	*Because the civilization of ancient Rome perished in consequence of the invasion of the barbarians,* we **are perhaps too apt to think** that civilization cannot perish in any other manner. (Alexis de Tocqueville)
3. dependent clause in the middle	His mother, *though he never really said so,* **found it difficult to understand him.**

Try It Out

It's time to test your newly found knowledge. Using the same passage from the *New York Times* we analyzed in the last chapter, underline all adverbs and circle the words they modify. Include single-word adverbs, phrases, and clauses.

The following appears from the March 11, 2001, edition of the *New York Times,* p. B1:

Daniel Barenboim is a storyteller, not a poet. He is a storyteller because the pieces he conducts have a dramatic motion; they are always emphatically going somewhere. But he is not a poet because he doesn't stop to bring details into a sharper focus: a phrase, the nuance of a single tone, the kind of perfection that can make an audience hold its breath.

Answer to Exercise

The **adverbs** appear in bold, the **word or words modified** in bold underline.

Daniel Barenboim **is** a storyteller, **not** a poet. He **is a storyteller because the pieces he conducts have a dramatic motion**; they **are** always emphatically **going** somewhere. But he **is not** a poet **because he doesn't stop to bring details into a sharper focus**: a phrase, the nuance of a single tone, the kind of perfection that can make an audience hold its breath.

Some of the clauses have verbal phrases in them, which in turn are modified by other adverbial phrases, so perhaps a table will more accurately show the adverbs and the words they modify.

Also, notice the two *not*s. One hides in the contraction *doesn't*. The word *not* is an adverb. You might have missed these two. I did when I first concocted the exercise.

Adverb, Phrase, or Clause	Words Modified
not	is
because the pieces he conducts have a dramatic motion	is a storyteller
always	are going
emphatically	are going
somewhere	are going
not	is
because he doesn't stop	is not a poet
to bring details	doesn't stop
does stop	not (in the contraction *doesn't*)
into sharper focus	to bring details

ADVERBS: A SUMMARY

In this chapter we met the last of the working words, the adverb. We've visited the noun, the verb, the adjective, and now the adverb. In this chapter, we learned that adverbs come in a variety of sizes: one-word adverbs, multiword phrases, and multiword clauses. We saw that adverbs modify not only verbs but adjectives, other adverbs, and entire sentences. We learned that most adverbs that are derived from adjectives form themselves with an *-ly* ending: *easy* (adjective) and *easily* (adverb). We also learned that some adjectives have identical adjective and adverb forms: *fast* (adjective) and *fast* (adverb), *clear* (adjective) and *clear* (adverb).

> **Adverbs are remarkably versatile. Not only do they modify verbs, adjectives, and adverbs, but they can modify entire clauses. Furthermore, when we decide where to put them in sentences, we find that they can move all over the place.**

Adverbs are remarkably versatile. Not only do they modify verbs, adjectives, and adverbs, but they can modify entire clauses. Furthermore, when we decide where to put them in sentences, we find that they can move all over the place.

In multiword verb forms, some conventions guide us in properly placing the adverb. We usually put the adverb between a helping verb and its main verb, contrary to ill-informed conventional wisdom.

Adverbs follow the same rules as adjectives when they form their comparative and superlative forms. We use *-er* or *more* for the comparative and *-est* or *most* for the superlative. The number of syllables usually dictates the choice, with the *-ly* adverbs requiring *more* and *most*.

Finally, phrases and clauses can enter our sentences and act as adverbs. The prepositional, present participial, and infinitive phrases can act adverbially. Dependent clauses do as well. Because adverbial structures are moveable, we can shift them around in the sentence to achieve a particular style or point of emphasis.

That completes the working words. Let's move on to the glue words: pronouns, conjunctions, and prepositions.

NOTES

1. *New Fowler,* p. 702.
2. *New Fowler,* p. 702.
3. *Garner Legal,* p. 409.
4. *Garner Oxford,* p. 172.
5. *Follett,* p. 18.

5

Pronouns:

Words Substituting for Words

Back at the dawn of grammatical time, one of our ancestors got tired of grunting out sentences like this:

> Igor ran quickly over to Igor's cave and took the moose Igor had slain with Igor's spear to Igor's wife.

The early tribes convened an emergency session of the Grammar Committee—Miss Hamrick presiding—and promptly invented pronouns so that they could say things a bit more smoothly:

> Igor ran quickly over to **his** cave and took the moose **he** had slain with **his** spear to **his** wife.

To make certain all schoolchildren could have yet another definition to memorize for English class, the Grammar Committee prescribed:

A pronoun is a word that takes the place of a noun (or noun phrase or clause).

As our discussion unfolds, we'll see that pronouns do quite a bit more than elbow nouns out of the way. But that's the standard definition we all learned in those gone-forever days of our youth.

PRONOUNS: SEVEN DIFFERENT VARIETIES

The first pronouns our forebears invented were the (1) *personal pronouns,* words that could substitute for *Igor, Amber,* and other members of the tribe. Then they invented (2) *reflexive and intensive pronouns,* those *-self* words enabling them to say, *Me, **Myself,** and I.* They went even further and devised other types of pronouns, which, as a student of grammar, you must, of course, master: (3) *indefinite pronouns* (like *everyone, everybody, anyone, one, none,* and others), (4) *demonstrative pronouns (this, that, these,* and *those),* (5) *relative pronouns (that, which, who, whom,* and *whose),* (6) *interrogative pronouns (who, whose, whom, which,* and *what),* and (7) *reciprocal pronouns (each other* and *one another).*

It's quite a list. It'll be quite a chapter. So in winter build a fire, in summer crack a beer, or fix some tea, and curl up with this Gothic romance that bares Igor and Amber's lust for lucid language. Intrigue awaits, for pronouns are fraught with danger, as many smart people get hopelessly entangled—invariably at cocktail parties—in trying to figure out the proper *case* of pronouns. I have cleverly revealed this universal problem in the title of this book: *A Grammar Book for You and I . . . Oops, Me!*

So, once and for all, let's straighten out the problems. Then you'll be able to breeze right through those sentences laying those *who-whom* traps that inevitably ensnare you just when you're trying to say something important to impress somebody.

Here's where we're going. We have seven stops to make: (1) personal pronouns, (2) reflexive and intensive pronouns, (3) indefinite pronouns, (4) demonstrative pronouns, (5) relative pronouns, (6) interrogative pronouns, and (7) reciprocal pronouns.

> **Intrigue awaits, for pronouns are fraught with danger, as many smart people get hopelessly entangled—invariably at cocktail parties—in trying to figure out the proper case of pronouns. Listen to them stumble over *who* and *whom*.**

1. PERSONAL PRONOUNS

Let's start with the personal pronouns, those that take the place of people or other living or once-living beings. Personal pronouns can refer to *Igor, Amber,* or *Amber's pet turtle.* We've already met some of the personal pronouns, for we used them to help us make it through verb conjugation: **I** write, **You** write, **He** or **She** writes.

Personal pronouns create four major pitfalls, obstacles all aspiring grammarians must learn to negotiate with ease: (1) *person,* (2) *number,* (3) *case,* and (4) *gender.* Let's look at each in turn, starting with the easiest.

Person: First, Second, and Third

Amber, Igor, and Miss Hamrick realized a long time ago that people mostly talk about only one thing—other people. That is, they gossip. They recognized, therefore, a universal truth: Only three people exist on earth.

> **The speaker became known as *first person;* the listener, as *second person;* the unfortunate soul whose reputation was being shredded, as *third person.***

When ordinary human discourse took place—when gossip was whispered in Amber and Igor's cave—we had only three players: (1) the speaker, (2) the listener, and (3) the unfortunate soul whose reputation was about to be skewered. The speaker became known as *first person;* the listener, as *second person;* and the, uh, skeweree, as *third person.* The tables below show the various personal pronouns, in first, second, and third persons.

As the system of personal pronouns became widely used, especially in Igor's cave, we began to hear all three persons appear . . . not in Igor's sweet nothin's but in his entreaties: *I'm telling you, my dear, that she forced me to do it.*

Number: Singular and Plural

When the Pronoun Committee met in Amber and Igor's cave, it realized another universal truth: Often there would be more than one speaker, more than one listener, and more than one unfortunate soul being talked about. So in addition to singular pronouns, the esteemed committee devised plural pronouns. The string of pronouns for the singular first person *I/me/my/mine* was joined by its plural counterpart *we/us/our/ours.* The singular second person *you/you/your/yours* gained its plural *you/you/ your/yours* (which turned out to be identical, but only if one ignores the southern *y'all/y'all/y'all's/y'alls* or the northern *youse/youse/youse's/youses*). And the singular third person *he-she-it/him-her-it/his-his, her-hers, its-its* received its plural *they/them/their-theirs.*

Is this getting hard to follow? Not to worry. The tables below will help.

Case: Subjective, Objective, Possessive

Remember the chapter on nouns? Remember those nuggets of information we tucked away for the future? Remember those paragraphs mentioning the *case of pronouns?* Well, the future is now.

Back in Amber and Igor's cave when the Pronoun Committee was devising its system of pronouns, it was visited by the Noun Committee. The Noun Committee pointed out that nouns have various functions to perform in sentences. Nouns act as subjects and subject complements, the Noun Committee pointed out. They act as objects. And they can possess stuff, a condition we show with possessive endings. Therefore, the Noun Committee preached, the pronouns you devise must reflect these different usages of nouns.

> **(1) Pronouns in the *subjective case* would replace nouns used as subjects and subject complements, (2) pronouns in the *objective case* would replace nouns used as objects of prepositions and objects of verbs, and (3) pronouns in the *possessive case* would replace nouns appearing with possessive endings.**

The Pronoun Committee responded by devising different forms of pronouns, forms that would reflect the function served by the noun being replaced. So the Pronoun Committee decided to develop three *cases:* (1) Pronouns in the *subjective case* would replace nouns used as subjects and subject complements, (2) pronouns in the *objective case* would replace nouns used as objects of prepositions and objects of verbs, and (3) pronouns in the *possessive case* would replace nouns appearing with possessive endings. All appear in the tables below.

Before putting all this together, let's visit the final pitfall of personal pronouns: *gender.*

Gender: Masculine and Feminine

Our forebears on the Pronoun Committee had a sinister goal in mind: to wreak havoc on people in the late 1900s and early 2000s. They invented one set of pronouns for men and another set for women, for they knew that one day we'd confront the problem of sexism in the written and spoken word and end up stumbling all over ourselves with *she/he, her/his,* and *her/him* (and, to be fair, *he/she, his/her,* and *him/her*). Thus, just to be a bunch of old meanies, the Pronoun Committee created the grammatical concept of *gender.*

Other languages have special endings to show whether nouns, pronouns, or adjectives reveal a masculine, feminine, or neuter entity. Fortunately, in English, the grammatical concept of gender shows up mostly in third-person singular pronouns.[1] And there it causes a great deal of trouble—clearly foreseen by the heartless Pronoun Committee. We'll get to the problem a bit later.

Back in Amber and Igor's cave, it didn't take long for the Pronoun Committee to realize that living things consisted of males and females. They figured that the personal pronoun replacing a noun denoting people or other living (or previously living) things should reveal whether that noun is male or female. They also realized that most nouns simply name things or ideas, which don't have any sexual identity. So they decided to break the world down into three groups: masculine, feminine, and neuter. (Actually, some of the other Pronoun Committees meeting in various countries of the world devised as many as 20 grammatical genders, but most languages settled on three.)

> **They invented one set of pronouns for men and another set for women, for they knew that one day we'd confront the problem of sexism in the written and spoken word and end up stumbling all over ourselves with *she/he, her/his,* and *her/him,* and, to be fair, *he/she, his/her,* and *him/her.***

So for third-person singular pronouns, the Pronoun Committee decided that *he/him/his/his* would reveal the gender of masculine nouns, *she/her/her/hers* would reveal the gender of feminine nouns, and *it/it/its/its* would take care of all nouns in the neuter category.

Now let's put it all together. The first table below shows singular personal pronouns; the second, plural personal pronouns.

SINGULAR PERSONAL PRONOUNS

Person	Subjective Case	Objective Case	Possessive Case
First person	I	me	my/mine
Second person	you	you	your/yours
Third person	he (masculine)	him (masculine)	his/his (masculine)
	she (feminine)	her (feminine)	her/hers (feminine)
	it (neuter)	it (neuter)	its/its (neuter)

PLURAL PERSONAL PRONOUNS

Person	Subjective Case	Objective Case	Possessive Case
First Person	we	us	our/ours
Second Person	you	you	your/yours
Third Person	they	them	their/theirs

As you study the tables above, a question should form in your mind. Why does the possessive case have two forms? What's this *our/ours, my/mine* bit?

A pronoun in the possessive case can appear in two different ways in a sentence. Like the possessive noun, it can appear right before the word it modifies. Thus: **Susan's** house is on the corner. Here the possessive noun *Susan's* stands in the attributive position. We can say the same thing by using the third-person, possessive, feminine pronoun like this: **Her** house is on the corner. Here the possessive pronoun *her* also stands in the attributive position.

But we might have stated our sentence this way: **The house on the corner is Susan's.** Here the possessive noun stands in the predicative position; it is linked to the word it modifies *(house)* by a linking verb *(is)*. Recognizing this little twist, the Pronoun Committee came up with a predicative form of the possessive pronoun enabling us to say the same thing: **The house on the corner is hers.**

Thus:

> This is **my** house.
> This house is **mine.**
>
> This is **our** office.
> This office is **ours.**
>
> This is **your** car.
> This car is **yours.**

Botching *Your* and *Its*

I would be remiss in my duties as an early twenty-first-century reincarnation of Miss Hamrick if I did not pause and talk a bit about serious problems many people have with two words: *your* and *its.* Let's take *your* first.

For some reason, many people think that *your* means *you are.* Thus, on Internet chat boards, you'll see grotesque mistakes like this: *Your crazy. Your a moron. Your going to lose big time.* The word *your* is the second-person possessive pronoun. It must always precede a noun. It is not the combined subject-verb *you are.* It is not some weird contraction having no apostrophe. If the writer wishes to use a contraction for *you are,* the correct form is *you're.* I deal with this problem separately in chapter 21.

Even more people have trouble with *its.* Singular nouns form their possessives with an "apostrophe -*s.*" Plural nouns ending in -*s* form their possessives by adding just an apostrophe. Not a single personal pronoun forms its possessive with an apostrophe (some indefinite pronouns do, however, e.g., *other's*). Instead, for the third-person, singular, neuter pronoun *it,* we simply add -*s* to form the possessive. Thus, the possessive of *it* is *its:* The committee reached **its** decision. The novel finally revealed **its** plot.

> **People make horrible mistakes when trying to use the correct case of pronouns. You'll find a separate discussion in chapter 22.**

The word *it's* is a contraction of *it is:* **It's** a shame he couldn't join us. **It's** raining outside. You'll find a more detailed discussion of this problem in chapter 27.

In sum, neither *your* nor *its* can possibly act as a subject and verb. Both are possessive pronouns. By the same token *it's* cannot act as the possessive form of *it*. Instead the term *it's* acts as a subject-verb, for it serves as a contraction for the subject-verb pair *it is*.

Antecedents: Placement of Pronouns

When you use a pronoun, it will typically refer to a word somewhere close by. That is, the noun the pronoun replaces sits somewhere in the vicinity. This noun is called the *antecedent*. The prefix *ante* (meaning *before*) might make you think that the word the pronoun refers to necessarily comes before the pronoun. But it doesn't. True, a pronoun looks backward to its antecedent, but it can also look ahead to a referent placed later in the sentence.

> **No rule states that a pronoun must refer to the immediately preceding noun.**

The backward-looking pronouns are called *anaphoric;* the forward-looking ones, *cataphoric.* Thus, a cataphoric (forward-looking) pronoun would find its referent coming later in the sentence: After **his** discovery of New Zealand, **Captain Cook** went on to discover several Pacific islands.[2]

Unfortunately, many writers do not know they may use forward-looking pronouns and thus rob themselves of an interesting variation in their styles.

Furthermore, many writers develop very awkward styles because they have heard that pronouns must always refer to the most recent noun in the sentence. Nothing could be further from the truth. Read and learn from Mr. Burchfield, the editor of *New Fowler*. He states the rule on placing pronouns:

> It is clearly desirable that an anaphoric or cataphoric pronoun should be placed as near as the construction allows to the noun or noun phrase to which it refers, and in such a manner that there is no risk of ambiguity.[3]

No rule states that a pronoun must refer to the immediately preceding noun. Indeed, Mr. Burchfield's sentence itself confirms that the pronoun need not refer to the immediately preceding noun. Look at the **antecedent** (bold type) and all the **other nouns** (bold underlined type) coming between it and the ***ensuing pronoun*** (bold italic type):

> It is clearly desirable that an anaphoric or cataphoric **pronoun** (antecedent) should be placed as near as the **construction** (intervening noun) allows to the **noun** (intervening noun) or **noun phrase** (intervening noun) to which *it* (pronoun) refers, and in such a manner that there is no risk of ambiguity.

The antecedent to the word *it* is the word *pronoun,* yet three singular nouns come in between: *construction, noun,* and *noun phrase.* But the reader knows that *it* refers to the word *pronoun.*

Thus, the rule governing placement emphasizes the avoidance of ambiguity. No one can think that the statement *to which **it** refers* points to the three nouns (1) *construction,* (2) *noun,* or (3) *noun phrase.* The word *it* can only refer to the word *pronoun.*

Clarity reigns, and the reader is satisfied.

Antecedents: Agreement in Number and Gender

You must use a plural pronoun to refer to a plural noun, a singular pronoun to refer to a singular noun. This rule is called *agreement in number.* Thus: **The young women pursued their career goals.** That's easy, and few people make the mistake of using a singular pronoun to refer to a plural antecedent. Few if any people would write, **The young women pursued her career goals,** at least not any people I know.

But a lot of people I know do make the opposite mistake. They use a *plural* pronoun to refer to a *singular* antecedent. Fact is, almost everybody makes this mistake. As a matter of fact, you, dear reader, make this mistake. You might deny it vehemently, but I would wager any amount that you make this mistake at least several times each day. As a matter of fact, so many people use *they/their/them* to refer back to singular antecedents that the usage will one day be regarded as correct. I don't think we're there just yet, at least not when we use written words.

We are there in speech, however. After all, if an editor of an internationally known publishing company uses *they* to refer back to *person,* we can probably predict where the language is going:

> What is happening is that the younger the **person,** the more likely **they** are to turn to an online place for reference.[4]

Why do people use plural pronouns to refer back to a generic, singular antecedent?

Sexism.

What's that got to do with it?

Everything.

When Amber, Igor, and Miss Hamrick developed our language, they dreamed up another rule: Pronouns must agree with the gender of the nouns they replace or refer to. A pronoun referring to a woman or girl must be the feminine pronoun, and a pronoun referring to a man or boy must be the masculine pronoun.

Of course, there's no problem when you know the sex of the person being referred to. But what about referring to a *type* of person? How could Igor refer to, say, a member of another tribe, who might be male or female? Igor faced a dilemma.

We know how he solved it. Igor is perhaps the quintessential male chauvinist pig in all of human history. After all, he appointed himself Chairman (that's the way he'd say it) of the Grammar Committee. When he devised the language, he made certain that masculine pronouns were the superior forms of speech. Thus, if Igor referred to a type of person, say a generic member of another tribe, invariably he would refer to that member with a masculine pronoun, even if the member could just as easily have been a woman.

> **Igor is perhaps the quintessential male chauvinist pig in all of human history. After all, he appointed himself Chairman (that's the way he'd say it) of the Grammar Committee. When he devised the language, he made certain that masculine pronouns were the superior forms of speech.**

Thus, Igor would say, When we meet a **member** of that other tribe, let's give **him** a party. He certainly would not make a grammatical mistake and use the plural pronoun *them* to refer to the singular word *member*.

But that's what you do. That's what everybody does. These days, most people would say, When we meet a neighbor from that new development, let's give **them** a party. Or ... let's give **'em** a party.

Why do we say that? Because we don't want to be like Igor and just use *he* all the time. We want to avoid that cumbersome *he/she, his/her, him/her* or that tongue-twisting *he or she, his or her, him or her,* and so on. So we settle for:

> When a **policy holder** comes to me for service, I want to make sure **they** get the personal attention **they** deserve. —State Farm Insurance TV Advertisement

Policy holder is singular. *They* is plural. Under traditional rules of grammar, the two don't match.

Everybody makes this mistake.

Textbooks and institutions of higher learning take various approaches to this problem. In the olden days, books routinely used the masculine to refer to singular, generic antecedents:

> In many cases a mere **possessor** of land may be treated as if **he** were the owner for the purpose of awarding a particular form of legal or equitable relief.[5]

Others took an inclusive approach and used both:

> In a competency proceeding, a judge is asked to appoint a conservator to manage the property of a **person** who is no longer competent to manage it for **him or herself.** [This should probably read himself or herself. Or perhaps him- or herself.][6]

Still others took the inclusive approach to ridiculous extremes. A colleague of mine served on the law review of a major law school. The editor in chief instructed him and all other editors to change manuscripts of submitted articles to remove any vestiges of sexism. The solution? If a paragraph has a singular, generic antecedent, use the masculine. Then in the next paragraph having a singular, generic antecedent, switch to the feminine. Then to the masculine. Then to the feminine. This is a most unsat-

> **Problem solved: Make your antecedent plural. Refer to *people*, not *a person*. Refer to *readers*, not *a reader*. Talk about *neighbors*, not *a neighbor*. Then you can use *they*, *their/theirs*, *them*, and *themselves*.**

isfactory experience for the reader, I would imagine, despite the fairness achieved: *She* gets used to one pronoun, and then the writer switches on *him*.

In case you don't think people really do that, learn from the experience of Erik Wensberg, editor of Wilson Follett's *Modern American Usage*. He quotes an example of this back-and-forth approach:

> Likewise distracting is a writer who tells us how to be courteous to the blind: Speak when you enter a blind person's room. . . . Only then take **her** hand if **she** offers it to you. Let **her** know if you are leaving. . . . When showing a blind person to a chair, place **his** hand on the back. **He** will seat **himself**. . . . When changing a blind person's money, let **her** know what each bill is.[7]

And some texts now use the best solution of all. When generalizing, they make antecedents plural. They can then use third-person plural pronouns, which do not reveal gender:

> **Veterinarians** are encouraged to modify and adapt the sample forms included here to fit **their** needs.[8]

That's the solution I use. I try to refer to *people* instead of *a person;* to *readers,* not *a reader.* I'll talk about *neighbors,* not *a neighbor.* Then I can use *they, their/theirs, them,* and *themselves.* Problem solved.

Other tricks can help you avoid the problem:

1. When you need a possessive pronoun, don't write *his or her.* Instead, use an article so that the need for a pronoun goes away:

   > The writer should submit **his** manuscript.

   > The writer should submit **the** manuscript.

2. Just delete the phrase containing the pronoun. You might not need it:

   > When a doctor reviews the reports delivered **to him** each day . . .

   > When a doctor reviews the reports delivered each day . . .

3. Repeat the noun, if the two don't appear too close together:

> An applicant must complete the application form and include a complete employment history. **He or she** must also include ...

> An applicant must complete the application form and include a complete employment history. **The applicant** must also include ...

4. When writing instructions, use the second-person *you*.

> An applicant must complete the application form and include a complete employment history. **He or she** must also include ...

> You must complete the application form and include a complete employment history. **You** must also include ...

5. Try redesigning the sentence and use the relative pronoun *who:*

> If an applicant wants to obtain an interview, **he or she** must check the appropriate box on the application form.

> An applicant **who** wants to obtain an interview must check the appropriate box on the application form.

6. As mentioned above, make your antecedents plural:

> An applicant must complete the application form and include a complete employment history. **He or she** must also include ...

> Applicants must complete the application form and include a complete employment history. **They** must also include ...

But if you must refer to a singular, generic type of person, please avoid those language-destroying structures no one wants to read or say: *he/she, him/her, his/her,* or worse *(s)he.* Instead, use the masculine and stick with it. Or use the feminine and stick with it. Or, in rare cases, use the disjunctive *he or she.* Or, if you want to be ahead of the curve, go ahead and make the "mistake": use *they/their/them* to refer to a singular antecedent. If an editor of an internationally known publishing company can get away with it, so can you. At least in speech. In your master's thesis, however, follow traditional rules on agreement in number.

Two more points: First, the same problems of agreement in number and agreement in gender arise with the use of indefinite pronouns (*everybody, everyone,* etc.)—a topic covered below. Second, if the antecedent is a collective or group noun (*team, group, band, family,* etc.), you should use the singular pronoun *it* or *its* when the collective acts as a unit. Thus:

> The **band** practiced **its** marching technique.
> The **committee** reached **its** decision.
> When the **company** filed **its** complaint, **it** brought antitrust charges against Acme, Inc.

But (there's always a *but* when it comes to grammar) if the members of the group are acting individually, you should use the plural pronoun *they, their,* or *them.* Take a look at some examples Mr. Follett provides:

> The **family** discussed **their** differences all the time and wherever **they** went.
> One by one the **jury** wrote **their** votes on slips of paper. [9]

We'll return to the problem of gender and number when we discuss the indefinite pronouns below. But that takes care of the personal pronouns, so let's move on to the others.

2. REFLEXIVE AND INTENSIVE PRONOUNS

These are the reflexive *-self* pronouns, and we use them in the objective function to handle situations where the subject and the object of the sentence are the same person. Repeat after me:

> We use the reflexive *-self* pronouns *in the objective function* when the subject and object of the sentence are the same.

Also, these reflexive pronouns will immediately follow a verb or a preposition. *You* might repeat that to *yourself* 10 times or so.

Suppose Amber inflicted some injury on Amber; the subject (Amber) and the object (Amber) are the same. If I say, Amber hurt **her** or She hurt **her,** you have no clue about whether Amber hurt Amber or Amber hurt somebody else. To solve this problem, Amber, Igor, and Miss Hamrick developed the reflexive pronoun so that action could reflect back on the actor.

REFLEXIVE AND INTENSIVE PRONOUNS

Person	Singular	Plural
First	myself	ourselves
Second	yourself	yourselves
Third	himself herself itself	themselves

Thus, study these examples where the subject and object refer to the same person or people:

> **Amber** hurt **herself.**
> **We** gave **ourselves** a party.
> Do **yourself** a favor. (The implied subject is *you.*)

As mentioned above, the reflexive *-self* pronoun should follow either the verb or a preposition:

> **He** punished **himself** for his stupidity. (Follows the verb *punished.*)
> **She** gave a present to **herself.** (Follows the preposition *to.*)

Remember two things: (1) Use the *-self* pronoun only when the subject of the sentence and an object in the sentence are one and the same, and (2) never use a *-self* pronoun as a subject, only as an object.

The reflexive *-self* pronoun should not be used unless the person referred to and the subject are one and the same. When two people are involved so that the subject and object are not the same, in formal settings it's incorrect to use the reflexive pronoun and say:

| **Wrong:** | He hurt **myself.** |
| **Right:** | He hurt **me.** |

| **Wrong:** | The opponent sent the report to Fred and **myself.** |
| **Right:** | The opponent sent the report to Fred and **me.** |

| **Wrong:** | Please research this issue for Jane and **myself.** |
| **Right:** | Please research this issue for Jane and **me.** |

The reflexive pronouns should always serve as objects, never as subjects. In formal settings, it is a grammatical mistake to use a reflexive pronoun as the subject of a sentence:

| **Wrong:** | The committee and **myself** will decide this issue. |
| **Right:** | The committee and **I** will decide this issue. |

So remember two things: (1) Use the -*self* pronoun only when the subject of the sentence and an object in the sentence are one and the same, and (2) never use a -*self* pronoun as a subject, only as an object:

| **Wrong:** | Jane and **myself** enjoyed the dinner at your house. |
| **Right:** | Jane and **I** enjoyed the dinner at your house. |

Finally, these pronouns also serve as *intensives,* structures enabling us to emphasize. We use them to repeat the noun referred to. In formal style, we put the -*self* word directly after the noun. In less formal settings, we can move it to the end of the clause:

| **Formal:** | I **myself** finished the report. |
| | The judge **herself** wrote the majority opinion. |

| **Informal:** | I finished the report **myself.** |
| | The judge wrote the majority opinion **herself.** |

3. INDEFINITE PRONOUNS

Oodles of indefinite pronouns enable us to refer to any one, any two, several, or all of a group or class of persons or things or ideas. As shown in the list below, some of the pronouns have possessive forms. Unlike the personal pronouns, the indefinite pronouns form their possessives by adding "apostrophe -s." Only one has a plural form *(others)*.

Indefinite Pronouns

all	everybody ('s)	none
another ('s)	everyone ('s)	nothing
any	everything	one ('s)
anybody ('s)	few	other ('s)
anyone ('s)	many	others (others')
anything	most	several
both	much	some
each	neither ('s)	somebody ('s)
each one ('s)	no one ('s)	something
either ('s)	nobody ('s)	such

Any of these words can act as a subject, complement, or object. So distinctions in case exist only in the possessive, shown by the possessive ending.

In formal settings, all these words ending in *-one* or *-body* are singular. You should therefore use singular verbs. And, in formal settings, when referring back to them, you should use singular pronouns:

Formal

Wrong: **Everybody** is entitled to **their** own opinion. (One day, even highly literate Americans will regard this usage as correct.)

Right: **Everybody** is entitled to **his** own opinion. (But watch out for charges of sexism.)
   Everybody is entitled to **her** own opinion. (Ditto.)
   Everybody is entitled to **his or her** own opinion. (A tongue twister.)

Informal

Right: **Everybody** is entitled to **their** own opinion. (This usage will one day prevail.)

We could go on at some length debating the use of the plural pronouns *they/their/them* to refer to the distinctly singular *everybody* or other indefinite pronouns. Those who wish to pursue the issue should read Mr. Follett's *Modern American Usage,* 31–33 (rev. ed. 1998) and Mr. Garner's *Oxford Dictionary of American Usage and Style,* 300–303 (2000). Mr. Follett wishes to retain the traditional approach of using the figurative (and singular) *he/him/his* to refer to indefinite pronouns (and any other singular generic antecedent). But it's a debate Mr. Follett is not likely to win, for he identifies some formidable opposition:

> The *Random House Handbook* [recommends] that a student writing an essay substitute *she* for the figurative *he* throughout; the reader "will become quickly adjusted to the change," the authors assert. The *Harbrace College Handbook* adds that the writer avoiding the figurative *he* can change a sentence from the active to the passive voice; but the authors immediately warn that statements in the passive tend to be wordy and weak.

Mr. Follett then tries out the passive-voice solution on one of his test sentences showing the problems of referring back to indefinite pronouns:

Anyone driving tonight had better keep **his** eyes on the road.

The passive voice yields:

Eyes had better be kept on the road by anyone driving tonight.

Yuck.

Making the antecedent plural and abandoning the singular indefinite pronoun *anyone* solves the problem:

Any people driving tonight had better keep **their** eyes on the road.

In informal settings, breaking the old rule also works:

Anyone driving tonight had better keep **their** eyes on the road.

In the future, it will likely be regarded as correct to use third-person plural pronouns *they/their/them* to refer back to singular indefinite pronouns. In fact, the trend shows that *they/their/them* will correctly refer back not only to singular indefinite pronouns but also to any generic singular antecedent noun. This might send chills up and down the spines of the purists, but no amount of protest will hold back this trend. In the words of Mr. Garner:

> Speakers of American English resist this development more than speakers of British English, in which the indeterminate *they* is already more or less standard. That it sets many literate Americans' teeth on edge is an unfortunate setback to what promises to be the ultimate solution to the problem.[10]

None: *Singular or Plural?*

The indefinite pronoun *none* requires some separate discussion. A myth has emerged that *none* always requires a singular verb. Not true. The word *none* can take the singular or the plural. In the words of *New Fowler:*

> It is a mistake to suppose that the pronoun *[none]* is singular only and must at all costs be followed by singular verbs or pronouns. . . . At all times since the reign of King Alfred the choice of plural or singular . . . has been governed by the surrounding words or by the notional sense.[11]

You'll produce the more emphatic statement by using the singular. Look at this example of the singular by T. S. Eliot, which appears in *New Fowler:*

> . . . a fear which we cannot know, which we cannot face, which **none understands.**

The use of the singular *none* in that statement says *not a bloody one understands this terrible fear.* But compare this example of the plural from the *New Yorker,* which also appears in *New Fowler:*

> She also says that though she had many affairs, **none were** lighthearted romances.

In this statement, the writer wants a plural-like generality, stated succinctly by the plural word *romances*. Consider the ineffectiveness of the singular:

> She also says that though she had many affairs, **none was** a light-hearted romance.

Also, sometimes *none* logically requires a plural:

> **None** of the women **meet** after work.

A myth has emerged that *none* always requires a singular verb. Not so.

It takes at least two to meet, now doesn't it?

Each: *Singular or Plural?*
The pronoun *each* is always singular and takes a singular verb. Thus:

> **Each** of the golfers **wants** to win the PGA.
> **Each** of us **wishes** for success.

When the pronoun *each* is referred to by another pronoun, that other pronoun must appear in the singular. Thus:

> **Each** of the NFL players wants to increase **his** bonus.
> We must recognize that **each** has identified **his or her** own priorities.

Sometimes, however, the pronoun *each* acts in apposition to a plural subject. In that case, the verb must be plural, for the grammatical subject always determines the number of the verb:

> The **coach and** the **quarterback** <u>each</u> **want** to win the championship.

4. DEMONSTRATIVE PRONOUNS
We have four demonstrative pronouns in our language: *this* and *that* and their plurals *these* and *those*. When these words act as subjects or objects,

that is, when they replace a noun, they are called *demonstrative pronouns.* But they can also act as adjectives when they accompany a noun; they are then called *demonstrative adjectives.*

Let's see some examples of each use.

Demonstrative Pronouns
This is where he works.
That is a very bad idea.
These are the times that try men's souls.
Those were the days, my friends.

Demonstrative Adjectives
This issue has troubled us in the past.
That approach will fail.
These cases should resolve the controversy.
Those packages arrived late.

People often ask about the differences between *this* and *that,* and *these* and *those.* The words *this* and its plural *these* refer to people, objects, or ideas close in time or space, while *that* and its plural *those* refer to people, objects, or ideas more remote in time or space. For example:

That game last night was more exciting than **this** one tonight.

The close-in-space factor can measure the proximity of the referent in the writing itself. Thus, you might refer to **these** issues just discussed as compared with **those** issues mentioned in the introduction.

When you use demonstrative pronouns as subjects or objects, beware the problem of vagueness. Make certain the pronoun has an identifiable referent—either a noun or a specific idea. Too often writers ignore this rule. Read the following passage written by a federal court and figure out what *these* refers to:

Officials at [border] checkpoints ... have been granted increasingly intrusive power in connection with the search of vehicles at these checkpoints, without any requirement of probable cause. *These* include the power to stop and question occupants about aliens and to search in automobile cavities that could conceal aliens. [12]

We can, of course, figure out that the plural *these* was meant to refer to the singular *power*. But the lack of care momentarily threw us off base.

Also beware the writing instructor who says that a demonstrative pronoun, when used as a subject or object, must always be accompanied by a noun. The advice is not only wrong but definitionally impossible: How can a demonstrative pronoun be accompanied by a noun? It can't. If it is, then it's no longer a pronoun but a demonstrative adjective.

> **All great writers use *this* or *that* or *these* or *those* as subjects. They simply make sure the word has an identifiable referent.**

All great writers use *this* or *that* or *these* or *those* as subjects. They simply make sure the word has an identifiable referent. Perhaps they use this test: When they use the word *this* as the subject of a sentence, they ask themselves, "This what?" If the answer readily comes to mind, the usage is sound. [13] The use of *this* as a subject works in this passage by an esteemed professor at Harvard Law School:

> In civilized society men must be able to assume that they may control, for purposes beneficial to themselves, what they have discovered and appropriated to their own use, what they have created by their own labor, and what they have acquired under the existing social and economic order. *This* is a jural postulate of civilized society as we know it. [14]

(Law professors love to talk about "jural postulates.") In the passage, the word *this* refers to the entire idea, *people can cash in on stuff they create*. The reader immediately knows what the professor is referring to and does not have to rummage around in the preceding sentences in search of the word or idea he had in mind.

Now for some real fun, the relative pronouns: *that, which, who, whom,* and *whose.*

5. RELATIVE PRONOUNS

Amber, Igor, and Miss Hamrick must have had a bad night when they concocted relative pronouns. Or perhaps they intentionally devised a system that would stump even the smartest writers. Actually, truth be known, the system is quite ingenious. You just need to understand it. When you do, you'll never make a mistake again.

Smart people get confused over relative pronouns. They use *which* when it feels good and *that* when it sounds right, and totally come apart when trying to sort out *who/whom/whose*.

Let's see if we can set things straight on the proper use of *that, which, who, whom,* and *whose.*

These five words share three characteristics: (1) They introduce a dependent adjectival clause, (2) they serve a grammatical function in that clause, and (3) they refer to a particular noun in the main sentence. Take a look:

The fund **that you identified** soared in value.

The relative pronoun *that* (1) introduces the dependent clause **that you identified,** (2) serves as the object of *identified,* and (3) refers to the noun *fund* in the main sentence. The entire clause **that you identified** is an adjectival clause modifying *fund.*

Let's look at another:

The fund **that soared in value** won the award.

Check out the three functions: The word *that* (1) introduces the dependent clause **that soared in value,** (2) acts as the subject of the clause, and (3) refers to the noun *fund* in the main sentence.

Note the differences in these two *that* clauses. The first (**that you** identified) has its own independent subject *you.* But the second (**that** soared in value) has no independent subject; instead the word *that* acts as the subject. We'll see the relevance of this distinction in chapter 14, "Word War IV, Clauses vs. Phrases."

The words *that* and *which* do not change their form depending on the function they serve in the sentence. The word *that* can act as an object or a subject, and its form stays the same. The same is true for *which*.[15]

Grammatical Function	Example
subject of clause	The book **that arrived** at the store sold out in one day.
subject of clause	This report, **which details** the problems, will explain all.
object of clause	The book **that I described** sold out in one day.
object of clause	This report, **which she wrote,** will explain all.

I must point out, however, that when a possessive form is called for by the sentence, the word *that* has to bow out and rely on *which* to borrow a preposition to show possession. An example will show what I mean:

Congress passed the statute, **the purpose of which** was to lower taxes.

The words *which* and *that* have no possessive form. Here the *of which* is showing the state of the statute's possessing a *purpose*. We cannot say, *that's purpose* or *which's purpose*. We have to use *which,* flip it over, and connect it to *statute* by using the *of which* form. The word *that* will not accommodate a preceding preposition.

Of course, if you write lots of reports crammed with *of whiches,* you won't further your career. So Miss Hamrick, Igor, and Amber made a deal with the personal relative pronouns. The *who/whom/whose* combo, with its possessive *whose,* agreed to allow *that* and *which* to borrow *whose* when they need to show possession. Thus, it is grammatically correct to write:

Congress passed the statute, **whose purpose** was to lower taxes.

Amber, Igor, and Miss Hamrick dreamed up *that* and *which* when they wanted to refer to inanimate objects and abstractions. But they also dreamed up a set of relative pronouns *(who, whom, whose)* to refer to people. These words exhibit the condition of *case,* which you've already mastered. The word *who* is the subjective case; *whom,* the objective; and *whose,* the possessive.

Choosing the correct word—usually choosing between *who* and *whom*—becomes a herculean task, especially at social functions when you're trying to impress people. So let's learn to get it right once and for all. The key lies in identifying the grammatical function served by the relative pronoun.

Who vs. Whom

Here's a trick that'll force you to use the correct word 100 percent of the time. Identify the subjectless clause. The what? The subjectless clause.

Remember the two clauses above? One clause (that **you** identified) has its own subject, the word *you.* But the other clause (**that** soared in value) has no independent subject. The word *that* must act as the subject. That's a subjectless clause.

In clauses referring to people, whenever you spot a subjectless clause—and you must do it in a nanosecond—the word *who* is always correct. Why? Because the clause needs a subject and the subject must appear in the subjective case *(who).* When you spot a clause that already has a subject, the word *whom* (or perhaps *whose)* will always be correct. Why? Because the clause likely needs an object and the object must appear in the objective case *(whom).* If the clause has both its subject and its object, then it might very well need the possessive case *(whose).*

Let's see the trick in action. Which of the following clauses are subjectless?

1. The child **who/whom** did the homework received the top grade.
2. The child **who/whom** the teacher selected had done the homework.
3. The child **who/whom** was chosen by the coach hit a home run.
4. The child **who/whom** the coach chose hit a home run.

Numbers 1 and 3 have no subjects and thus require *who*—the subjective case. Numbers 2 and 4 already have subjects and thus require *whom*—the objective case. Pay attention to the clauses and their **subjects** (bold underlined type), their **verbs** (bold italic type), and their **<u>objects</u>** (bold underlined italic type):

1. The child **<u>who</u>** **did** the **<u>homework</u>** received the top grade.
2. The child **<u>whom</u>** **<u>the teacher</u>** **selected** had done the homework.
3. The child **<u>who</u>** **was chosen** by the coach hit a home run.
4. The child **<u>whom</u>** **<u>the coach</u>** **chose** hit a home run.

When the verbs in the clauses (here, *did* and *was chosen*) have no subject, you must supply it with the word *who*—the subjective case. And when the verbs in the clauses (here, *selected* and *chose*) already have a subject, the verb then wants an object, which you supply with the word *whom*—the objective case.

> **Whenever you spot a subjectless clause—and you must do it in a nanosecond—the word *who* is always correct. And when you spot a clause that already has a subject, the word *whom* (or perhaps *whose*) will always be correct.**

The clauses having their subject-verb pair intact won't always beg for a direct object for the verb. The object you supply might well be an object of a preposition. But the subjectless-clause trick still works to determine the need for *who*. Note the **prepositional phrase** (bold type):

The child **to who/whom** **<u>the teacher</u>** **paid** the most **<u>attention</u>** tended to succeed.

Here the clause has its subject *teacher.* Indeed, the verb *paid* has its own direct object *attention.* The clause demands an object for the preposition *to.* Hence, you use the objective case *whom:*

The child **to whom** **<u>the teacher</u>** **paid** the most **<u>attention</u>** made good grades.

Parenthetically, please note that *whom* follows the preposition and opens the clause. Such is the formal construction. In informal settings, however, you may move the preposition to close the clause. And please don't let anyone tell you that you may not end a clause or a sentence with a preposition. A preposition is often a good word to end a sentence with. We'll discuss this myth in chapter 7.

Thus, in our sample sentence, in informal settings, you may write:

> The child **whom <u>the teacher</u> *paid*** the most *<u>attention</u>* **to** made good grades.

You'll use the possessive case *whose* in those clauses that have their subject and their verbal object already satisfied and don't need an object of a preposition. Thus:

> The child **who/whom/whose *<u>homework</u>* <u>the teacher</u> *graded*** first received an A.

Here the verb *graded* is satisfied; it has its subject *teacher* and its object *homework*. Thus, you must supply the possessive case *whose:*

> The child **whose *<u>homework</u>* <u>the teacher</u> *graded*** first received an A.

The Relatives: Mixing Them Up
We use *who-whom-whose* to refer to humans and *that-which* to refer to inanimate objects and abstractions. Thus:

> The woman **who became** CEO was admired by all.
> The idea **that she suggested** ultimately succeeded.
> The report **that she wrote** cinched the deal.

Living things closely associated with humans often receive the honor of *who-whom-whose:*

> Amber affectionately stroked her **pet turtle, <u>who</u>** curled up in front of the fire.

but:

> Igor stomped on the **cockroach <u>that</u>** crawled along the floor.

Sometimes, however, we use *that* to refer to people, usually a generic type of person:

> The **writers that** learn these rules will improve their work.

Or you could use *that* to refer in a restrictive way to an identifiable person:

> The **child that** made the A addressed the class.

These days we never use *which* to refer to a person. Such usages as "Our Father, *which* art in heaven" are archaic.

Finally, as noted above, when an inanimate object or abstraction needs to show possession in a clause, we can either use the rather stuffy *of which* or we can borrow from the personal relative pronouns and use *whose:*

> It was an idea **whose time** had come.

Surely no one would write:

> It was an idea **the time of which** had come.

That vs. *Which*

Now we open the proverbial can of worms. Some people on earth know the differences between *that* and *which*. I'm one of them. So is your boss. Enough discerning readers out there do know the differences. So it'll pay dividends for you to use these words correctly. Think of them as your tickets into a rather exclusive circle, if not The Writers Club itself.

You'll have a general idea of the differences between *that* and *which* when you finish reading this section. But you won't become a true expert until you read not only this section but chapter 14 as well. In that chapter on clauses vs. phrases, we'll explore this matter more deeply.

First of all, both words introduce adjectival clauses, that is, entire clauses that modify a noun in your sentence. Adjectival clauses come in two basic models: restrictive clauses and nonrestrictive clauses. We might also refer to restrictive clauses as *defining clauses* and nonrestrictive clauses as *nondefining clauses*.

Suppose the noun in your sentence is the noun *books*. Suppose you modify *books* with a restrictive clause. That restrictive clause takes a look at *books* and says,

"Now, which books is this writer talking about? From the context of the stuff he has written so far, we don't know the specific books he's referring to."

"Therefore, this writer needs me to identify the precise books he's talking about. Now watch me point out which books. Watch me *define* which books. Here I go," says the restrictive clause:

Everybody should read the books that the critics recommend.

Here the clause that the critics recommend singles out which books the writer is talking about and defines them. Thus, the clause is a restrictive or defining clause.

Now suppose the writer has already revealed the identity of the books. From context the reader knows which books the writer is referring to. The writer might have written: "Children profit from the Harry Potter series." And then the writer adds:

Everybody should read the books, which the critics recommend.

Now the clause is not identifying which books the writer is writing about. The reader already knows which books—the Harry Potter series. The clause, therefore, is not defining the books. The clause is thus nonrestrictive or nondefining. The correct pronoun is *which,* and the clause *must be set off from the rest of the sentence by commas*. Do I need to repeat that, or does the bold italics type drive the point home?

In sum, the word *that* introduces a restrictive clause. Ironically, this clause always answers this question: Which book? *That* book. Which books? *That* group of books. On the other hand, the word *which* introduces a nonrestrictive clause. It must always be set off by commas.

> **In sum, the word *that* introduces a restrictive clause. Ironically, this clause always answers this question: Which book? *That* book. The word *which* introduces a nonrestrictive clause. It must always be set off by commas.**

We'll explore the differences between *that* and *which* more thoroughly in chapter 14. After a while, you'll automatically choose the correct word and punctuate the sentence with any necessary commas to set off any nonrestrictive clauses. In that chapter, we'll also see how the grandfathers of the plain-English movement, Messrs. Strunk and White, gave some very careless advice in their book, *The Elements of Style,* and as a result caused all sorts of problems.

6. INTERROGATIVE PRONOUNS

Amber, Igor, and Miss Hamrick had lots of questions they wanted to ask, so they convened the Grammar Committee and devised ways to interrogate members of the tribe. First, they decided to form questions by including an auxiliary verb and then putting the auxiliary before the subject. Voila!

> **Are** <u>you</u> **going** to the party?
> **Will** <u>you</u> **visit** your brother?
> **Do** <u>you</u> **want** a birthday present?

Pretty clever, our cave-dwelling Grammar Committee. Then they decided to borrow some of the relative pronouns to use for question asking: *who, whom, whose,* and *which.* (The word *that* just didn't work.) To this list they added the word *what* and came up with a list of interrogative pronouns:

who	**Who's** on first?
whom	**Whom** should we call?
whose	**Whose** turn is it?
which	**Which** runner won the race?
what	**What** time is it?

Sensing that other shades of meanings must show up in questions posed by astute questioners, the committee then borrowed some adverbs: *why, where, when,* and *how.*

why	**Why** did you retire so early?
where	**Where** did Steve get his new car?

when   **When** will this nightmare ever end?

how   **How** will this nightmare ever end?

The difference between relative pronouns and adverbs acting as inter-rogatives lies in the function they serve in the sentence. The pronoun will serve as a subject *(who)* or object *(whom)* or show possession *(whose)*, as pronouns are wont to do. The adverb, not surprisingly, will act as an adverb. Let's see these different functions:

Who came to the party?	*Who* acts as the subject of the verb *came*.
Whom should we call?	*Whom* acts as the object of the verb *call*.
Whose position did he fill?	*Whose* acts as the posses-sor of the noun *position*.
Where did Steve get his new car?	*Where* is an adverb modi-fying the verb *get*.

A final thought on the use of questions, for we have two kinds, direct and indirect. A direct question appears in quotation marks and ends with a question mark inside the closing quotation marks:

Fred asked, "Where did Steve get his new car?"

Indirect questions are different. They appear as a statement, have no quotation marks, and don't even end with a question mark:

Fred asked where Steve got his new car.

The same is true for indirect questions that politely ask a favor:

Will you please send the report as soon as possible.

Now, the seventh and final kind of pronoun will take just a few sentences.

7. RECIPROCAL PRONOUNS

We have only two of these pronouns, and they come in pairs: *each other* and *one another*. We use them to show some sort of a relationship between two or more people or larger groups. Like this:

> The two teams enjoyed the competition between **each other.**

The reciprocals have possessives, formed by adding "apostrophe -*s.*" Each of these possessive expressions is singular:

> **Wrong:**   Jane and Fred tired of criticizing **each others'** political views.
>
> **Right:**   Jane and Fred tired of criticizing **each other's** political views.

In formal settings you should use *each other* to refer to two people or two groups; *one another,* to three or more. In less formal settings, we use the terms interchangeably.

> **Formal:**   The two law students disliked **each other** immensely.
>   All the class members disliked **one another.**
>
> **Informal:** The two law students disliked **one another** immensely.

PRONOMINAL PHOBIA

As we conclude our discussion of the seven kinds of pronouns, I should pause to point out a problem with the writing styles of many people, particularly professionals. For some unknown reason, professional people like to repeat professional people's nouns and not use professional people's pronouns because professional people think that professional people achieve a high degree of accuracy in professional people's work by repeating professional people's nouns.

Whew. See what I mean?

Why the fear of pronouns, folks? Isn't it much better to use the pronoun whenever its antecedent is crystal clear? Of course it is. Why? Because the use of a pronoun forces the reader to fill in the mental blank and identify the antecedent. This mental task forces the reader to pay attention. Thus we write:

> For some unknown reason, **professional people** like to repeat **their** nouns and not use **their** pronouns because **they** think **they** achieve a high degree of accuracy in **their** work by repeating **their** nouns.

Lawyers, yielding to their overwhelming urge to appear to write with precision, have a particularly difficult time condescending to use a pronoun now and again. Bryan Garner urges lawyers to overcome this fear. He wants legal writers to ease up on the problem of "ambiguous referents," in one sentence making it humorously plain that a pronoun does not have to refer to the immediately preceding noun:

> "It is not simply that referential pronouns are avoided only where their use could raise genuine confusion; [in legal writing] they seem to be eschewed as a species." [Citation omitted.] The result is often a sentence that no native speaker of English—other than a lawyer—would ever perpetrate, such as: "Then Tina became very lethargic, at which time Tina was taken to the emergency room."
>
> Why the fear of pronouns? Because lawyers have *overlearned* the lesson that pronouns sometimes have ambiguous referents. That being so, they (the lawyers, not the referents) swear off using them (the pronouns, not the lawyers) altogether.[16]

In Garner's last sentence, he facetiously adds the parentheticals, which, of course, are totally unnecessary:

> Why the fear of pronouns? Because lawyers have overlearned the lesson that pronouns sometimes have ambiguous referents. That being so, **they** swear off using **them** altogether.

From context, it's plain what *they* refers to. Equally so, it's plain what *them* refers to.

PRONOUNS: A SUMMARY

You must commit to memory some of the basic rules governing the correct use of pronouns. A summary looks like this:

1. *Personal Pronouns.* Personal pronouns appear in three cases: subjective, objective, and possessive. Good writers make certain they use the proper case, so you must review the chapter on nouns and relearn the grammatical functions of subjects (subjective case), subject complements (subjective case), direct objects (objective case), objects of verbal phrases (objective case), and objects of prepositions (objective case). You'll use possessive case for those pronouns replacing nouns that would appear with possessive endings.

   Pay attention to the rules on agreement in number and agreement in gender. When you have a generic antecedent, try to make it plural to avoid having to pick *he* over *she* or *she* over

   > **We have seven types of pronouns: (1) personal, (2) reflexive and intensive, (3) indefinite, (4) demonstrative, (5) relative, (6) interrogative, and (7) reciprocal.**

   he. Picking one over the other might be viewed as sexist writing. As the language continues to evolve, the plural pronouns *they/their/ them* will one day be regarded as the proper pronouns to use when referring back to singular, generic antecedents. Be aware of your audience. In formal settings, follow the old, traditional rule of agreement in number.

2. *Reflexive and Intensive Pronouns.* Avoid using the reflexive -*self* pronouns as subjects of sentences. Make sure you use the reflexive only when the subject of the sentence and an object are the same person.

3. *Indefinite Pronouns.* When using indefinite pronouns, pay attention to the rules governing agreement in number. The word *everybody* is singular and, in formal settings, requires a later singular pronoun (*he* or *she, him* or *her, his* or *her, his* or *hers*). These days, however, you can use the plural pronouns *they/their/them* to refer back to singular indefinite pronouns. To avoid sexism, don't use the

indefinite pronoun; instead, try to make the antecedent plural (use *people, persons,* or type of group, such as *writers*) so that you may then use *they, their,* or *them.*

4. **Demonstrative Pronouns.** Be careful when using demonstrative pronouns, especially *this,* as subjects of sentences. Make sure the *this* has a readily identifiable antecedent, either a noun, noun phrase, or entire idea. Ask yourself, "this what?" If an answer immediately comes to mind, the usage is probably okay.

5. **Relative Pronouns.** These words introduce clauses, and the issue of case shows up for those relatives referring to people. You must learn to distinguish between *who* (subjective), *whom* (objective), and *whose* (possessive). Watch for verbs in the clauses that have no other word acting as the subject; these will always require *who.* If the verb has some other subject, *whom* or sometimes *whose* is always correct.

   Learn the differences between *that* (introduces restrictive clause) and *which* (introduces nonrestrictive clause and is set off by commas). We'll return to these tricky words in chapter 14, "Word War IV: Clauses vs. Phrases."

6. **Interrogative Pronouns.** We borrow four of the relatives *(who, whom, whose,* and *which)* and add *what* to yield the interrogative pronouns, which enable us to ask questions. (We also use certain adverbs to assist in forming our questions: *why, when, where,* and *how.)*

7. **Reciprocal Pronouns.** Finally, we have two sets of pronouns that help us refer to two people or groups or to three or more people or groups: *each other* and *one another.* These do have possessive forms, but only in the singular: *each other's* and *one another's.*

Let's move on to the glue words. First, conjunctions, and then, prepositions.

NOTES

1. We used to give female names to hurricanes, but we've fixed that. And we must still deal with *mailman* and *workman.* But new words are entering the language, so that a *mail carrier* describes a male or female person who carries the mail and *worker* describes men and women who work.

2. This example appears in *New Fowler,* p. 134.
3. *New Fowler,* p. 629.
4. "Dueling Dictionaries," *Washington Post,* June 28, 2001, p. C4, col. 5.
5. Roger A. Cunningham, *The Law of Property,* p. 10 (1984).
6. Paul Berman and Michael Asimow, *Reel Justice,* p. 102 (1996).
7. *Follett,* p. 33.
8. James F. Wilson, *Law and Ethics of the Veterinary Profession,* p. 248 (1990).
9. *Follett,* p. 31.
10. *Garner Oxford,* p. 302.
11. *New Fowler,* p. 526.
12. *United States v. Oyarzun,* 760 F.2d 570, 577 (5th Cir. 1985).
13. You'll find this approach suggested in *Garner Legal,* p. 260 and *Garner Oxford,* p. 259.
14. Roscoe Pound, *An Introduction to the Philosophy of Law,* p. 108 (1922; repr. 1975) (quoted in *Garner Legal,* p. 260).
15. In these examples, we assume that the "report" is necessarily one already identified to the reader. Hence the use of the nonrestrictive, "comma *which*" clause. The "book," we assume, needs to be identified to the reader. Hence the use of the restrictive *that* clause. See the upcoming discussion on *that* vs. *which.*
16. *Garner Legal,* p. 702.

6

Conjunctions: Words That Join

During one of the early meetings of the Grammar Committee, Miss Hamrick pointed out that members of the tribe needed a way to express more than one thing. "They might have two things to say," she astutely observed. "Or three," Igor responded. After considerable study, the committee discovered the need for words that would join one sentence with another, or one part of a sentence with another part, or one word with another word. After rejecting the potential name of *Sticky Words,* the Grammar Committee settled on: *conjunctions.*

Conjunctions join words to words, phrases to phrases, or clauses to clauses. They come in three different varieties: (1) coordinating conjunctions, (2) correlative conjunctions, and (3) subordinating conjunctions.

1. COORDINATING CONJUNCTIONS

We have seven basic coordinating conjunctions, and you can remember them by referring to the acronym BOY FANS.

B	*But*	F	*For*
O	*Or*	A	*And*
Y	*Yet*	N	*Nor*
		S	*So*

These conjunctions join words, phrases, or clauses. As we'll discuss more fully below, when you use them, you must make absolutely certain each element in the series (of words, phrases, or clauses) is grammatically equal to all other elements in the same series. They must be grammatically equal not only in function but in form. We call this requirement the rule of *parallel construction* and explore it in detail in chapter 18, "Sentence Shapes: The Art of Parallel Structure."

Let's see how coordinating conjunctions enable us to expand the types of sentences we can build.

Structures Joined	Conjunction	Example
Two sentences	*and*	**John hit the ball, <u>and</u> he ran to first base.**
Two dependent *that* clauses	*and*	The book **that you enjoyed <u>and</u> that won the award** has finally arrived at the store.
Two adverbial clauses	*and*	He enjoyed the movie **because his favorite actor starred <u>and</u> because the special effects required computer technology.**
Three prepositional phrases	*but*	John hit the ball **over the pitcher's head, between the legs of the short stop, <u>but</u> into the waiting glove of the outfielder.**
Two subjects	*and*	**Lincoln <u>and</u> Jefferson** rank among our greatest presidents.
Two verbs	*but*	Susan **waited** for two hours **<u>but</u>** then **decided** to leave.
Two direct objects	*or*	Jane wants the **apple <u>or</u>** the **orange.**

Notice in the examples above that each series contains elements grammatically identical in function and form. If you violate this rule of parallel construction, you have produced what some grammarians call a *shifted construction;* others call it a *nonparallel construction.* Look at this example:

He likes **running <u>and</u> to play soccer.**

Here, both elements of the series perform the same grammatical function: direct object of the verb *likes*. But they appear in different forms, one as an *-ing* verb (present participle) acting as a noun (that is, a gerund), the other as a *to* verb (infinitive) acting as a noun. To follow the rule, we would write:

He likes **running <u>and</u> playing soccer.**
He likes **to run <u>and</u> to play soccer.**

2. CORRELATIVE CONJUNCTIONS

The second kind of conjunction is the correlative conjunction, which comes in pairs of words. Here are the most commonly used:

Correlative Conjunctions
either . . . or
neither . . . nor
not . . . but
not only . . . but (also)
both . . . and

Powerful writers use these conjunctions all the time. Here's Mr. Churchill:

But **neither** King Charles **nor** the Roundhead executive had the slightest intention of giving way upon the two main points.[1]

Here's Mr. Churchill again:

This was **not** a butchery, **but** a ceremony, a sacrifice, or, if we may borrow from the Spanish Inquisition, "an act of faith."[2]

And again:

He used arguments **not** of law **but** of revolution.[3]

The trick to using correlative conjunctions lies in two key points: (1) Make sure you follow the rule of parallel construction, and (2) try using these conjunctions to join a wide variety of structures. Below we'll learn more about parallel structure and the use of correlative conjunctions.

3. SUBORDINATING CONJUNCTIONS

The final type of conjunction introduces subordinate clauses. We have a rather long list of these words, called *subordinating conjunctions.* Notice our friend, the word *that.* As a subordinating conjunction, it introduces a noun clause, as in: **He said that he would come.** Here it acts as a subordinating conjunction, not as a relative pronoun and not as a demonstrative pronoun.

Subordinating Conjunctions

after	how	unless
although	if	until
as	in order that	what
as far as	provided that	whatever
as if	since	when
as long as	so (that)	whenever
as though	that	where
because	though	wherever
before	till	while

Each of these words introduces a subordinate clause, which may act as a subject, object, adjective, or adverb. Take a look:

Clause	Function	Example
That he won the award	subject	**That** he won the award did not surprise us.
that she would win	direct object	She said **that** she would win.
where she lives	adjective	Let's meet on the street **where** she lives.
whenever the bell rings	adverb	The rat reacts **whenever** the bell rings.

Botching *as far as*

Many smart people flub the use of the subordinating conjunction *as far as*. Keep in mind that the expression serves as a subordinating conjunction. That is, it joins a clause. What must be in the clause to make it a clause? Right. A conjugated verb. That's the source of the flub: People leave out the necessary verb, which is often the verb *is concerned*.

Thus, you'll hear people say or see people write:

As far as success, I feel sure I can make it.

In that sentence, the *as far as* is not a subordinating conjunction, but a preposition, the topic of the next chapter. Some guides allow this use in informal speech and informal writing, but I would urge you to join those who cherish the language and insist on using the expression as a subordinating conjunction:

As far as success **is concerned,** I feel sure I can make it.

Of course, when tempted to use the *as far as* expression without the required verb, you might very well want to produce the meaning of a preposition, and plenty of good ones come to mind: *on, concerning, regarding,* and others.

So perhaps you do mean *concerning* or *regarding* (two verb-like expressions that have transformed themselves into full-blown prepositions). If so, simply say so:

Regarding success, I feel sure I can make it.

PARALLEL CONSTRUCTION

Though we'll study parallel construction in chapter 18, I must introduce the concept here, for producing a parallel series requires the use of two of the conjunctions we just discussed: coordinating conjunctions and correlative conjunctions.

Basically, to follow the rule, you must make certain each element in the series that is joined with a conjunction appears in the same grammatical structure and performs the same grammatical function.

In the above discussion on coordinating conjunctions, I provided some examples of parallel structure. Here they are again. Notice how I double or triple (1) entire sentences, (2) dependent *that* clauses, (3) adverbial clauses, (4) prepositional phrases, (5) subjects, (6) verbs, and (7) verbal objects. The list of possibilities could go on and on.

Structures Joined	Conjunction	Example
1. Two sentences	*and*	**John hit the ball, <u>and</u> he ran to first base.**
2. Two *that* clauses	*and*	The book **that you enjoyed <u>and</u> that won the award** has finally arrived at the store.
3. Two adverbial clauses	*and*	He enjoyed the movie **because his favorite actor starred <u>and</u> because the special effects required computer technology.**
4. Three prepositional phrases	*but*	John hit the ball **over the pitcher's head, between the legs of the short stop, <u>but</u> into the waiting glove of the outfielder.**
5. Two subjects	*and*	**Lincoln <u>and</u> Jefferson** rank among our greatest presidents.
6. Two verbs	*but*	Susan **waited** for two hours **<u>but</u>** then **decided** to leave.
7. Two direct objects	*or*	Jane wants the **apple <u>or</u>** the **orange.**

Parallel Structure and Correlative Conjunctions

The rule of parallel construction creates a trap for unwary writers trying to use correlative conjunctions. As shown above, these words come in pairs *(neither . . . nor, either . . . or, not . . . but, not only . . . but (also),*

> To follow the rule of parallel construction, make certain each element in the series joined with a conjunction appears in the same grammatical structure and performs the same grammatical function.

both . . . and). To use them correctly, you must ensure that the structure joined by the first word of the pair is a grammatical mirror image of the structure joined by the second word of the pair.

If you wanted to use the *not only . . . but (also)* correlative conjunction, you should follow this model:

not only **X** but (also) **Y**
X = Y (in grammatical function)
X = Y (in grammatical form)

The key lies in the placement of the words. Carefully line up the first structure after the words *not only* and then the second structure performing the same grammatical function immediately after the *but* or *but also.* Like this:

not only **[noun acting as subject]** *but* **[noun acting as subject]**

Not only the CEO but the entire Board of Directors attended the press conference.

not only **[verb]** *but also* **[verb]**

The reporter **not only** contacted her sources **but also** spent many hours in the library.

not only **[prepositional phrase]** *but* **[prepositional phrase]**

He retraced his steps **not only along the trail but throughout the camp.**

not only **[entire sentence]** *but* **[entire sentence]**

Not only did the court reverse the lower court, but it sent a message to the police.

In the final example, when you use correlative conjunctions to join entire sentences, you'll have to use an auxiliary verb with the first sentence *(did)* and invert it, placing the subject between the auxiliary *(did)* and the main verb *(reverse)* (not only **did** <u>the court</u> **reverse** . . .). If you wrote the following, you'd produce a nonparallel construction:

> The court **not only** reversed the lower court, **but** it sent a message to the police.

Here the *not only* joins just the verb while the *but* joins an entire independent clause. Remember the formula X = Y. Here, "verb" does not equal "entire clause."

Many writers botch the use of correlative conjunctions, making mistakes like this:

> Wrong: She **not only** wanted a hamburger **but** french fries.
> Right: She wanted **not only** a hamburger **but** french fries.

In the above example the first part of the pair, *not only,* joins the verb *wanted.* But the second part of the pair, *but,* joins the direct object *french fries.* The rule of parallel constructions forbids the joining of a verb with a noun.

This rule of parallel construction applies to all the correlative conjunctions. Make sure the structure joined with the first word mirrors the structure joined with the second word. Some examples:

> Wrong: **Either you must wear** your suit **or** your **tux.**
> Right: **Either you must wear** your suit **or you must wear** your tux.
> Right: You must wear **either** your **suit or** your **tux.**
>
> Wrong: The coach **neither** wanted to lose **nor** to tie.
> Right: The coach wanted **neither** to lose **nor** to tie.

Never Start a Sentence with a Conjunction
Poppycock!

Not only can you start sentences with a conjunction, but you must—if you ever want to become a good writer, that is.

Reread the previous sentence. What words started it? The words *Not only*. What kind of words are they? Right. The correlative conjunction *not only . . . but*.

One does not have to look far for support of the proper rule. You may certainly use *and* or *but* or any other coordinating or correlative conjunction to start a sentence.

Here's Wilson Follett:

A prejudice lingers from a bygone time that sentences should not begin with *and*. The supposed rule is without foundation in grammar, logic, or art. *And* can join separate sentences and their meanings just as *but* can both join sentences and disjoin meanings.[4]

Here's Henry Fowler:

There is a persistent belief that it is improper to begin a sentence with *And*, but this prohibition has been cheerfully ignored by standard authors from Anglo-Saxon times onwards. An initial *And* is a useful aid to writers as the narrative continues. The *[Oxford English Dictionary]* provides examples from the 9th century to the 19th century, including one from Shakespeare's *King John:* Arthur. *Must you with hot Irons, burne out both mine eyes?* Hubert. *Young Boy, I must.* Arthur. *And will you?* Hubert. *And I will.*[5]

And one does not have to look far to identify other great writers who use conjunctions as sentence starters. Justice Oliver Wendell Holmes, for one, was not at all shy about starting a sentence with *And:*

Courts proceed step by step. **And** we now have to consider whether the cautious statement in the former case marked the limit of the law.[6]

Here's Justice Holmes again, this time using *But* to start a sentence:

But to many people the superfluous is necessary, and it seems to me that Government does not go beyond its sphere in attempting to make life livable for them.[7]

Here's Justice Hugo Black:

> The Framers knew, better perhaps than we do today, the risks they
> were taking. They knew that free speech might be the friend of
> change and revolution. **But** they also knew that it is always the
> deadliest enemy of tyranny.[8]

Here's Justice Robert Jackson, regarded by many as one of the best
writers ever to sit on the Supreme Court:

> This diversification of appellate authority inevitably produces con-
> flict of decision, even if review is limited to questions of law. **But**
> conflicts are multiplied by treating as questions of law what really
> are disputes over proper accounting.[9]

And here's the *Washington Post,* in its lead editorial on June 25, 2001,
appropriately entitled "And Now to Spend":

> **So** now it's spending time, and you guessed it: They're spending
> anyway. **Nor** is it the case ... that only profligate Democrats are
> pushing for increases while virtuous Republicans resist. When the
> Democrats took control of the Senate, Republicans were quick to say
> that there went fiscal discipline. **But** in fact they're both at it; spend-
> ing is the most bipartisan activity in Washington. **And** most of the
> action thus far has been in the Republican House.[10]

Need more proof? Read the first sentence in the third paragraph of the
Gettysburg Address. Surely President Lincoln knew how to arrange his
words:

> **But,** in a larger sense, we can not dedicate—we can not con-
> secrate—we can not hallow—this ground. The brave men, living and
> dead, who struggled here, have consecrated it, far above our poor
> power to add or detract.

Have we finally put that myth to rest?

Good. When you exercise your new writing muscles and use conjunctions to start sentences, make certain you do not put a comma immediately after the conjunction. Note all of the

> **Never start a sentence with a conjunction. Poppycock!**

examples above. You will use a comma when you begin a parenthetical pause, as Lincoln did with his "in a larger sense." But a single comma does not follow the conjunction beginning a sentence.

So go ahead and start sentences with conjunctions. *For* your writing will improve dramatically. *And* you'll help your reader along as you move from sentence to sentence. *But* if you have trouble convincing your colleagues or professors of the superiority of this style, just buy each a copy of *Oops, Me!*

Abandon "However" as a Sentence Starter

Look at the sentences above, the ones starting with *But*. Imagine how awful they would sound if the writer had started them with *However* followed by a comma. No applause for Justice Black if he had written:

> The Framers knew, better perhaps than we do today, the risks they were taking. They knew that free speech might be the friend of change and revolution. **However,** they also knew that it is always the deadliest enemy of tyranny.[11]

Strunk & White urges writers to shun *however* at the beginning of a sentence:

Avoid starting a sentence with *however* when the meaning is "nevertheless." The word usually serves better when not in first position.

Example: The roads were almost impassable. However, we at last succeeded in reaching camp.

Correction: The roads were almost impassable. At last, however, we succeeded in reaching camp.

When *however* comes first, it means "in whatever way" or "to whatever extent."

Examples: However you advise him, he will probably do as he thinks best. However discouraging the prospect, he never lost heart.[12]

Strunk & White could have expanded this advice by urging the use of *But* as a way to start a sentence and to show contrast at its beginning.

A Word about *Nor*

The conjunction *nor* can serve either as a coordinating conjunction or as part of the correlative conjunction *neither . . . nor.* As a coordinating conjunction, it can join a complete independent clause. When used in this way, it continues the negative state in the preceding clause (usually shown by *not, no, never,* etc.). Here we see its role in continuing a negative state.

He left and I never saw him again, nor did I regret it.[13]

The word *nor* also joins elements in a series within a given clause. It can appear even if a negative state already exists. At least according to *Random House,* the word *nor* can follow other negatives:

They won't wait for you, nor for me, nor for anybody.[14]

Personally, I prefer to use the word *or* when a negative has already been established in the sentence or clause. Bryan Garner concurs:

Where the negative of a clause has already appeared and a disjunctive conjunction is needed, *or* is generally better than *nor.* The initial negative carries through to all the elements in an enumeration.[15]

In *Garner Legal,* we find this example:

When on the witness stand at the trial of this case, he could not see the trial judge *nor* [read *or*] the examiner who was five feet away.[16]

In *Garner Oxford,* this example appears:

There have been no bombings *nor* [read *or*] armed attacks by one side against the other.[17]

Thus, if I had to edit the *Random House* example of *nor* joining elements in a series when a negative has already been established, I would opt for *or:*

They won't wait for you, **or** for me, **or** for anybody.

Finally, notice in the editorial by the *Washington Post* that the writer began a sentence with *Nor.* Notice also the need to *invert* the sentence: "**Nor is it** the case ...." Here the subject *it* follows the verb *is.* The same will hold true for the action verb in a sentence begun by *Nor.* You will have to use an auxiliary verb and put the subject between the auxiliary and the main verb. Study the *Random House* example above: "... nor **did** I **regret** it." Try it out. Whenever you begin a clause with *Nor,* you'll have to invert the clause, by putting the subject before the verb *to be* or by using an auxiliary (*will, do, have,* others) and putting the subject between the auxiliary and the main verb. We saw the same need to invert when we started a sentence with the correlative conjunction *not only . . . but (also).*

JOINED SUBJECTS: SINGULAR OR PLURAL

Before winding up our discussion of conjunctions, we need to visit the notion of subject-verb agreement in number. When you write a plural subject, you must use a plural verb. When you write a singular subject, you must use a singular verb. As a general rule, when you join subjects with the conjunction *and,* you form a plural subject, which requires a plural verb.

> The **critic and** the **author** sometimes **agree.**

Often, however, two singular nouns joined with *and* produce a subject singular in sense, which calls for a singular verb. This often happens when a prepositional phrase follows the second noun but modifies the entire singular idea. Look at this example, which comes from *New Fowler:*

> The **usefulness and credibility of such an arms control agreement hinges** on the reliability of seismic technology.[18]

Beware of words that join but do not qualify as true conjunctions and thus do not form plural subjects. These words include *as well as, together with, not to mention,* and others. Again, another example from *New Fowler:*

A very profitable **company** such as British Telecom, **along with** many other **companies** in the UK, **is** not prepared to pay a reasonable amount.[19]

The problem of subject-verb agreement also crops up when you use correlative conjunctions. When you use *neither . . . nor* to join two subjects of a clause, you will confront the problem of number. Must the verb appear in the singular or the plural? When *neither . . . nor* joins two singular subjects, the verb must be singular as well. Like this:

Neither the **player nor** the **coach wants** to lose the game.

But if the *neither . . . nor* expression joins two plural subjects, then the verb must be plural as well.

Neither the **players nor** the **coaches want** to lose the game.

The problem arises, naturally enough, when you use *neither . . . nor* to join a singular subject and a plural subject. What then? What happens, for example, when our subject appears like this:

Neither the **players nor** the **coach** ...

> **The number of the verb is governed by the number of the noun closer to the verb. If that noun is singular, then the verb is singular. If that noun is plural, then the verb is plural.**

Do we use a singular verb or a plural verb? Grammarians differ in their answers. One group insist that writers should avoid such structures, that they should "write around" the problem. Following this group's advice would yield this:

The players do not want to lose the game, and neither does the coach.

I find this approach way too restrictive. For example, that solution forces me to use the *do not* expression when I would prefer to use the *neither . . . nor* structure to express the negative condition.

Thus, I follow the advice of the second group of grammarians. Their advice makes sense, preserves the **neither . . . nor** expression, and gives the writer greater versatility. It goes like this: The number of the verb is governed by the number of the noun closer to the verb. If that noun is singular, then the verb is singular. If that noun is plural, then the verb is plural. Take a look at the following two sentences:

Neither the **players nor** the <u>**coach wants**</u> to lose the game.
Neither the **coach nor** the <u>**players want**</u> to lose the game.

See how it works? In the first sentence, the singular noun *coach* requires the singular verb *wants.* But in the second sentence, the plural noun *players* requires the plural verb *want.* Whichever noun is closer governs the number of the verb.

We'll study the problem of subject-verb disagreement in more detail in chapter 19.

CONJUNCTIONS: A SUMMARY

We have three kinds of conjunctions: coordinating, correlative, and subordinating. We have seen that coordinating and correlative conjunctions join two or three or four or more clauses, phrases, or words. The structures joined must be grammatically and functionally identical. Otherwise you'll write a nonparallel construction and won't look too smart to your professor or boss.

> And if your professor or boss objects, you may cite *New Fowler* and *Follett* as proof positive that great writers have been starting sentences with conjunctions for hundreds of years.

We destroyed a myth along the way. Of course you may begin sentences with conjunctions. When you do, you'll join company with Wilson Follett; Henry Fowler; Justices Holmes, Black, and Jackson; the *Washington Post;* and President Lincoln. Not bad company. And if your professor or boss objects, you may cite *New Fowler* and *Follett* as proof positive that great writers have been starting sentences with conjunctions for hundreds of years.

We also saw in this chapter that good writers use a wide variety of conjunctions to join a wide variety of structures. We'll return to this idea in chapter 18, "Sentence Shapes: The Art of Parallel Structure."

Now onward and, one hopes, forever upward, to more dabs of glue, the prepositions.

NOTES

1. Winston S. Churchill, *A History of the English Speaking Peoples,* vol. 2, p. 257 (Dodd, Mead & Co. 1960).
2. Churchill, *A History,* vol. 2, p. 279.
3. Churchill, *A History,* vol. 2, p. 220.
4. *Follett,* p. 27.
5. *New Fowler,* p. 52.
6. *Johnson v. United States,* 228 U.S. 457, 458 (1913).
7. *Tyson & Brother v. Banton,* 273 U.S. 418, 447 (1927).
8. Hugo Black, *The Bill of Rights,* 35 N.Y.U. L. Rev. 865, 880–81 (1960).
9. *Dobson v. Commissioner,* 320 U.S. 489, 4998-99 (1943).
10. "And Now to Spend," *Washington Post,* June 25, 2001, p. A14.
11. Hugo Black, *The Bill of Rights,* 35 N.Y.U. L. Rev. 865, 880–81 (1960).
12. *Strunk & White,* pp. 48–49.
13. *Random House,* p. 1321.
14. *Random House,* p. 1321.
15. *Garner Legal,* p. 597 and *Garner Oxford,* p. 230.
16. *Garner Legal,* p. 597.
17. *Garner Oxford,* p. 230.
18. *New Fowler,* p. 34.
19. *New Fowler,* p. 35.

7

Prepositions: Words That Glue

When we studied nouns, we saw their need for quite a bit of help to jump up on the back of a sentence and stay there. Verbs serve as the primary source of glue helping nouns stick to sentences. Verbs will stick nouns acting as subjects, direct objects, indirect objects, complements, and verbal objects.

The other big dab of glue sticking nouns to sentences is the preposition. Fact is, "noun sticking" is the preposition's primary reason for being.

So one day in Amber and Igor's cave, Igor was trying to construct a sentence:

I want to put the urn . . . table.

He looked at the urn and then at the table and figured he would put the urn *on* the table. Then he tried to put it *under* the table, *next to* the table, *above* the table, *away from* the table. He found he could put the urn all over the place in relation to the table, and the words he invented to describe those relationships he promptly dubbed: *prepositions.*

After all, what else could he call them?

Thus, to stick the noun *urn* on the back of the sentence, Igor needed a preposition to pull it off. As the language of the tribe grew, so did the list of prepositions, which enabled speakers, and later writers, to express a wide array of relationships between the noun (or pronoun) stuck to the sentence and the sentence itself.

> **There are three types of prepositions: (1) simple prepositions, (2) marginal prepositions, and (3) compound prepositions.**

Amber, Igor, Miss Hamrick, and the Preposition Committee actually devised three types of prepositions: (1) simple prepositions, (2) marginal prepositions, and (3) compound prepositions.

1. SIMPLE PREPOSITIONS

In the English language we have approximately 70 simple prepositions. About half of them have two syllables *(under, over, behind, without)* or more *(underneath, notwithstanding)*.

Here's just a partial list of simple prepositions:

Simple Prepositions

about	between	onto
above	beyond	to
after	for	toward
against	in	under
at	into	up
before	of	upon
behind	off	with
beside	on	without

Notice that many of these words show location *(on, off, behind, under,* etc.), some show time *(before, after)*, while others show less concrete relationships *(of, for, to, with)*.

2. MARGINAL PREPOSITIONS

Marginal prepositions act like prepositions but derive from other word classes, primarily verb forms:

Marginal Prepositions

barring	considering
concerning	pending

3. COMPOUND PREPOSITIONS

These come in two varieties: (1) two-word prepositions and (2) three-word prepositions. The two-word varieties include *pursuant to, according to, because of,* and others. The three-word varieties include *with respect to, in regard to, in accordance with,* and others.

Compound prepositions, such as *with respect to,* tend to get a bit fuzzy, so we should use them only when prepositions with more concrete meaning fail to capture exactly what we're trying to say. Before reviewing this list, you might want to pause and enjoy the grumbles of Henry Fowler on the wordiness and fuzziness of compound prepositions:

> Taken as a whole, [compound prepositions] are almost the worst element in modern English, stuffing up what is written with a compost of nouny abstractions. To young writers the discovery of these forms of speech, which are used very little in talk and very much in print, brings an expansive sense of increased power; they think they have acquired with far less trouble than they expected the trick of dressing up what they may have to say in the right costume for public exhibition. Later they know better, and realize that it is feebleness instead of power that they have been developing; but by that time the fatal ease that the compound-preposition style gives (to the writer, that is) has become too dear to be sacrificed.[1]

The most recent edition, *New Fowler,* however, says that this "colourful view no longer seems to be supported by the facts."[2]

I beg to differ with *New Fowler.* Especially in my profession—the law—and in government, writers do stuff up what they write with flimsy compound prepositions, the most favorite being *with respect to.* In one paper I reviewed, written by an attorney at a federal agency, I found seven *with respect to*'s in a single paragraph. Now that kind of style produces exactly the "compost of nouny abstractions" Fowler, and all good writers, would seek to avoid.

So study this list of compound prepositions (and other wordy strings of prepositional phrases and subordinating conjunctions) with corresponding simpler expressions that just might say the same thing:

Compound	Simple
at that point in time	then
at this point in time	now

Compound	Simple
by means of	by
by reason of	because of
by virtue of	by, under
during the course of	during
for the purposes of [+ noun]	for
for the purposes of [+ gerund]	infinitive phrase
for the reason that	because
from the point of view of	from, for
in accordance with	by, under
inasmuch as	since
in a manner similar to	like
in excess of	more than, over
in favor of	for
in order to	to
in receipt of	received
in relation to	about, concerning
in routine fashion	routinely
in terms of	in
in the event that	if
in the nature of	like
in the immediate vicinity of	near
in close proximity with	near
on the basis of	by, from
prior to	before
pursuant to	under, according to
similar to	like
subsequent to	after
with a view to	to
with reference to	about, concerning
with regard to	about, concerning
with respect to	on, about, for, in, concerning, with, to, *or some verbal expression*

THE PREPOSITIONAL PHRASE

The prepositional phrase consists of two major parts: (1) the preposition and (2) the object of the preposition. The object is the noun (or pronoun) attached to the sentence by the preposition. That noun might be a true noun, a noun phrase, or a noun clause. The entire unit then acts in two major ways: (1) as an adjective or (2) as an adverb.

Below is a table of various types of prepositional phrases. Note especially that various noun forms can serve as the object of the preposition.

PREPOSITIONAL PHRASES

Preposition	Object	Type of Noun	Example and Function of Prepositional Phrase
under	the table	true noun	The book **under the table** belongs to Sam. (adjectival prepositional phrase)
of	winning with class	*-ing* verb phrase (gerund)	He became the model **of winning with class.** (adjectival prepositional phrase)
of	whether this case applies	noun clause	The question **of whether this case applies** troubled the court. (adjectival prepositional phrase)
because of	his diligence	true noun	**Because of his diligence,** he won the debate. (adverbial prepositional phrase)
according to	scientific principles	true noun	He conducted the experiment **according to scientific principles.** (adverbial prepositional phrase)

Oops, *Me!*

A reminder. Whenever a pronoun serves as the object of a preposition, it *must* appear in the objective case. The correct title to this book, therefore, is *A Grammar Book for You and Me*. So please heed this advice from Henry Fowler:

After a preposition the objective form of a pronoun . . . must always be used: *believe in* him; *between* us; *for* them. This is especially important when two pronouns are linked by *and* or *or: between you and* me (not *I*); *a gift from my brother and* me (not *I*); *I asked if there was any chance of* him (not *he*) *and Gina reconciling.*[3]

ENDING SENTENCES OR CLAUSES WITH PREPOSITIONS

Here we have another myth, which I briefly mentioned in chapter 5: *Never* end a sentence or clause with a preposition. Actually, a sound rule would urge you to avoid ending sentences or clauses with prepositions in formal settings, as long as you don't end up writing awkward sentences.

Following the rule, we would write:

> These are the arguments **on** which the student relied.

But I know some excellent writers who would ignore the old rule and write:

> These are the arguments the student relied **on.**

Sometimes you simply must end the sentence with a preposition:

> What are you talking **about?**

Surely, not even a pedant would inquire:

> **About** what are you talking?

Great writers have been ending sentences and clauses with prepositions for centuries. According to *New Fowler:*

> Anyone who is in doubt about the frequency of occurrences over the centuries of prepositions placed at the end of clauses or sentences may wish to browse in the *Oxford English Dictionary* for *about, by, for, from,* etc.[4]

New Fowler suggests that the formality of the setting should govern. In highly formal pieces, like a master's thesis, you should try to avoid ending clauses with prepositions. But even in these formal settings, sentences sometimes demand a preposition at the end. In 1981, the *London Review of Books* wrote: "The conflict would be hard to live with." Surely if this work includes such structures, your master's thesis may, too. Thus, you need not write, "The conflict would be hard with which to live."

Sir Winston Churchill had his own opinion on the matter. In the words of his biographer:

> A junior civil servant had tortuously reworded a sentence to avoid ending with a preposition. The prime minister scrawled across the page: "This is nonsense up with which I will not put."[5]

But don't overdo it. *New Fowler* quotes a correspondent in 1923 showing how absurd sentences can become when they end with prepositions:

Child: I want to be read **to.**
Nurse: What book do you want to be read **to <u>out of</u>**?
Child: *Robinson Crusoe.*

Nurse returns with *Swiss Family Robinson.*

Child: What did you bring me that book to be read **to <u>out of</u> for**?[6]

PREPOSITIONS AS OTHER PARTS OF SPEECH

Many words that serve as prepositions also serve as other parts of speech. The word *up,* for example, acts as a preposition:

He looked **<u>up</u> the tree** (prepositional phrase).

But the word *up* can also serve as an adverb:

He looked **<u>up</u>** (adverb modifying *looked*).

And the word *up* can join a verb to form what's called a "complement verb," a verb consisting of a verb and a merged preposition *(drop out, dredge up)*:

He **looked <u>up</u>** the word (part of complement verb *look up*).

Some words can act as a preposition and a subordinating conjunction:

He left **after** **the movie** (prepositional phrase).
After **the movie ended,** he left (subordinating conjunction).

And the word doing the most damage to the communicative "skills" of young people today happens to be a preposition, and a noun, and a verb, and an adjective, and an adverb, and a conjunction, and an interjection. The word *like* serves as seven of the eight parts of speech (it isn't a pronoun).

> **The word *like* wrecks the speaking and writing "abilities" of young people today.**

This word does so much damage that we'll visit it again in chapter 31, which is entitled "Like, I'mlike gonna like learn how to like talk." For now, here it is as a preposition, a noun, and a verb:

He runs **like** a rabbit (prepositional phrase).
They grow oranges and the **like** (noun).
She **likes** to play soccer (verb).

PREPOSITIONS: A SUMMARY

In this chapter, you've learned all about the preposition, whose primary role in life is to stick nouns on sentences. You met three basic kinds: simple, marginal, and compound. You learned that skilled writers don't use too many compound prepositions like *with respect to* and *in regard to*.

You learned that the preposition, when it sticks a noun on a sentence, forms a structure called the prepositional phrase. The noun stuck on the sentence is the object of the preposition. And if you stick a personal pronoun on a sentence with a preposition, that pronoun must appear in the objective case.

The noun sticking to a preposition might be a true noun, a noun phrase, or a noun clause.

You learned that a preposition is often a good word to end a sentence *with*.

Finally, you learned that words serving as prepositions can often serve as other parts of speech as well.

We now proceed to a very short chapter on the eighth and final part of speech—the interjection.

NOTES
1. *Fowler,* p. 102.
2. *New Fowler,* p. 167.
3. *New Fowler,* p. 617.
4. *New Fowler,* p. 617.
5. William Manchester, *The Last Lion: Visions of Glory,* vol. 1, p. 31 (1983).
6. *New Fowler,* p. 618.

8

Interjections: Words That Exclaim

Like wow!
 Rats.
 Damn!
 Oh!

These and other words of surprise are interjections. Use them in speech and creative writing. Leave them out of your master's thesis.

And stop using the word *like* as a substitute for thought.

Enough!

PART**TWO**

Wars of the Words

When we learned grammar in grade school, we thought of it as an endless list of rules to be broken only by offenders willing to incur the disapproval of Miss Hamrick. Grammar just wasn't a positive thing. It caused us to get our knuckles rapped. It caused us to get "corrected." In public.

Grammar was not a Kodak Moment.

But from grammar springs a theory of style. With grammatical knowledge, we can begin to look at writing and try to figure out what makes good writing good and bad writing bad. We can become savvy critics not only by deducing some things ourselves but by looking carefully at the types of words good writers choose, the types of structures they use, and the various ways they manipulate those structures to achieve certain effects. When we see patterns emerge, we can then begin to do what they do. And then maybe, just maybe, we can join their elite club.

We embark on this journey by witnessing some clashes in our language: The Wars of the Words. We want to learn about the tension between nouns and verbs, the problem presented by the verb *to be,* the proverbial battle between the active and passive voice, and the spat between clauses and phrases.

Right now—in business, accounting, law, science, the military, government, and academe—the nouns are winning. *Be*'s have taken over. The passive voice rules. The clause is king.

Part II of this book seeks to reverse all that. Good writers have known for hundreds of years that verbs should triumph over nouns, that *not to be* answers that haunting question posed so long ago, that the active voice should usually reign supreme, and that no one has ever written a well-claused paper.

First we'll spend two chapters looking more deeply into the functions of nouns and verbs. Then we'll get ready to rumble and watch the Wars of the Words.

9

Nouns: What They Do

In chapter 1, we explored the major functions of nouns in our language: subjects, complements, and objects. In this chapter, we want to review these roles and expand the list of functions nouns serve.

THE TEN FUNCTIONS OF NOUNS
1. Subjects of Sentences

The **professor** is the expert, so he gave the class his views on the importance of learning to write papers clearly.

2. Subject Complements ("Predicate Nouns" or "Predicate Nominatives")

The professor is the **expert,** so he gave the class his views on the importance of learning to write papers clearly.

3. Direct Objects of Transitive Verbs

The professor is the expert, so he gave the class his **views** on the importance of learning to write papers clearly.

4. Objects of Verbal Phrases

> The professor is the expert, so he gave the class his views on the importance of learning to write **papers** clearly.

5. Indirect Objects

To become an accomplished writer, you must learn all functions of the noun, for the mark of the ace writer is the ability to use a wide variety of structures in a wide variety of ways. So let's learn a function of nouns we skipped over in chapter 1.

Shake hands with the *indirect object,* a person or thing secondarily affected by the action of the verb, the direct object being primarily affected. The indirect object appears in the sentence as a noun (or pronoun) unconnected by a preposition. It is positioned between the verb and the direct object. Like this:

> The professor is the expert, so he **gave** the **class** his **views** on the importance of learning to write papers clearly.

Note that the direct object of the transitive verb *gave* is the word *views.* The *class,* on the other hand, is "the person for whom or to whom something is done or given," to quote Miss Hamrick's definition burned into our memories in the 1950s. If you want to move the indirect object to a place after the verb, you'll have to turn it into the object of a prepositional phrase:

> The professor is the expert, so he gave his views **to the class** on the importance of learning to write papers clearly.

The First Five: Verb Dependent

Take a look at the first five functions of nouns: (1) subject of the **verb**, (2) complement of the linking **verb**, (3) direct object of the transitive **verb**, (4) object of a **verbal** phrase, and (5) indirect object secondarily affected by the **verb**. Anything stand out? What happens in all five situations if you take the verb away? The noun loses its ability to function in the sentence. The noun needs the verb to exist. Hmmmm. I wonder if this fact should affect our writing style in any way.

6. Objects of Prepositions

The professor is the expert, so he gave the class his views on the **importance** of learning to write papers clearly.

The First Six: Dependent Nouns

A noun has a hard time jumping up on the back of a sentence, without some help. It turns to the verb for its first five functions, to the preposition for its sixth. Its remaining functions do show some independence, for you can wad up a noun, throw it at your sentence, and have it stick all by itself—without the help of a verb or preposition.

But now hold on to this thought: Nouns primarily need verbs to exist in a sentence. Take the verb away, and the noun disappears as well. And consider this: If writers don't use many verbs or verbal phrases, how else can they get nouns to stick on their sentences? Check out function number 6 above. In chapter 11, "Word War I: Nouns vs. Verbs," we'll learn about the Preposition Parade. If you don't use verbs, you must use lots of prepositions.

So stay with me. I'm trying to build your knowledge so that you can then engage in an analysis of a powerful writing style. To understand it, you must know all about nouns.

Now let's look at some noun structures that can hang directly on sentences, all by themselves, without prepositions or verbs.

7. Noun Appositives

These structures always show up in the style of powerful writers. A noun appositive is a noun or noun phrase that restates or identifies another noun or noun phrase. Sometimes it is set off by commas and sometimes not. Ordinarily, the appositive immediately follows the noun it restates, but in some cases it can begin a sentence and then point directly to the grammatical subject of the sentence. Let's look at several of these variations, the **appositives** appearing in bold:

Appositive	Comments
The White House, **home of the president,** is closely guarded.	Appositive, set off by commas, immediately follows the noun.

Appositive	Comments
A graduate of Carolina, Michael Jordan became a star.	Appositive introduces the sentence and restates the upcoming grammatical subject.
Singing sensation **Britney Spears** sold the most albums.	This formulation, originally used in America, now appears through-out the English-speaking world, especially in newspapers. Here's the formula: "title or descriptive label + personal name."
Jane's brother **Fred** came to dinner.	A restrictive appositive with no commas. Jane has more than one brother. Here the appositive identi-fies which one came to dinner.
Susan's brother, **Jack,** came to dinner.	A nonrestrictive appositive with commas. Susan has only one brother, and his name is Jack.

8. Noun Modifiers

Nouns often modify other nouns, as in *noun modifier* or *sentence struc-ture*. We have thousands of terms where a first noun modifies an ensuing noun: **hot-dog** bun, **football** game, **college** course, **chair** legs, and many more.

Unfortunately, these days, many writers have gone berserk and now shorten everything down to a chain of nouns so long that nobody can figure out what is modifying what. The tendency shows up especially in the sciences, engineering, the defense establishment, business schools, the legal profession, academe, and bureaucracies in general.

Noun chains represent one of the biggest impediments to reading ever devised. They can consist of two words (noun chain), three words (noun chain use), four words (noun chain use reduction), five words (noun chain use reduction technique), and so on. Of course, when readers encounter one of these expressions, they don't know how to read it until the expression ends, for the first noun might satisfy the sentence, the second noun might satisfy the sentence, the third noun might satisfy the sentence, and so on.

Think about the following flows of words entering your brain. In each instance, your brain is satisfied with each ensuing noun, and it's not until you reach the end that you realize that the teacher *relies on an exercise:*

> The teacher relies on a **noun** ....
> The teacher relies on a noun **chain** ....
> The teacher relies on a noun chain **use** ....
> The teacher relies on a noun chain use **reduction** ....
> The teacher relies on a noun chain use reduction **technique** ....
> The teacher relies on a noun chain use reduction technique **exercise.**

Dean Richard Wydick, whom I referred to in an earlier chapter, wrote the wonderful little book *Plain English for Lawyers.* In it, he observes:

> A long chain of nouns used as adjectives is likely to strangle the reader. That is, noun chains create *noun chain reader strangulation problems.* Bureaucrats love noun chains. They write about *draft laboratory animal rights protection regulations* and about *public service research dissemination program proposals.*[1]

I realize that noun chains overwhelmingly tempt many technical, scientific, legal, military, academic, and bureaucratic writers, but they really do hurt our writing. If the noun chain has achieved the status of a term of art, then perhaps you should keep it. But you should not fall into the trap of thinking that all these structures merit professional worship. Typically, they run so far out of control that the inevitable acronym must step in to try to salvage the situation and take its place.

> **Noun chains represent one of the biggest impediments to reading ever devised.**

Soon the language will collapse down into strings of abbreviations, a condition Bryan Garner calls *initialese.*[2] The tendency shows up in the writing of judges:

> The following facts cannot be found in the complaint: REDCO's previous dealing with TOI, REDCO's reasons for conducting an EFP, Merrill's inability to find REDCO an EFP partner, REDCO's intro-

duction of TOI to Merrill, Hutton and NYME's lack of knowledge of TOI's default until June 11, and NYME's instigation of a <u>rules compliance investigation</u> after June 11.[3]

In the above passage, why the noun chain *rules compliance investigation* was not dubbed *an RCI* will forever remain a mystery.

Initialese also shows up in writing intended to be scholarly. Mr. Garner, as we might imagine, has his hard-hitting opinion on the matter:

> This kind of writing might be thought more scholarly than ordinary, straightforward prose. It isn't. Rather, it's tiresome and inconsiderate writing; it betrays the writer's thoughtlessness toward the reader and a puerile fascination with the insubstantial trappings of scholarship.[4]

Ponder this "scholarship," ironically appearing in a journal on linguistics:

> SLIP, like VALP and ECC, is a defeasible constraint that is obeyed by all the types of head-nexus phrase considered thus far. It guarantees that (except in SLASH-binding contexts that we turn to in a moment) the SLASH value of a phrase is the SLASH value of its head-daughter.[5]

Don't ask.

I guess I should anoint my "noun chain use reduction technique exercise" as an, uh, NCURTE (pronounced "In-curt"). Then I can appear scholarly. And cool.

To fix the problem of noun chains—and thus to nix the need for all these initials—you'll have to bring in two kinds of words: verbs and prepositions. Why? Because, as we saw in chapters 2 and 7, verbs and prepositions are the primary helping hands nouns need to get on the back of a sentence.

Focus on the noun completing the sentence. Put it up front so that it satisfies the noun urge. Then figure out what you're trying to say, bring in the verbs and prepositions, and watch the noun chain disappear. Let's take my ridiculous example above:

> The teacher relies on **a** noun chain use reduction technique **exercise.**

Notice that the *teacher relies on **an exercise***. The word *exercise* completes the thought. Thus, put it up front:

> The **teacher relies on** an **exercise** as a technique to reduce the use of noun chains.

Let's use shorter words:

> The teacher uses an exercise as a way to reduce the use of noun chains.

Or:

> The teacher uses an exercise to help writers reduce their use of noun chains.

Or:

> The teacher uses an exercise to help writers cut out noun chains.

In the first revision, look at the prepositions *as* and *of*. Notice the verbal phrase *to reduce*. They make up the cure to noun chains: verbs and prepositions. And put the thought-completing noun up front. Sometimes you'll use more words, but you need them to produce a smooth and readable style.

Then—all you scholars out there just dying to coin an NCURTE— after you introduce the idea the

> To get rid of noun chains, identify the noun completing the thought and put it up front.

first time, you can refer to it as the "noun-chain exercise" and then in later sentences simply as the "exercise." If you're not careful, the rest of us mortals out here in the real world will SLIP you a VALP and perhaps even SLASH your ECC. So there.

9. Noun Adverbs
Words we think of as nouns often act like adverbs. Consider these sentences, with the noun adverb appearing in bold type:

He went **home.**

She got a promotion **yesterday.**

10. Noun Absolutes

You cannot read an award-winning novel and fail to find oodles of noun absolutes. Neither can you listen to National Public Radio's *All Things Considered,* ESPN's *Sports Center,* or CNN's *Moneyline* and not hear an array of these structures. All good writers use noun absolutes, so it'll pay you to learn what they're all about.

> **You cannot read an award-winning novel and fail to find oodles of noun absolutes.**

Basically, a noun absolute is a phrase. It is therefore not a clause. Thus, it does not have a conjugated verb in it. It might very well have a verbal, in the form of a present participle (*-ing* verb), past participle (*-ed* verb), or sometimes an infinitive (*to* verb). Anchoring the structure is a noun (or a pronoun). Usually—but not always—this noun or pronoun points directly to a referent in the sentence.

The opportunity to use a noun absolute typically arises when you've stated a plurality, that is, you've identified a bunch of things or circumstances, and you then want to give some examples. If you're an ESPN sports announcer, you might say:

> Several top seeds bit the dust last night. **Duke lost** to Florida, and **Kansas fell** to Seton Hall.

The "top seeds" is your plurality. Duke's and Florida's losses are your examples. Look how the noun absolute condenses everything into a single sentence:

> Several top seeds bit the dust last night, **Duke <u>losing</u>** to Florida and **Kansas <u>falling</u>** to Seton Hall.

The noun absolute comes in five different forms. Basically, the structure consists of a noun (or pronoun) plus five types of words or phrases, four describing the noun, one restating it.

Commit to memory these examples of the five basic types of noun absolutes. The **nouns** (or **pronouns**) anchoring the structure appear in bold, the **added structure** in bold underlined type.

1. **Noun (or pronoun) + True Adjective or Adjectival Phrase**

   His **research** <u>complete,</u> he began to write his report.

   Her **face** <u>red with embarrassment,</u> the senator finally found her place in her notes and continued her speech, the **crowd** <u>uneasy with her discomfort</u>.

Notice in these first examples two of the noun absolutes have "referents" in the sentence. The phrase *his research complete* refers to *he* in the sentence. The phrase *her face red with embarrassment* refers to *the senator*. But look at the noun absolute phrase ending the second example. The phrase *the crowd uneasy with her discomfort* has no referent in the sentence. So a noun absolute phrase usually—but not always—refers to another noun or pronoun in the main sentence.

2. **Noun (or pronoun) + Present Participle**

   The parties raised $500,000, the **founder** <u>paying</u> $400,000, the **others** <u>contributing</u> $100,000.

   His **tires** <u>screeching</u> on the pavement, John braked to avoid the pedestrian.

3. **Noun (or pronoun) + Past Participle**

   These **issues** <u>resolved,</u> the agency turned its attention to other matters.

   That <u>said</u>, the chair then turned her attention to the treasurer's report.

   His **face** <u>twisted in hatred</u>, the killer wildly hurled the hammer at his victim's head.

4. Noun (or pronoun) + Prepositional Phrase

In one of my writing courses presented at a federal agency, I was explaining the noun absolute phrase to a class of lawyers. One of the lawyers said, "Well, I'm currently working on a novel. I like to pattern my style after Hemingway's, and I can't imagine that he'd use such a structure."

The issue was joined, as lawyers are wont to say.

I didn't have to do much homework. Here's the *first sentence* of *For Whom the Bell Tolls:*

He lay flat on the brown, pine-needled floor of the forest, his **chin on his folded arms**, and high overhead the wind blew in the tops of the pine trees.

5. Noun (or pronoun) + Noun

Our opponent has chosen to ignore scientific principles, his **theories** a **wish list** of insupportable propositions.

The defendant knew he'd survive the trial, his **sister** the only **witness** to the murder.

Many of these structures have become widely known sayings in our language, culture, and even our law. In the following examples, the **noun** or **pronoun** appears in bold, the **added structure** in bold underlined type:

All **things considered**, the business managed to survive.

Other **things being equal**, the proposition will withstand scrutiny.

Weather permitting, we'll convene the class in the park.

The case was televised to the world, **Judge Ito presiding**.

A well-regulated **militia being necessary to the national defense**, the right to bear arms, shall not be infringed.[6]

Right now, you should tuck away a thought for the upcoming chapter on clause cutting: chapter 14, "Word War IV: Clauses vs. Phrases." Look

10 FUNCTIONS OF NOUNS

1. Subjects of sentences
2. Subject complements ("predicate noun" or "predicate nominative")
3. Direct objects of transitive verbs
4. Objects of verbal phrases
5. Indirect objects
6. Objects of prepositions
7. Noun appositives
8. Noun modifiers
9. Noun adverbs
10. Noun absolutes

at the five structures we add to a noun to yield the five types of noun absolutes. Commit them to memory:

1. adjective or adjectival phrase
2. present participial phrase (*-ing* phrase)
3. past participial phrase (*-ed* phrase)
4. prepositional phrase
5. noun appositive

In chapter 14, we're going to learn about the fine art of clause cutting. We'll see the same five structures appear with clauses that use the verb *to be*. We'll also see them reappear in another powerful structure, the *truncated clause*. Stay tuned.

THAT'S WHAT NOUNS DO: A SUMMARY

Those are the ten biggies. You must know them cold. You must be able to take any sentence, identify all nouns in the sentence, and specify the function each noun serves.

As you can see, the noun does some heavy lifting in our language. In fact, when coupled with the verb, the noun reveals our main idea to our readers. It makes a great deal of sense to use the noun to communicate noun-like information, doesn't it?

But would it make much sense to use the noun to communicate verb-like information? Especially when we have the verb sitting there—ready, willing, and able to do the job?

So let's revisit the verb, and, with no disrespect to the noun, proclaim the verb the most powerful of the eight parts of speech.

NOTES

1. Richard Wydick, *Plain English for Lawyers,* p. 61 (2d ed. 1985).
2. *Garner Legal,* p. 447.
3. *Ryder Energy Distribution Corp. v. Merrill Lynch Commodities, Inc.,* 748 F.2d 774 (2d Cir. 1984), quoted in *Garner Legal,* p. 447.
4. *Garner Oxford,* p. 2.
5. Quoted in *Garner Oxford,* p. 3.
6. United States Constitution, Second Amendment.

10

Verbs: What They Do

'm setting you up for the next chapter, "Word War I: Nouns vs. Verbs." In the last chapter, we looked more deeply at what nouns do in our language. We saw that nouns often need verbs to exist in the sentence. And if verbs are scarce, then to get nouns onto the back of the sentence, the writer must necessarily turn to prepositions and noun modifiers.

In this chapter we look once again at the verb. We want to see what it does and how it acts in our sentences. In chapter 9, we saw that nouns perform ten basic functions in our language. Here we'll see that verbs perform five. You might then conclude that nouns have more power than verbs because they can do double the number of things. But you'd be wrong, for as we will see, verbs can do it all. They can act as verbs, they can act as nouns, they can act as adjectives, and they can act as adverbs.

Using just verbs, you can write an entire sentence: <u>Learning to win has been thrilling</u>.

REVIEW: FOUR KINDS OF MAIN VERBS
Remember that all verbs break down into four categories: (1) action transitive, (2) action intransitive, (3) verb *to be*, and (4) linking verbs. Numbers 1 and 2 are action verbs; numbers 3 and 4, no-action verbs.

These four kinds of verbs enable us to write four basic types of sentences:

1a. Subject   + Transitive Verb   + Direct Object
    (Actor)   in the active voice   (Recipient)

1b. Subject   + Transitive Verb   + Actor Phrase
    (Recipient)   in the passive voice   (Actor)

2. Subject   + Intransitive Verb   + Phrase

3. Subject   + Verb *to be*   + Complement, Adjective,
                                          or Phrase

4. Subject   + Linking Verb   + Complement, Adjective,
                                          or Phrase

That's it, folks. Every English sentence falls into one of these categories, which vary with the type of verb chosen. When we get to chapter 15, we'll see how all writers begin with one of these types of sentences and then develop their styles by using subordination, parallel structure, and noun substitutes.

REVIEW: A FIFTH KIND OF VERB

Don't forget. We do have a fifth kind of verb, the auxiliary verb. Three are primary auxiliaries: *be, do,* and *have.* The verb *to be* enables us to form the progressive tense (**I am** writing) and the passive voice (**The book was** written by me). The verb *do* enables us to ask questions (**Do** you write?), to emphasize (Please **do** come for dinner), and to negate (She **did** not respond). And the verb *have* enables us to form the perfect tenses (You **have** written a book). Then, thirteen modal auxiliaries enable us to show various conditions, abilities, and obligations: *can, could, dare, may, might, must, need, ought (to), shall, should, used (to), will,* and *would.*

> **Verbs can do it all. They can act as verbs, as nouns, as adjectives, and as adverbs.**

REVIEW: CHAPTER 2

If you feel shaky about the concepts of conjugation, person, number, participles, and infinitives, you might go back right now and reread chapter 2. For now we're going to explore the ways the verb helps us improve our writing.

THE MANY AND VARIED FORMS AND FUNCTIONS OF VERBS
Verbs appear in five basic ways in our language, and in those various ways they can perform a wide variety of functions in the English sentence. Here are the five things verbs do in the English language. You must commit them to memory if you're ever to become a member of The Writers Club:

1. Conjugated verb
2. Infinitive phrase
3. Present participial phrase
4. Past participial phrase
5. Participial adjectives

Let's look closely at these forms and the many functions they perform.

> **FIVE FORMS OF VERBS**
>
> 1. **Conjugated verb**
> 2. **Infinitive phrase**
> 3. **Present participial phrase**
> 4. **Past participial phrase**
> 5. **Participial adjectives**

1. Conjugated Verb
In the list above I drew a line under the first form—the conjugated verb. It sits alone. It performs the most crucial role in all of English: It forms the sentence. Without the conjugated verb, we would have no complete grammatical sentences.

When conjugated, the verb forms two kinds of clauses. The *independent clause* can stand alone as a complete sentence. Ordinarily, it starts with a capital letter and ends with a period or other terminal punctuation. The independent clause, with its basic three-part message, is our starting point when we begin to write.

The *dependent clause* cannot exist by itself. It must attach itself to an independent clause. Consider these dependent clauses, with the **conjugated verbs** in bold (one clause has a clause within a clause):

> that **try** men's souls
> that our flag **was** still there
> and that government of the people, by the people, for the people,
>   **shall not perish** from this earth
> which they who **fought** here **have** thus far so nobly **advanced**

> **The conjugated verb forms two kinds of clauses: *independent* and *dependent*.**

None of those clauses can stand on its own. Instead, each needs an independent clause as a prop. When we get to chapter 14, "Word War IV: Clauses vs. Phrases," we'll learn what functions dependent clauses can serve in our sentences. There we'll see that they can act as nouns, adjectives, and adverbs.

So that's the conjugated verb. It forms independent clauses (which have all the attributes of complete sentences) and dependent clauses (which do not). Now let's look at the other forms and functions of verbs.

2. Infinitive Phrase

Remember the definition from chapter 2: The infinitive form of a verb is the word you would ordinarily look up in the dictionary. Its bare form is just the word by itself: *write*. Its *periphrastic* form consists of the infinitive preceded by the preposition *to: to write*. The bare infinitive appears in conjugations with the modal auxiliaries: I should **write,** I must **write,** I will **write.** The *"to"* form is needed for the modal *ought:* I ought **to write.**

> **The infinitive phrase gives us the ability to take a verb-like idea and use it as (1) a noun, (2) an adjective, or (3) an adverb.**

But we're not so interested in the use of infinitives to form certain conjugations. Instead, we want to see how they work on their own, as one of the three verbal phrases: infinitive, present participial, and past participial. The infinitive phrase gives us the ability to take a verb-like idea and use it as (1) a noun, (2) an adjective, or (3) an adverb. Thus, to increase the power of your writing, you must use infinitive phrases.

Just look at the four infinitive phrases in the preceding paragraph and the functions they perform:

Phrase	Function
use of infinitives **to form** certain conjugations	adjective modifying *use*
we want **to see** how they work	noun, the direct object of *want*

Phrase	**Function**
the ability **to take** a verb-like idea	adjective modifying *ability*
To increase the power of your prose, you must use infinitive phrases.	adverb modifying *must use*

Notice in the four phrases above that the verbs are transitive. Thus, the phrases themselves have objects:

> to form certain **conjugations**
> to see **how they work** (here the clause *how they work* acts as a noun)
> to take a verb-like **idea**
> to increase the **power** of your prose

To Split or Not to Split

Perhaps no "rule" of grammar sparks more controversy than the "rule" against splitting infinitives. Leading experts on the English language, however, point out that the split infinitive appeared in the great works of English as early as the fourteenth century, with two constructions appearing in the works of Chaucer.

The problem of the split infinitive only comes up when the infinitive appears with the preposition *to* and an accompanying adverb or adverbial phrase. If you put these adverbial words between the *to* and the verb, you have split the infinitive. If you keep the *to* and the verb together, you have refused to split the infinitive, and you must put the adverbial expression

Why the big fuss over splitting infinitives?

in one of three places: (1) before the infinitive, (2) after the infinitive, or (3) sometimes at the very end of the expression. Most writers prefer the before-the-infinitive and end-of-the-expression approaches.

Before the Infinitive

I had no wish <u>**actually**</u> **to read** it.

After the Infinitive

It became urgent **to demarcate <u>accurately</u>** Alaska's eastern boundary.

End of the Expression

For investors **to take a risk <u>voluntarily</u>**, they must first know the risks involved.

So why the big fuss over splitting infinitives? Tempers originally flared, no doubt, because of the relationship between English and Latin. In Latin, an infinitive verb appears as one word. For example, *to love* is *amâre,* and *to grow* is *crescere.* Thus, in Latin, one simply cannot split up the infinitive; it is already connected, it is indivisible. Consequently, in the early history of the English language, split infinitives rarely appeared in writing. But in 1812 Byron penned, **"to <u>slowly</u> trace** the forest's shady scene," and in 1895 Hardy wrote, "She wants **to <u>honestly and legally</u> marry** that man."

Barriers began to crumble.

So what, then, is the current state of the "rule"?

We can profit from the views of R. W. Burchfield, editor of *New Fowler:*

There can be no doubt that there continues to be a noticeable reluc-tance to split infinitives both in the national press and in the work of many of our most respected writers. Thus in a 1987 issue of the *Daily Telegraph* [we find]: *there will be a further disposition **seriously to underestimate** the strength . . . of the United States.* . . . Such placing of the adverb is overwhelmingly the norm at present.[1]

Thus, according to Henry Fowler, keeper of the Queen's English, top writers *reluctantly* split infinitives. But they do indeed split. Let's pick up with Mr. Burchfield's remarks:

When Bernard Levin, the well-known columnist in *The Times,* wrote (24 Oct. 1991) *he was in Vilnius to **formally** close down the headquarters of the Lithuanian KGB,* the use [of the split infinitive prompted an outcry and] called for special comment in the Diary of that newspaper two days later . . . : "The most diligent search can find no modern grammarian to pedantically, to dogmatically, to invariably condemn a split infinitive." These lighthearted comments draw attention to the irrational nervousness that many people feel when they are in danger of breaking a terrible taboo.[2]

Mr. Burchfield continues: "What then are the present-day facts?" He points out that most writers try to avoid splitting and place the adverb before the infinitive. Examples abound:

Before-the-Infinitive Approach

The threat of abolition enabled the Livingstone Administration **briefly to ride** the inevitable wave of popular indignation it caused.
—*London Review of Books,* 1987.

I had no wish **actually to read** it.   —C. Rumens, 1987.

Burchfield points out that writers less commonly put the adverb after the infinitive:

After-the-Infinitive Approach

It became urgent **to demarcate accurately** Alaska's eastern boundary   —*Georgr. Journal,* 1983.

Little or no effort has been made **to explicate clearly** the mechanisms through which these needs [can be satisfied]
—*European Sociological Review,* 1986.

But Burchfield cautions against "rigid adherence to a policy of non-splitting," for it "can sometimes lead to unnaturalness or ambiguity":

Unnatural

[England and the U.S. made a grave mistake] in not combining **to forbid flatly** hostilities.

Ambiguous (What does *flatly* modify? *combining? to forbid?*)

[England and the U.S. made a grave mistake] in not combining **flatly to forbid** hostilities.

Go ahead and split it

[England and the U.S. made a grave mistake] in not combining **to
flatly forbid** hostilities.

Burchfield further points out the trend among top writers to split
infinitives, where their objectives might be to avoid unnaturalness, to
avoid ambiguity, or perhaps even to stress the adverb. Following are
some examples from Burchfield's "substantial file . . . collected since
1987":

Examples of Splitting

That's when you have **to really watch** yourself
—Quarto, 1981 (UK).

It led Cheshires **to finally abandon** publishing fiction at all
—B. Oakley, 1985 (Australia).

The goal is **to further exclude** Arafat
—U.S. News & World Report, 1986 (United States).

Other leading authorities agree that the "rule" against splitting infinitives is not really a rule but a preference. Messrs. Strunk and White have
this to say:

There is precedent from the fourteenth century down for inter-
posing an adverb between *to* and the infinitive it governs, but the
construction should be avoided unless the writer wishes to place
unusual stress on the adverb.[3]

Elsewhere, the same authors observe that more than "unusual stress
on the adverb" can justify splitting the infinitive. Sometimes splitting
produces a better sentence:

The split infinitive is another trick of rhetoric in which the ear must
be quicker than the handbook. Some infinitives seem to improve on
being split . . . . "I cannot bring myself to really like the fellow." The
sentence is relaxed, the meaning is clear, the violation is harmless
and scarcely perceptible. Put the other way, the sentence becomes
stiff, needlessly formal.[4]

The Views of the OED

In 1998, the *Oxford English Dictionary* ended the centuries-old ban on splitting infinitives. Take a look at this press release:

> OLD SAYBROOK, Conn. (AP), October 26, 1998,—It's time to officially abandon the rule against the split infinitive.
>
> Oxford dictionaries, makers of the self-proclaimed "last word on words," has ended its centuries-old ban on splitting infinitives.
>
> Some language purists are unhappy with the change. They say the infinitive—a verb with "to" in front of it—always should remain joined. For example, the infinitive "to jump" should be modified as "to jump quickly," they say, and never "to quickly jump."
>
> "I do think it's a great sadness that the Oxford dictionary is doing this," said Loftus Jestin, head of the English department at Central Connecticut State University. "Hearing split infinitives is like listening to Mozart when the pianist keeps hitting all the wrong notes."
>
> "I do not dine with those who split infinitives," said Samuel Pickering, a University of Connecticut English professor who is considered to be the inspiration for the lead role in "The Dead Poets Society."
>
> The change is included in the new Oxford American Desk Dictionary, which came out last month. The dictionary says the prohibition on split infinitives can lead to "awkward, stilted sentences."
>
> Frank Abate, editor in chief of Oxford's U.S. dictionaries program in Old Saybrook, says the rule is arbitrary. The rule has its basis in Latin, and as Abate points out, we don't speak Latin.
>
> "There's essentially no validity to it," Abate said.
>
> Random House, Strunk and White and others already have given their approval to split infinitives.
>
> But this is Oxford after all, publisher of the venerable unabridged Oxford English Dictionary—the hallowed 20-volume, 138-pound, 21,730-page O.E.D. It is considered by many the authority on the King's English.
>
> Oxford University Press first lifted the moratorium in its British edition last year.
>
> Cindy Butos, assistant director of the writing center at Trinity College in Hartford, is thrilled with the change.
>
> "I think it's terrific," she said. She said it frees people from an unnecessary rule that doesn't contribute to the English language.

So what's the best advice? You can follow the rule in *New Fowler:* Split to stress the adverb, to avoid ambiguity, or to avoid writing a construction

> **"Hearing split infinitives is like listening to Mozart when the pianist keeps hitting all the wrong notes."**
> **—Loftus Jestin, Central Connecticut State University.**
>
> **"I don't dine with those who split infinitives."**
> **—Samuel Pickering, University of Connecticut.**

that simply sounds unnatural. Or if you want to split them all, you have the *Oxford English Dictionary* on your side.

But if you write for one who does not dine with those who split infinitives or for one who likens them to Mozart played with the wrong notes, I'd advise you not to split.

When the Infinitive Phrase Shows Tense and Voice

Elsewhere, I've stated that the conjugated verb shows three things: tense, person, and number. I've also stated that verbal phrases like the infinitive phrase do not show tense. Well, that's true for what's called the simple infinitive: *to ride*. We don't know anything about tense.

But infinitive phrases can appear in ways that reveal a time dimension. (They will still not reveal person and number.) Study the following phrases and note how tense is seemingly revealed. Note also the ability to express the phrase in the passive voice:

to ride the horse (active)
the horse **to be ridden** (passive)
to be riding the horse (progressive)
to have ridden the horse (perfect)
the horse **to have been ridden** (perfect passive)
to have been riding the horse (perfect progressive)

Infinitive Phrases: Check Your Style

You need to check your own writing style to see how often you use infinitive phrases. You also need to figure out whether you use them to serve all possible functions: noun, adjective, adverb. Powerful writers use them all the time. You should, too.

3. Present Participial Phrase

Every verb has a present participle. Just add *-ing* as an ending. If a silent *-e* ends the word, then drop it: *writing*. If a consonant ends the word, you'll sometimes have to double it: *beginning, occurring* (check the dictionary).

The present participle, which I call "the *-ing* verb," shows up in verb conjugation. Add it to any form of the verb *to be* and you get the progressive tense: We **are studying** ways to improve our writing styles; we **should have been studying** grammar in high school.

> The *-ing* verb forms the present participial phrase, which can then act as an adjective, as an adverb, and as a noun.

But the *-ing* verb also serves other vital roles. It can form the present participial phrase, which can then act as an adjective, an adverb, and a noun. When the *-ing* verb does act as a noun, it gets a special name: *gerund*. Let's take a look at examples of each:

Present Participial Phrase	Function
Running five miles a day improved the woman's health.	noun, subject of sentence
The woman **running five miles a day** improved her health.	adjective, modifying *woman*
Running five miles a day, the woman improved her health	adjective modifying *woman;* or adverb, modifying *improved*
The woman improved her health **running five miles a day.**	adverb, modifying *improved*
The woman improved her health by **running five miles a day.**	noun, object of preposition *by*

Above you can see the amazing versatility of the verb form. We can take the same words—*running five miles a day*—and simply by manipulating the location of the *-ing* phrase and the structure of the sentence produce different sentences with different functions of the phrase.

A Special Note on Gerunds:
Possessive Nouns and Possessive Case of Pronouns
Get ready for a can of worms, for we are about to discuss what Henry Fowler called "fused participles."

Compare these two sentences:

1. **She cannot tolerate** a <u>**baby**</u> going without food.
2. **She cannot tolerate** a <u>**baby's**</u> going without food.

Now what is it she cannot tolerate? A *baby?* Or the *going without food?* Take a look at the verb *cannot tolerate.* It's transitive, right? Yes, and it needs an object. That object must be a noun. So which noun completes the thought? The noun *baby?* Or the noun-gerund *going without food?*

The answer is quite obvious: She cannot tolerate the *going without food.* Fact is, from the statement, we can see that she is quite fond of babies and wants to protect them. But if we write *baby going* and not *baby's going,* the word *baby* initially tells the reader what she cannot tolerate: She can't tolerate the baby. But then the present participle ushers in the exactly opposite thought: Actually she loves babies.

> A fused participle consists of a noun or pronoun followed by an *-ing* verb. The entire unit is then plopped down in a sentence to serve as a noun. We might call it a *Noun Combo.*

The two words *baby going* form what Henry Fowler called a *fused participle.* Together, as a unit, they would have to serve the noun role of direct object of *cannot tolerate.* He became downright apoplectic over the construction, describing it as "grammatically indefensible" and saying that "the words defy grammatical analysis."[5]

A war of grammarians then broke out, Otto Jespersen saying that Fowler's analysis "is a typical specimen of the method of what I call the instinctive grammatical moralizer."[6] Wow, we wordsmiths can really get testy.

Does everybody reading this book see what a "fused participle" is? A fused participle consists of a noun or pronoun followed by an *-ing* verb. The entire unit is then plopped down in a sentence to serve as a noun. We might call it a *Noun Combo.*

What Fowler found so objectionable, and I tend to agree with him, is that a fused participle does defy grammatical analysis. To make the structure work, we have to recognize the structure—Noun Combo—as grammatically unique and grammatically accurate. In that form, the entire unit will sometimes fit in the sentence and serve as a noun. The problem with accepting this structure willy-nilly is this: It often not only defies grammatical analysis but directly contradicts what the writer is trying to say. In other words, sometimes the fused participle works and sometimes it doesn't. And meaning can shift dramatically, depending on whether the noun (or pronoun) appears in the possessive.

Writers, therefore, should (1) understand the problem, (2) learn how to analyze the situation facing them, and (3) come up with the correct construction.

Let's look at another example. Suppose you go home for the weekend to visit Mom and Dad. Your room is just as you left it, complete with wall posters of the latest rock stars and sports figures. Mom likes it that way. You have a great weekend, going out Saturday night and seeing some old high-school friends. Then, on Sunday, at the crack of noon, you awaken to a wonderful aroma: Mom is downstairs frying chicken. You leap out of bed, ready to meet the day, don your robe and slippers, go downstairs, head for the kitchen, and say to Mom,

"Wow! What a great way to wake up! I smelled you frying chicken."

Now if your mom had Miss Hamrick as her English teacher, she's likely to clean your clock with a spare frying pan. Look at what you said. Look at the three-part sentence. Recognize that the verb *smelled* is transitive and needs a direct object. I'll put the **subject** in bold, the **verb** in bold italic, and the **<u>direct object</u>** in bold underline:

I _smelled_ <u>you</u> frying chicken.

Of course, if your mom has been frying chicken all morning, perhaps that's the correct statement. But Mom doesn't like your grammar, for obvious reasons. Focus on the present participial phrase *frying chicken.* In your statement, this phrase is perfectly happy to sit there and act as an adjective modifying the pronoun *you.* In fact, in your statement, that's the function you've given to the phrase *frying chicken.* It's an adjectival phrase. The word *you* appears in the objective case and thus serves as the direct object of *smelled.*

But remember that the -*ing* verb can also act as a noun. It is then called a gerund. And maybe, just maybe, what you smelled was not Mom but *the frying of chicken.* Thus, you need to get *frying chicken* to serve as the object of *smelled.* To make that happen, look at what you have to do:

I *smelled* YOUR <u>frying chicken.</u>

By switching the objective case *you* to the possessive case *your,* you now allow *frying chicken* to act as the noun—as the direct object of the transitive verb *smelled.* The possessive-case *your* then possesses that noun. The possessive-case *your* possesses the *-ing* phrase, that is, the gerund.

The above is a traditional grammatical analysis. And that analysis is what prompted Fowler to say that fused participles defy grammatical analysis. For to get the fused participle to act properly in the sentence, you have to treat it as a separate and legitimate noun form—a Noun Combo. In other words, the direct object of the sentence must be the entire phrase, *you frying chicken.* So with a fused participle, our sentence would look like this:

I *smelled* <u>you frying chicken.</u>

Three Questions to Answer

Whenever you use a noun or pronoun followed by an *-ing* verb, you must figure out whether the issue of the fused participle even arises. Figure out what noun function you need in your sentence. Is it a direct object? An object of a preposition? A subject? Focus on the noun or pronoun. Then you must make one of three decisions about the use of the possessive:

1. Does the noun or pronoun serve that noun function and convey your meaning, and does the *-ing* verb therefore just modify the noun or pronoun? If so, do not use the possessive.
2. Does the *-ing* verb serve the noun role? If so, use the possessive.
3. Does the combination of the noun (or pronoun) and *-ing* verb state your meaning? If so, use the fused participle (don't use the possessive form).

Here are the three situations, along with their solutions:

1. Noun or Pronoun Serves Noun Role (Direct Object)

If so, don't make the noun or pronoun possessive:

> **She *saw* <u>the woman</u>** running down the street.

Here she saw the woman, not the running. The *-ing* verb *running* is clearly adjectival and modifies *woman*.

Does everyone see that this is not a fused participle? We're not using the combination *woman running*. We're using *woman* as the direct object and *running down the street* as an adjective modifying *woman*.

2. The *-ing* Verb Serves Noun Role (Direct Object)

If so, make the noun or pronoun possessive:

> **They *hated* OUR <u>digging up the yard</u>.**

Here they hated the *digging,* so we use the possessive case *our* to force the *-ing* verb to serve the role of the noun. We hope they didn't hate *us*. Hence, we avoid using the objective case *us,* which would produce this:

> **They *hated* US <u>digging up the yard</u>.**

3. Noun Combo Conveys Meaning and Serves Noun Role (Object of Preposition)

If so, don't make the noun or pronoun possessive. Let the fused participle stay:

> Many will question the wisdom **of <u>government departments straying</u>** into competitive commercial areas.[7]

Here the Noun Combo *government departments straying* is what many are questioning the wisdom of. The structure—the fused participle—acts as the object of the preposition *of*.

The key to successfully handling these structures lies in your ability to analyze the structure of the sentence and the different meanings it will convey if you make the noun or pronoun possessive and let the -*ing* verb act as the noun. Look at this example from *Strunk & White:*[8]

> Do you mind **me** asking a question?
> Do you mind **my** asking a question?

The two sentences convey quite different meanings. In the first *(me asking)*, the speaker is asking whether she, as opposed to someone else, may ask a question. In the second *(my asking)*, according to *Strunk & White,* "the issue is whether a question may be asked at all."

From the experts, we can glean some categories of situations where one style (possessive noun or pronoun) or the other (nonpossessive noun or pronoun) tends to dominate. Mr. Burchfield, the editor of *New Fowler,* has identified various examples of "current practice." He notes, however, that the choice is often a personal one. I would note, however, that the choice should primarily depend on grammatical analysis, which will reveal your meaning.

POSSESSIVE OR NONPOSSESSIVE

Word Before -*ing* Verb	Use Possessive	Use Non-possessive	Example
proper name	•		He wondered if he should be angry about **Nancy's having failed** to call him on time.
personal noun (e.g., brother, baby, son)	•		He did not like his **son's driving** with beer in the car.
nonpersonal noun (e.g., house, tree)		•	They enjoyed talking about the **house being** haunted.
plural nonpersonal noun		•	They expressed no opinion about the **jewels losing** their value.

Word Before *-ing* Verb	Use Possessive	Use Non-possessive	Example
personal pronouns (practice is evenly divided, but analyze grammar and meaning)	•	•	I do not understand **him making** that mistake. We appreciate **your stand-ing** in line to buy our tickets for us.
indefinite pronouns (e.g., something, everyone, anyone)		• •	These facts are a symptom of **something going wrong** with the banking system. Is there a problem with **everyone leaving** now?[9]
personal pronoun as first word in sentence	• (always)		**My interrupting** the class was frowned on. (Not: **Me** interrupting the class ....) (Not: **I** interrupting the class ....)

This topic is not an easy one to discuss. But it is definitely worth discussing, for in America today, many people do not seem to know that a noun or pronoun in its possessive form is often necessary to enable them to say exactly what they want to say. If they aren't careful, they might end up smelling their moms frying chicken.

You need a fairly high degree of grammatical knowledge to get through this discussion. **Your reading** this book should equip you with the necessary concepts.

4. Past Participial Phrase

Every verb has a past participle, which we form by adding *-ed* for regular verbs and some other ending for irregular verbs. For the *-ed* verbs, we sometimes have to double up an ending consonant *(occurred)* (check the dictionary).

Past participles show up in two places in verb conjugation. When coupled with the primary auxiliary *have,* they form the perfect tense: The committee **has decided** this issue. When coupled with the primary auxiliary *to be,* they form the passive voice: The tapes **were hidden** by the president of the United States.

> **The past participle forms the past participial phrase, which serves only as an adjective.**

But in addition to these conjugated forms, the past participle forms the past participial phrase. It invariably serves as an adjective, not as an adverb, and not as a noun. Look at these examples:

Past Participial Phrase	Function
Enacted in 1964, the Civil Rights Act moved power from the states to the federal government.	adjective modifying *Civil Rights Act*
The woman's stamina, **improved by her running five miles a day,** enabled her to battle the disease.	adjective modifying *stamina*
The package **delivered by UPS** contained the child's birthday present.	adjective modifying *package*
Thus armed, James granted a dispensation to the Curate of Putney.[10]	adjective modifying *James*

Three comments: First, notice that these adjectival phrases can either precede or follow the nouns they modify. Second, notice that commas surround a nonrestrictive phrase (improved by her running five miles a day) but don't appear with a restrictive phrase (delivered by UPS). And third, notice that the past participial phrase is really the remnant of a chopped-down passive-voice clause; these would read: . . . stamina, **which was improved** by her running five miles a day, and . . . package **that was delivered by UPS.** We'll learn in chapter 14 that phrases usually produce a cleaner style than clauses.

5. Participial Adjectives

We come to the end of the list of the functions of verbs. One-word participles, either present or past, serve as wonderful adjectives. Think about the images these verbal adjectives can paint in your writing:

> the **smoking** gun
> the **torn** pocket
> the sad, **twisted** face
> the **winning** poker hand

and

> the **conjugated** verb

THAT'S WHAT VERBS DO: A SUMMARY

Verbs fulfill five functions in our language. In their conjugated form, they enable us to form clauses, either as complete sentences or as dependent clauses. They also appear as infinitives (*to* verbs), as present participles (*-ing* verbs), and as past participles (ordinarily *-ed* verbs). In these three forms, they appear as phrases. And, in their *-ing* and *-ed* forms, they can appear as single-word adjectives.

We can use two of the verbal phrases (*to* phrase, *-ing* phrase) as nouns, adjectives, and adverbs. We can use the third verbal phrase (the *-ed* phrase) as an adjective. In short, verbs can perform the roles of all major parts of speech: nouns, verbs, adjectives, and adverbs.

That's power.

With so much versatility inherent in the verb form, one would think that writers would favor verb-based writing. The good writers do just that: They fashion their styles around the verb. But soft, fluffy writers shy away from verbs. Instead, they prefer the noun form.

So the time has come to see the first great tension in our language, the tension between verb-based writing and a condition called "nominalization," which I call "nouniness."

It's time to begin Word War I: Nouns vs. Verbs. Say hello to the idea of "nouniness." And then, when you finish the chapter, it'll be time to say goodbye to nouniness, once and for all.

NOTES

1. *New Fowler,* p. 737.
2. *New Fowler,* p. 737.
3. *Strunk & White,* p. 58.
4. *Strunk & White,* p. 78.
5. *New Fowler,* p. 609.
6. *New Fowler,* p. 609.
7. Quoted in *New Fowler,* p. 610.
8. *Strunk & White,* p. 13.
9. I recall a sentence in the chapter on adverbs by Mr. Follett: "These principles were practiced for many generations without *anyone's* **having** to think about them." *Follett,* p. 18. Usage does vary, even among the experts.
10. Winston S. Churchill, *A History of the English Speaking Peoples,* vol. 2, p. 392 (Dodd, Mead & Co. 1960).

Word War I: Nouns vs. Verbs

THE NOUNS ARE WINNING

Read the words of the sociologist:[1]

> In the act of forging, an ephemeral personal reorganization occurs in response to situational interactors which may be recognized as a special symbolic process conceived to cover aspects of motivation, feeling, emotion, and the choice of adjustment alternatives. The personal differentiae we have set down here are the original broad limits within which a certain class of situations can impinge upon the person with the possibility of emergent forgery.

Read Mr. Wilson Follett's curt critique: "The sociologist offends."
Read the words of the college administrator:

The educational program of the college is a unique approach to the teaching of the liberal arts and sciences. While offering a new level of flexibility for maximum individual student growth, the curriculum welds together the natural sciences, social sciences, and the humanities into a unified whole throughout the entire three years.

Here's the critique of Mr. Follett: "Apart from the obvious surplusage, these *approaches to teaching* and *levels of flexibility for maximum individual student growth* are unanalyzed abstractions that do not acquire meaning

211

simply by being juxtaposed in familiar ways. The one question that must be put to any description, especially that of a college program, is: What goes on? With nothing but abstract nouns in series, clarity and vividness are unattainable."

Read the words of the science reporter. This time I'm going to put some words in **bold type**:

> The **prediction** of the **existence** of antiparticles was made by Dirac in 1927 and its **confirmation** was an important **reason** for the **construction** of the Bevatron at Berkeley in 1954. [30 words.]

See how Mr. Follett rewrites the passage:

> Dirac **predicted** in 1927 that antiparticles **exist**. Once this state-ment **was confirmed**, the Bevatron **was built** in 1954. [18 words.]

See the problem? All three writers love the noun. They hardly know that verbs even exist. All three inflict on their readers piles of words, which, when read, make the readers feel as if they must trudge through mud to get at the meaning, if any lies there at all. The writing tires them out. And the reason is: *nouniness.*

These writers—indeed, many writers—think they sound more impor-tant when they use nouns and avoid verbs. If you're in college, listen to your professors. Read their writing. See if they suffer from nouniness. If you're a professor, listen to your students. Read their writing. See if they suffer from nouniness. If you're in business or gov-ernment, look at reports and memos com-

These poor writers wouldn't know a verb if it jumped up and bit them.

ing across your desk or filling up your e-mail in-box. See if your colleagues and perhaps your boss have a bad noun habit.

If you're in science, law, or the military, I can guarantee that you'll encounter nouniness in everything you read. Wade through this passage quoted in *Garner Legal:*

> The **regulation** of **solicitation** involves the **consideration** of whether there are ample alternative **channels** for **communica-tion** of the **information.**[2]

Or check out this mess quoted in *Garner Oxford:*

All of the "classic" **assumptions** that are at the basis of the terms "culture" and "intercultural differences" find **expression** in this **intervention**. That is why the **situation** at the Center is not a **question** of **organizational** change.[3]

Whew. Is it fun trudging through those "clusters of *-ion* words"?

Experts in style uniformly agree that power comes from verbs, not from nouns hooked onto sentences by prepositions and flimsy verbs. Listen to Henry Fowler:

> Flabby English is full of abstract nouns; the commonest ending of abstract nouns is *-ion,* and to count the *-ion* words in what one has written, or, better, to cultivate an ear that without special orders challenges them as they come, is one of the simplest means of making oneself less unreadable. It is as an unfailing sign of a nouny abstract style that **a cluster of *-ion* words is chiefly to be dreaded.** But some nouny writers are so far from being awake to that aspect of it that they fall into a still more obvious danger, and **so stud their sentences with *-ions* that the mere sound becomes an offence.** [Examples omitted.] Writers given to over-working these words would be wise to try doing without them altogether; they would seldom find any great difficulty in it, and they would have a salutary exercise in clear thinking.[4]

Listen to Wilson Follett:

> Many abstract nouns in English end in *-tion,* and the effect on the ear of stringing several of them together is narcotic. The prose of science may be left to the scientists, who are more concerned with numbers and diagrams than with words. But the prose of journalists, business [professionals], scholars, lawyers, and civil servants amounts to a public act and becomes our intellectual environment. It should, if not enchant, at least inform without causing instant weariness and protracted boredom.[5]

WHAT IS NOUNINESS?

Don't get me wrong. I do not say for a minute that you should purge all nouns from your writing. Indeed, you couldn't do that and still talk, write, or even think. Instead, I urge you to look for structures that Bryan Garner calls "buried verbs."[6]

SIX FEATURES OF NOUNINESS
1. **Derivative nouns**
2. **Derivative adjectives**
3. **Homographs**
4. **Weak verbs**
5. **Auxiliary verb goo**
6. **The preposition parade**

These structures are usually nouns and sometimes adjectives. We have three major types: (1) derivative nouns, (2) derivative adjectives, and (3) homographs. Using them causes you to use even more words, for nouniness forces you to write with (4) oodles of weak verbs, (5) auxiliary verb goo, and (6) the preposition parade. These six features of nouniness, which cause wordiness, prompted Bryan Garner to say:

> Though long neglected in books about writing [not by yours, Bryan, and not by mine], buried verbs ought to be the sworn enemy of every serious writer. [7]

Repeat: *Buried verbs ought to be the sworn enemy of every serious writer.*
Again: ***Buried verbs ought to be the sworn enemy of every serious writer.***

Got it?

THE SIX FEATURES OF NOUNINESS

1. Derivative Nouns

As the name implies, derivative nouns are derived from something. Well, they are derived from verbs. Hiding inside them, you'll find a verb form, or, as Bryan Garner would say, *buried* in the derivative noun is a verb form, desperate to get out. You can spot derivative nouns by the suffixes added to the verb to yield the noun. Watch for these suffixes:

Suffix	Verb	Derivative Noun
-tion	circumvent	circumvention
-sion	compel	compulsion
-ment	state	statement
-ence	depend	dependence
-ance	comply	compliance
-ency	tend	tendency
-ancy	hesitate	hesitancy
-ity	identify	identity

The nouny writer never *states* something; the nouny writer *makes a statement*. The nouny writer never *concludes* anything; the nouny writer *reaches a conclusion*. The nouny writer never *hesitates;* the nouny writer *exhibits a hesitancy*. The nouny writer *has a preference for* nouns.

But good writers *prefer* verbs.

2. Derivative Adjectives

We can also convert verbs into derivative adjectives. Though using these adjectives does not fit within the moniker of "nouniness," it does represent the same sin of avoiding verb forms by burying verb meanings in other structures. Again, adding suffixes enables us to bury verbs in derivative adjectives:

Suffix	Verb	Derivative Adjective
-ent	depend	dependent
-ant	hestitate	hesitant
-ful	hope	hopeful
-able	prevent	preventable
-ive	operate	operative

The nouny writer never *prevents* anything; the nouny writer makes certain that *it is preventable*. The nouny writer never *hopes;* the nouny writer *is hopeful*. The nouny writer never *hesitates;* the nouny writer *is hesitant*.

3. Homographs

Words that are spelled the same but may or may not be pronounced the same are called *homographs*. Often, in such pairs, one word is a noun, the other a verb; the words are spelled the same and sometimes pronounced the same. An example of a noun-verb homograph that is pronounced the same is *change* (noun) and *change* (verb). An example of a noun-verb homograph that is not pronounced the same is *use* (noun) and *use* (verb).

> **"Buried verbs ought to be the sworn enemy of every serious writer."—Bryan Garner**

Naturally enough, the nouny writer will always choose the noun form and, for some inexplicable reason, shy away from the verb form. Watch for these pairs (there are others):

Noun Form	Verb Form
change	change
love	love
use	use
abuse	abuse
request	request

The nouny writer never *requests* anything; the nouny writer *submits a request*. The nouny writer will not *change the policy;* the nouny writer *makes a change in the policy*. The nouny writer never talks about *using a computer;* the nouny writer *engages in the use of a computer*.

4. Weak Verbs

The nouny style will force you to use weak verbs, and that doesn't make sense. After all, if you've got a perfectly good verb meaning you are burying in a noun (or adjective), why attach that verb-like meaning buried in that noun to the sentence with some mushy verb like *be, have, involve, reach,* and a host of others? If you want to say the verb *state,* don't reach for some other weak verb and say **make** *a statement*. If you want to say *compel,* don't reach for a weak verb and say *there is a compulsion*. If you want to say *he predicted,* don't reach for a weak verb and say *he* **made** *a prediction* or worse *there* **was** *a prediction* **made** *by him*. You've already got a verb. It's buried in the noun (or adjective). Use it. Other unnecessary words will fall from the sentence.

5. Auxiliary Verb Goo

Remember auxiliary verbs? Especially the modals, which allow us to express compulsion *(must),* ability *(can),* permission *(may),* doubt *(might),* and other conditions? Well, look what happens to the poor nouny writer. The nouny writer wants to say *we* **must stop** *contradicting our boss*. But the nouny writer would never utter the verb *stop*. Instead, we'd get long-winded nouns like *termination* or *cessation*. So the nouny writer uses *termination*. But the nouny writer still has to get in the meaning of the auxiliary verb *must*. Trouble is, the nouny writer has no verb that the auxiliary can attach to. Thus, the nouny writer builds a pile of "auxiliary verb goo." Watch how the nouny writer says *we must stop contradicting the boss*. The **auxiliary verb goo** appears in bold:

There is a requirement of our termination of contradictions with our superior.

See? The words *there is a requirement of* mean nothing more than *must*. The word *termination* means nothing more than *stop:*

We **must stop** contradicting our boss.

In the nouny style, watch for these expressions:

Auxiliary Verb Goo	Auxiliary Verb
requirement	must
obligation	must
possible	can (could), may, might
possibility	can (could), may, might

6. The Preposition Parade

The nouny style will cause you to use scads of prepositional phrases. Remember our discussion of noun forms; they depend on other words to stick to a sentence; if you don't use many verbs as noun stickers, then you must turn to prepositions as the primary means of sticking nouns onto sentences. There's no other way you could possibly write or talk.

Nouny writers, of course, use very few verbs and thus must turn to the preposition as the means of sticking their nouns onto sentences.

If you come up to me and say, "Hey, Ed, I've got a 30-word sentence with only two verbs in it," then I would respond, "Well, you must have oodles of prepositions sticking nouns to the sentence. Otherwise, you couldn't say very much."

Take a look at our science reporter's 30-word sentence quoted at the beginning of this chapter. I'll put the **two verb forms** in bold and the **eight prepositions** in bold underline:

The prediction **of** the existence **of** antiparticles **was made by** Dirac **in** 1927 and its confirmation **was** an important reason **for** the construction **of** the Bevatron **at** Berkeley **in** 1954. [30 words, 2 verbs, *8 prepositions*]

Now look at Mr. Follett's verb-based rewrite. The **verbs** appear in bold, the **two prepositions** in bold underline:

> Dirac **predicted <u>in</u>** 1927 that antiparticles **exist.** Once this statement **was confirmed,** the Bevatron **was built <u>in</u>** 1954. [18 words, 4 verbs, *2 prepositions*]

WRITE WITH VERBS
AND YOUR WRITING WILL COME ALIVE

Nouny writing stays on an abstract plane. In it, nobody ever *does* anything. Your readers cannot visualize your concepts as they unfold. Instead, they must wade through noun-hooked-to-noun-hooked-to-noun-hooked-to-noun. Somewhere in there lies a verb. And an idea.

You *decide.* (*You reach a* **decision.**)

Which style *does* a better job of *expressing* what the writer *wants* to *say* to the reader? (*Which passage has a greater* **ability** *for the* **expression** *of the message that is the* **desire** *of the writer for* **communication** *to the reader?*)

You should *prefer* verbs. (*You should exhibit a* **preference** *for verbs.*)

Convinced? I hope so.

Now, in the next chapter, let's answer Hamlet's centuries-old question: *To be or not to be, that is the question.*

Not *to be.* That is the answer.

NOTES

1. The following examples of writing by a sociologist, a college administrator, and a science reporter appear in *Follett,* pp. 206–207. Mr. Follett's critique follows each example.
2. *Garner Legal,* p. 602.
3. *Garner Oxford,* p. 232.
4. *Fowler,* pp. 640–41 (bold emphasis added).
5. *Follett,* p. 206.
6. *Garner Legal,* pp. 122–23; *Garner Oxford,* pp. 49–50.
7. *Garner Legal,* p. 123; *Garner Oxford,* p. 50.

12

Word War II: *To Be* or Not *To Be*

People attending my courses in writing often ask if one simple trick can help improve their writing. I always respond, "Yes, try using fewer forms of the verb *to be.*"

If you write as many people do, you probably use the verb *to be* as the focal point of many sentences. When you choose the verb *to be,* you use up the most important part of the English sentence—the verb—and say very little. The other two parts—the subject and the noun or adjective following the *be*—must then carry the information you wish to convey. And, as a rule, nouns and adjectives don't do much to capture and hold the reader's attention, a task more adeptly carried out by the action verb.

OVERUSE OF *TO BE*

Let's look at a real-world example of overusing *to be,* one drawn from the law. First, attend a quick course on the "hearsay rule." This rule of evidence prevents a lawyer from introducing written or oral evidence penned or spoken by someone not in the courtroom. The absent writer or speaker cannot come forward for cross-examination. Thus, the law excludes that evidence, because the opposing side cannot attack it by cross-examining the witness.

But the hearsay rule does permit some exceptions. For example, a lawyer may admit documents that qualify as "business records." In the following passage from a brief submitted to a federal court, the writer explains the theory behind the business-records exception to the hearsay rule. Unfortunately, the writer of the brief has a severe habit of overusing the verb *to be*. The 11 **be's** appear in bold (I have changed the facts to protect the guilty):

> The reason for excluding business records from the hearsay rule **is** their circumstantial guarantee of trustworthiness. If a business **is to be** successful, there **must be** accurate records on which it can rely to carry out its activities.
>
> In the instant case, Exhibit A **is** a profit and loss statement. The making of a profit **was** a key consideration of the Benevolent Society in holding these bake sales. This document **was** prepared to record the result of the sale. The trustworthiness of Exhibit A **is** ensured by its intended usage by the Benevolent Society. It **is** respondent's position that Rule 803(6) **is** applicable and Exhibit A **is** admissible.

The tone of that kind of writing puts the reader in a cat-like coma.

But a factor other than tone should prompt you to reduce your use of the verb *to be:* getting rid of fuzzy abstraction. When you force yourself to use action verbs, typically you will toss abstraction aside. In each sentence, you create a concrete image, even when the subject matter itself forms part of an abstract whole, as it so often does in academic, business, legal, and scientific writing.

> **When you use action verbs, you'll toss abstraction aside. Abstraction, especially fuzzy abstraction, gets in the way of winning points with your professor, your boss, your potential customer, or other important readers.**

Abstraction, especially fuzzy abstraction, gets in the way of winning points with your professor, boss, potential customer, or other important readers. Their eyes glaze over, their minds cloud as they plod through yet another pile of abstract words. Careful writers seek to clarify their thoughts and avoid abstraction. They pull it off by refusing to use the main dab of glue that fastens abstract words to the already-overloaded sentence: the verb *to be.*

THE *E-PRIMERS*

The goals of clear writing and clear thinking prompted some members of the International Society for General Semantics to form a new language called *E-Prime*. As described by Cullen Murphy in the February 1992 issue of the *Atlantic Monthly*, the language of *E-Prime* has one simple but ambitious principle: Eradicate all forms of the verb *to be* from all language, written and spoken. According to Mr. Murphy, the "general semanticists believe that the very structure of language can influence or distort our perceptions, and they contend that a failure to observe the many ways in which language can do this results in an inability to apprehend the meaning not only of other people's words but of one's own as well. This, of course, causes problems, the size of which can range from the most minor misunderstanding to complete metaphysical disarray, and the problems, naturally, spill over into the realm of behavior."[1]

To rid their language of abstraction, the *E-Primers* cull all forms of *be*'s as main verbs in their sentences. They avoid the eight forms of the word—*am, is, are, was, were, be, being,* and *been*—whether those words appear fully spelled or as parts of contractions such as *I'm, it's,* or *there's*. The diehard *E-Primers* go even further and obliterate all forms of *to be* used as an auxiliary verb. They would therefore abolish all forms of the passive voice, as in **the case was decided,** and the progressive tense, as in **the man was carrying a package** or **we will be deciding this issue tomorrow.**

Do the *E-Primers* offer sound advice for the busy writer who must struggle daily with expressing complex ideas? Yes and no. Pedagogically, the *E-Primers* have discovered a trick. But linguistically, they go too far. Should you reduce your use of the verb *to be?* Without doubt. Should you abolish the word altogether? Hardly.

SWATTING YOUR *BE'S*

To gain practice, and to improve your writing dramatically, you should go on a *be* hunt. In fact, you should use your word processor to search for the eight culprits: *am, is, are, was, were, be, being,* and *been*. As you find these words, determine how you use them and see if you can say the same thing more clearly and vividly with action verbs.

To make it happen, try these mental tricks:

Show *being* through *doing*

Whenever I sit down to write, I put on my "doing helmet." As my sentences unfold, I constantly ask myself this question: *Who or what does what to whom or what?* I then try to show what something *is* by what it *does*. If you do this too, will your writing *be* better? Yes, but your writing will also *improve*. See how it works?

Bring the actor back into the writing

No one populates this sentence: There **are** only a few scholarly articles that have addressed this issue. Bring back the actors: Only a **few scholars** have addressed this issue.

Let ideas *act*

Oliver Wendell Holmes once wrote: "And we now have to consider whether the cautious statement in the former case *marked* the limit of the law."² Can a statement literally *mark* a limit of the law? No. But note the figurative image Holmes achieved by using the action verb.

Use linking verbs

As we saw in chapter 2, linking verbs include the sense verbs *(looks, sounds, feels, smells,* and *tastes)* and other verbs *(appears, becomes, continues, grows, proves, remains, seems,* and others). These verbs link to adjectives or nouns or sometimes adverbial phrases, e.g., he looks awful (adjective), she feels bad (adjective), she seems an honest woman (noun), the document appears in the appendix (adverbial phrase). Thus, instead of writing, The committee **was adamant in its refusal** to change its decision, write, The committee **remained adamant** and declined to change its decision. Or without a linking verb: The committee **adamantly refused** to change its decision.

Edit out nouniness

In the last chapter we saw the damage that nouniness inflicts on our style. When we use derivative nouns, derivative adjectives, and noun-verb homographs in our writing, we often hang them on our good friend, the verb *to be*. Thus: The senator **was <u>hesitant</u>.** Or: There **was** a <u>conclusion</u> to the case.

If you'll declare war on these stuffy and weak derivative nouns and adjectives—those that bury the more powerful verb—you'll simultaneously destroy many *be*'s. Thus, instead of writing, The senator **was** hesitant (derivative adjective), write, The senator **hesitated.** Don't pile up nouns like this: The meeting **was** because of our **desire** for the **achievement** of the **improvement** of our mutual **understanding.** Instead, use verbs and write, We **met** because we **wanted** to **understand** each other better.

Use intransitive verbs

Intransitive action verbs show motion or location of a person or thing. Thus, instead of writing, The pulse **is then divided** and **is switched** to two circuits, write, The pulse **then splits** and **moves** to two circuits. The English language offers hundreds of intransitive verbs: *stands, serves, moves, enters, leaves, remains, moves, stays, lies, proceeds,* and so on.

Fake it

The English language has many words that can substitute for the verb *to be.* Instead of writing, The event **was** before the deadline, write, The event **preceded** the deadline. In an article, Professor Charles White-bread of the USC Law Center wrote, "The juvenile court judge **emerges** as the best possible transfer decision maker." Not "**is** the best possible transfer decision maker."

Let's use some of these mental tricks to revise the above passage on the hearsay rule. The writer could have obliterated all 11 *be*'s. I'll put the verbs in **bold**:

> The law of evidence **excludes** business records from the hearsay rule because they **guarantee** a certain minimum level of trustworthiness. **To succeed,** a business **must keep** accurate records of its daily business dealings, records **deemed** reliable by the business itself and by its customers, suppliers, and lenders.
>
> In the current case, Exhibit A **amounts to** a typical profit-and-loss statement. **Motivated** by a desire **to raise** funds, the Benevolent Society **held** these annual bake sales and carefully **recorded**

their financial results in the document now **called** Exhibit A. The Society **viewed** the document as a business document and **relied** on it to plan future sales. Thus, the finder of fact **may rely** on the document as trustworthy. As a result, under Rule 803(6), the court **should admit** Exhibit A as a valid exception to the hearsay rule.

KICKING THE HABIT

If you have a *be* habit—in your speech or your writing—you might heed the words of Dean Richard Wydick in his book, *Plain English for Lawyers:*

> Avoid Cosmic Detachment
> When you find yourself struggling to express a complex . . . idea, remember to ask yourself [this] key question . . . : "Who is doing what to whom?" Bring those living creatures into your writing— make them move around and do things to each other. Suddenly abstraction will evaporate, and your writing will come alive.[3]

Most professions and disciplines have squeezed the life out of writing by insisting on the heavy use of *be*'s and their inevitable nouny abstractions. Various professions practically demand that their members enter a trance-like state of addiction to the verb *to be* and adopt a slew of other bad habits. Breaking those habits will require a lot of work. But you will experience the long-term reward of becoming a potent writer, and speaker, when you make it through a paragraph, a page, or even an entire paper or speech without using a single form of the verb *to be*.

As you read this chapter, notice that I never use the verb *to be*.

So you think that one cannot possibly write this way? Well, let me prove the point. Simply reread the 1,962 words I've used in this chapter. When you do, you'll search the text (not the examples or quotations) and find not one single construction of the verb *to be*. How did I do it? By showing *doing*, not *being*. By letting actors act. By letting ideas act. By making the action verb the key event in all sentences.

Try writing a paper of 2,000 words with zero constructions of the verb *to be*.

Two things will happen. You will probably get an *A*. And you will make a mad dash to the medicine cabinet for Exedrin to relieve a massive migraine.

EPILOGUE

Just for fun, look over a representative list of the verbs and verbals I used in this chapter.

achieved	fastens	populates
adopt	focusing	pull it off
already-overloaded	force	qualify
breaking	getting rid	recorded
bring back	glaze over	reread
bury	hang	squeezed
carried out	inflicts	swatting
cloud	kicking	think
deals	link	totaling
declare	motivated	try
destroy	obliterated	viewed
drawn	opposing	winning
edit out	overusing	wish
excludes	penned	
fake	plod	

NOTES

1. Cullen Murphy, *"To Be* in Their Bonnets," *Atlantic Monthly,* February 1992, p. 18.
2. *Johnson v. United States,* 228 U.S. 457, 458 (1913) (emphasis added).
3. Richard C. Wydick, *Plain English for Lawyers,* p. 63 (Carolina Academic Press 1992).

13

Word War III: Active vs. Passive

These days, the passive voice has a very bad reputation. Conventional wisdom has it that writers should *never* use the passive voice. The examples seem endless. A secretary of one of the federal departments banned the passive voice in any correspondence going out over his signature. Interestingly, his edict stated, "The active voice *is preferred*."

Another head of an independent federal agency condemned the passive voice in a memorandum to all agency employees. His memo began, "The active voice *is used* exclusively in the federal government."

Indeed, the fathers of the plain-language movement in America, Messrs. Strunk and White, admonish writers to use the active voice. They say, "Many a tame sentence of description *can be made* lively and emphatic by substituting a transitive in the active voice."[1]

And many books on writing criticize the passive voice by saying, "More often than not, the passive *is best avoided*."[2]

What's going on here?

Why do these critics of the passive voice use the passive voice to criticize the passive voice? Perhaps they intentionally tease their readers with admonitions against the passive couched in the passive itself.

While teaching courses in effective writing throughout the country, I have found that many people know the rule—*Prefer the active voice and avoid the passive*—but, when pressed, find it difficult to articulate just what the passive voice is, describe why they should avoid it, or identify when they might profitably use it.

It might pay us, then, to review the differences between the active and passive voice, analyze the conventional wisdom, and identify those situations where the passive voice *is preferred.*

PASSIVE VOICE: WHERE IT ALL BEGAN

One bright summer day, Amber and Igor returned to their cave with bags of wild, succulent berries. When they entered the cave, they saw their little three-year-old daughter, Stephanie, cowering in the corner, sucking her thumb, and clutching her security moose skin. Stephanie tried not to look at the earthenware in the middle of the cave. There it sat, in three pieces, with the words "Cookie Jar" chiseled on the biggest surviving piece.

In a moment of brilliant linguistic insight, little Stephanie said:

The cookie jar was broken.

Thus was uttered the first recorded passive-voice construction in all of human history. Ten thousand years later, the headlines of the *Washington Post* would blare out the latest quotation from yet another high government official:

Mistakes Were Made!

And so we humans invented the passive voice as a way of saying that *something was done* without having to reveal *whodunit.*

Amber and Igor promptly called Miss Hamrick on her cell phone and hastily assembled a meeting of the Verb Committee to announce this astounding discovery.

VOICE: TRANSITIVE VS. INTRANSITIVE VERBS

In your quest to become an expert in voice, you must first distinguish between transitive and intransitive verbs, a topic we covered in chapter 2. Only transitive verbs have voice. Pure intransitive verbs have no voice at all. Voice has to do with the relationship that a transitive verb has with a noun. A transitive verb, please recall, is quite capable of picking up a noun—that is, of attaching a noun to itself—without any help from any other word. The noun it picks up is called its direct object.

The transitive verb *hit,* for example, has no difficulty attaching itself to the noun *ball.* Thus, the quintessential sentence—John hit the ball—has *John* as its subject, *hit* as its transitive verb in the active voice, and *ball* as its direct object. But the intransitive verb *proceed* cannot attach itself to the noun *investigation.* You simply cannot *proceed the investigation.* The intransitive verb must turn to the preposition for help in picking up a noun: The board proceeded **with** the investigation.

If the verb you select to use is transitive, you then have a question to answer: Should you put it in the active voice or the passive voice? Many writers don't strategically answer that question. Instead, from a set of habits imbedded by their profession—government, military, academe, law, science—most writers routinely turn to the passive voice. Or, from conventional wisdom, some writers routinely turn to the active voice, ignoring those situations where the passive voice is preferred.

FORMING THE PASSIVE VOICE

To form the passive voice, take any form of the verb *to be* and add the past participle of the transitive verb. Don't protest and say you don't know the past participles of all transitive verbs, for you do. Just complete the trick sentence we learned in chapter 2, and you'll identify the past participle of the transitive verb: *I have [verb].* Just plug in the verb and you'll form the present perfect tense, which, as you know, also uses the past participle.

The past participles of regular verbs end in *-ed (decided), -t (dealt),* or *-d (heard).* The past participles of irregular verbs, however, end some other way: *-n (shown), -lt (felt, built),* and others.

Before forming some passive constructions, let's look at some active-voice sentences in various tenses. The <u>**subjects**</u> appear in bold underline, the ***active-voice verbs*** in bold italics, the **direct objects** in bold:

> ***Active-Voice Sentences***
> The <u>**committee**</u> ***decided*** this **issue** (past tense).
> <u>**Congress**</u> ***will enact*** the **statute** (future tense).

The **intern** *has witnessed* this **medical procedure** (present perfect tense).

John *is showing* the **movie** (present progressive tense).

The **contractor** *was building* the **stadium** (past progressive tense).

Notice that these active-voice sentences occur in many different tenses, shown parenthetically above. In all, regardless of tense, the **subject** does something to the **direct object**. The *verb*, appearing in the active voice, forces the agent of the verbal activity to stand as the subject of the sentence, whereas the recipient of the verbal activity serves as the direct object of the sentence. The *do-or* is the subject. The *do-ee* is the direct object. In these active-voice sentences, the grammatical subject is *active*.

We can, of course, take the same sentences, flip them over, and write them in the *passive voice*. When we do, what

> **To form the passive voice, take any form of the verb** *to be* **and add the past participle of the transitive verb.**

used to be the direct object becomes the **subject** of the sentence. What used to be the subject in the active-voice sentence now trots to the end of the sentence and sits there as the **object of the preposition** *by*. The tense, you will note, does not change. Just the voice. In these passive-voice sentences, the grammatical subject is *passive:*

Passive-Voice Sentences

This **issue** *was decided* by the **committee** (past tense).

The **statute** *will be enacted* by **Congress** (future tense).

This **medical procedure** *has been witnessed* by the **intern** (present perfect tense).

The **movie** *is being shown* by **John** (present progressive tense).

The **stadium** *was being built* by the **contractor** (past progressive tense).

If you look carefully at the above passive-voice constructions, you'll see that all use the past participle of the transitive verb (*decided, enacted, witnessed, shown,* and *built*). The constructions simply form their tenses through the conjugation of the verb *to be,* i.e., *was, will be, has been, is being,* and *was being.*

A CONJUGATION IN THE PASSIVE VOICE
In chapter 2, we conjugated regular and irregular verbs in the six major tenses. Here's a conjugation of the verb *to write:*

> **present:** I write, you write, he/she/it writes, we write, you write, they write
>
> **past:** I wrote, you wrote, he/she/it wrote, we wrote, you wrote, they wrote
>
> **future:** I will (shall) write, you will write, he/she/it will write, we will (shall) write, you will write, they will write
>
> **present perfect:** I have written, you have written, he/she/it has written, we have written, you have written, they have written
>
> **past perfect:** I had written, you had written, he/she/it had written, we had written, you had written, they had written
>
> **future perfect:** I will (shall) have written, you will have written, he/she/it will have written, we will (shall) have written, you will have written, they will have written

We then conjugated a verb in the six progressive tenses. Here's the verb *to write:*

> **present progressive:** I am writing, you are writing, he/she/it is writing, we are writing, you are writing, they are writing
>
> **past progressive:** I was writing, you were writing, he/she/it was writing, we were writing, you were writing, they were writing
>
> **future progressive:** I will (shall) be writing, you will be writing, he/she/it will be writing, we will (shall) be writing, you will be writing, they will be writing
>
> **present perfect progressive:** I have been writing, you have been writing, he/she/it has been writing, we have been writing, you have been writing, they have been writing
>
> **past perfect progressive:** I had been writing, you had been writing, he/she/it had been writing, we had been writing, you had been writing, they had been writing

> **future perfect progressive:** I will (shall) have been writing, you will have been writing, he/she/it will have been writing, we will (shall) have been writing, you will have been writing, they will have been writing

We should now look at a complete conjugation of a transitive verb in the passive voice. As you will see, you can convert the six main tenses into passive constructions. But you can only convert two of the progressive tenses into the passive voice: the present progressive and the past progressive. There is no future progressive passive. There are no perfect progressive passives.

Let's conjugate the transitive verb *show* in both voices: active and passive. We'll put the subject-actor *John* to the left for the active-voice constructions. John trots to the end of the sentences in the passive constructions. The word *movie* serves as the direct object of the active-voice constructions and as the subject of the passive-voice constructions. Take a look:

	Active	**Passive**
	shows	is shown
	showed	was shown
	will show	will be shown
John	has shown **the movie.**	has been shown
	had shown	had been shown
	will have shown	**The movie** will have been shown **by John.**
	is showing	is being shown
	was showing	was being shown
	will be showing	?
	has been showing	?
	had been showing	?
	will have been showing	?

Again, notice the absence of any passive progressive tenses beyond past progressive *(was being shown)*. If we had future progressive passive, it would appear like this: *will be being shown*. Present perfect progressive passive would yield: *has been being shown*. Those constructions just don't exist in the language.

I said as much in a book I wrote for lawyers in the 1980s: *Mightier than the Sword—Powerful Writing in the Legal Profession*. Then one day I got a rather nasty letter from some English professor at a small college in a state I won't name. He tore into me, saying "Oh yeah? What's wrong with the future progressive passive, *will be being shown?*" I soothingly wrote back: "There's nothing wrong with the construction, sir. It simply doesn't exist, except perhaps in [name of state]." Whew. Writing a book on writing takes guts.

At the time, I couldn't find any authority for my statement. But now I can cite Thomas Kane:

> In the *progressive* aspect, passives are formed *only* *for the present and past tenses*. The formula is: the appropriate tense form of *be* + *being* + the past participle of the main verb:
>
> | Present | *is being shown* |
> | Past | *was being shown*[3] |

THE CONVENTIONAL WISDOM

So is the conventional wisdom correct? Should a writer prefer the active voice over the passive? We can frame the answer as a rule: Favor the active over the passive unless you can find a good reason not to. In fact, many writers, suffering from a longstanding habit of passive-voice writing, should seek to break free by trying to write every sentence in the active voice. Then, with caution, these former addicts can try a few passives to achieve various objectives.

But you must proceed with caution. Without doubt, traditional scientific, legal, bureaucratic, and academic writing favors the passive to such a degree that most writers inevitably succumb to the addiction and end up writing like this:

> The original, duplicate, and triplicate copies of the enclosed agreement **should be signed and dated,** as indicated with the corporate name, followed by the signature of an authorized corporate officer or an authorized representative. After it **has been executed** in triplicate, the signed original and copies of the agreement **must be returned** to this office within thirty days. If the signed original and copies of the agreement **are not received** by this office within

thirty days, it **will be assumed** that it **is no longer desired** by you to enter into a closing agreement and, accordingly, our files in regard to this matter **will be closed** without further action.

Rancid.

Surely the heavy passive-voice style of that passage will not tempt the Pulitzer Committee to pick up the phone and award the prize. Surely the active voice does a better job:

> You must sign and date the original and two copies of the enclosed agreement. Use the corporate name and follow it with the signature of the person authorized to sign for the corporation. Then return the original and two copies to this office within thirty days. If we do not receive them by that time, we will assume that you no longer want to enter into a closing agreement and will close our files on this matter without further action.

A CONTRARIAN VIEW: WHEN THE PASSIVE *IS PREFERRED*

I believe that the passive voice is justified in seven situations. Virtually all have to do with the relative importance of the identity of the actor vis-à-vis the recipient of the action. When the actor is the focus of your subject matter, you should use the active voice, which places the actor as the grammatical subject. But when the result, that is, the recipient of the action, becomes your focus, you should use the passive voice, which places the recipient as the grammatical subject. Sometimes you want to flip-flop a sentence and place the actor at the end, a feat achievable only by using the passive voice.

> **PASSIVE IS PREFERRED**
>
> 1. **Generalizing**
> 2. **Actor is punch**
> 3. **Actor is irrelevant**
> 4. **Actor is unknown**
> 5. **Hide the actor**
> 6. **Avoid sexist writing**
> 7. **Recipient is subject**

1. **When you are generalizing and want to avoid overusing the pronoun *one***

    Remember back in college or graduate school when professors would *one* you to death: "*One* might point out, mightn't *one*, that

one's best approach concerns the use of *one's* . . . ." In the faculty
lounge one day, I even heard a professor inquire of a colleague,
"Where might *one* find the coffee cream?"

One should get a life. In the passive: Where **is** the coffee cream
found? Or why not the good old verb *to be:* Where in heck **is** the darn
coffee cream?

> **Passive:** Here are seven situations when the passive voice **is
> preferred.**
>
> **Active:** Here are seven situations when **one prefers** the pas-
> sive voice.

Don't get me wrong. I do not advise writers to obliterate the pronoun *one* as a handy device when generalizing. One should simply
seek a sense of balance.

2. **When the identity of the actor is the punch of the sentence
   and you want to place it at the end**

   According to the theories of "primacy" and "recency," the two
   most emphatic parts of a sentence are the beginning and the end.
   Often, you can achieve a sense of drama or intrigue by postponing
   the crucial information to the very end. If the emphatic information in a sentence is the actor, then the only way in the English language to make an actor trot to the tail end of a sentence is to use
   the passive voice.

> **Passive:** The tapes **were hidden** by the **president of the
> United States.**
>
> **Active:** The president of the United States **hid** the **tapes.**

3. **When the identity of the actor is irrelevant and you simply
   want to omit it**

   This situation often arises in many forms of writing. If you're
   writing about the enactment of a federal statute, then the enactor,
   of course, is Congress, a truly irrelevant bit of information. Or if
   you're writing about an issue confronting your company, often the
   decider of that issue is irrelevant. If the identity of the actor is irrelevant, then the only way in the English language to omit the actor
   altogether is to use the passive voice.

Passive: The ad campaign **was concocted** late last summer.
Active: The marketing department **concocted** the ad campaign late last summer.

4. When the identity of the actor is unknown

Perhaps you don't know who the actor was. If you follow conventional wisdom and always use the active voice, then you must use the word *somebody* as the subject of your sentence. Notice how the active-voice sentence is not very mysterious.

Passive: The files **were** mysteriously **destroyed.**
Active: Somebody mysteriously **destroyed** the files.

5. When you want to hide the identity of the actor

This is the cover-your-, uh, self approach. Perhaps you know who the actor is, but you ain't sayin'. You're like little Stephanie, who broke the cookie jar in Igor and Amber's cave:

Passive: I regret to inform you that your file **has been misplaced** (by me!).
Active: I regret to inform you that **I misplaced** your file.

6. When you want to avoid sexist writing but also want to avoid those horrible *s(he)'s, he/she's, him/her's,* and *his/her's*

A graduate student inevitably gets tangled up in her/his third-person singular pronouns when s(he) must refer to his/her singular antecedent in her/his master's thesis. Often, the passive voice offers him/her a way out of this morass:

Passive: An application **must be filed** with the personnel office. A complete educational background **should be included.**
Active: An applicant for employment **must file her/his** application with the personnel office. **He/she** should include **her/his** complete educational background.

7. When the recipient of the action is the focus

When you focus on the recipient of the action, you can keep the spotlight shining on your subject only by using the passive voice.

> **Passive:** Smith, because he knows the workings of the depart-
> ment, has lasted for more than a year. Nevertheless, **he** will
> probably be asked to resign.
>
> **Active:** Smith, because he knows the workings of the depart-
> ment, has lasted for more than a year. The **CEO,** nevertheless,
> will probably ask him to resign.

A DANGER LURKS

Carving out so many exceptions to the rule runs an obvious risk: The
exceptions might very well consume the rule. If you are a passive-voice
addict, then you'll be able to justify every passive construction. So remain
alert and guard against the onset of an overly passive writing style. As so
often seen in articles on effective writing:

> The passive voice is best avoided.

By one.

SUMMARY: THE FIRST THREE WARS OF THE WORDS

The last three chapters have reviewed the three biggest problems with
the style of many writers: "Word War I: Nouns vs. Verbs," "Word War II:
To Be or Not *To Be,*" and "Word War III: Active vs. Passive." Writers use
too many nouns and not enough action verbs, too many constructions of
the verb *to be,* and too many passive-voice constructions of transitive
verbs.

These three features characterize the styles of the scientist, the government worker, the military careerist, the lawyer, and many academics.
Just reread the sample passages at the beginning of chapter 11. Look at
the science reporter's sentence with all three problems identified in
brackets:

> The **prediction** [noun] of the **existence** [noun] of antiparticles
> **was made** [passive] by Dirac in 1927 and its **confirmation** [noun]
> **was** *[to be]* an important reason for the **construction** [noun] of
> the Bevatron at Berkeley in 1954.

When I encounter writing like that, I immediately know how to help
the writer. I focus on the three biggies: nouns, *be*'s, and passives.

In the early 1990s, I was teaching a course to a group of lawyers in Atlanta. The course took place in the Medical Arts Society, a beautiful old building in midtown Atlanta. We held the course in the library, lined floor to ceiling with medical books in old wooden bookcases. When I came to the part of the course dealing with the big three— nouns, *be*'s, and passives—I mentioned that those in the sciences and medicine had the most intractable habits of using these three structures. To prove it, I pulled a medical book off the shelf at random and read a passage aloud. The writer of the passage built every single sentence around the verb *to be* or a passive-voice action verb. Most of the meaning dwelled in derivative nouns, derivative adjectives, and noun-verb homographs. The style was slow and sluggish.

> **Writers use too many nouns and not enough action verbs, too many constructions of the verb *to be*, and too many passive-voice constructions of transitive verbs.**

No wonder it takes seven years to become a doctor.

If you want to improve your writing right now, you must focus on the verb form. You must resist the urge to put your meaning in buried verbs. Instead, free them up and let them act like verbs. When you do, put most of them in the active voice. And all the while, declare war on the verb *to be*. Challenge yourself to see how many sentences, how many paragraphs, how many pages you can write without using a single *be*. Practice speaking without using the verb *to be* at all.

If you want a real challenge, try what I do in my courses on effective writing.

When teaching lawyers how to improve their writing, I always use a trick when I get to the part of the course dealing with the verb *to be* and the passive voice. I'll casually ask if someone has the correct time, as if I want to plan the timing of the next section. Someone will say, "10:30." I'll then begin my lecture on the overuse of the verb *to be*. After about 10 minutes, I'll stop and ask the same person, "What time do you have now." "10:37" comes the answer. I continue the lecture. Then I ask the time again. "10:48." And so on.

Slowly it begins to dawn on the class. They realize that my oral lecture lacks any constructions of the verb *to be* or the passive voice. They then sit up and take notice, waiting to pounce. In the summer of 2000, I set my record at a New York law firm. In that lecture, I went for 20 straight minutes without using a single construction of the verb *to be* or the passive voice. Then, just this summer, I broke that record at a Washington law firm by speaking for 21 minutes without using a single form of *to be*.

Inevitably I will slip and out comes a *be* or a passive. But I've gotten pretty good at it, and the exercise has improved my ability to speak in a way that keeps the attention of students already on the edge of their seats as they anxiously await a discussion of the nonexistent future perfect progressive in the passive voice. Yeah, right.

Now you try that out when you talk. The exercise alone will challenge your mental faculties. And when you get good at it, you'll speak—and write—much more forcefully.

Now we move to yet another big problem of modern, stuffy style: overusing clauses.

NOTES
1. *Strunk & White,* p. 18.
2. Richard K. Neumann Jr., *Legal Reasoning and Legal Writing,* p. 70 (Little Brown & Co. 1990).
3. *Kane,* p. 680.

14

Word War IV: Clauses vs. Phrases

Ever hear of a well-claused article? No, and you won't. You will hear, however, of a well-*phrased* article.

Many writers use way too many clauses. They introduce them with lots of *thats* and *whiches*.

Truth be known, many writers don't know the differences between *that* and *which,* the relative pronouns we touched on briefly in chapter 5. When confronted with the choice, they use either the coin-toss approach (heads *that,* tails *which*), the fairness doctrine (50 percent *that,* 50 percent *which*), or the sounds-best approach ("*which* sounds like the word my professor would use, so I'll go with *which*"). The resulting mishmash threatens precision and diminishes credibility in the eyes of readers who know correct usage.

Powerful writers do know the differences between *that* and *which.* But even when they use the words correctly, they stay alert for leaner structures to replace *that* and *which* clauses whenever possible. It's a two-part exercise: Let's first learn the differences between *that* and *which,* and then explore the fine art of cutting cumbersome clauses down to leaner phrases.

> **First we'll learn the differences between *that* and *which,* and then explore the fine art of cutting clauses down to phrases.**

THAT VS. *WHICH*

The confusion between *that* and *which* arises only in the context of adjectival clauses, that is, clauses modifying a noun or pronoun. We don't need to fret about the noun clause, which can also use *that* as its beginning word: The professor said **that** attendance is not mandatory. In that sentence, the word *that* starts a noun clause, not an adjectival clause. The noun clause acts as the direct object of the transitive verb *said*. Do not confuse the two. Instead, focus on the clause modifying a noun.

When you modify a noun in your sentence, you must do so either restrictively or nonrestrictively. Let's suppose you need to modify the noun *cows*. Let's suppose you own a cattle ranch, either because you like cows or because you read somewhere that farming is cool. Let's further suppose that a violent thunderstorm strikes your ranch one summer night. The next morning, your ranch manager—a noted grammarian—knocks on the door of the big house and says one of two things:

1. The cows **that** *slept in the barn* survived.
2. The cows, **which** *slept in the barn,* survived.

To analyze which statement you hope is true, we must call on a pie chart for help.

THE COW PIE CHART

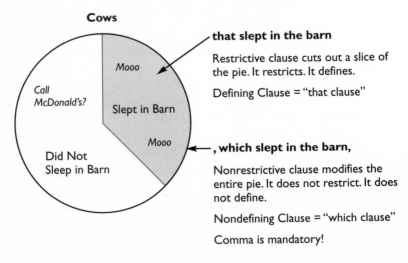

Cows

Mooo

Call McDonald's?

Slept in Barn

Mooo

Did Not Sleep in Barn

that slept in the barn

Restrictive clause cuts out a slice of the pie. It restricts. It defines.

Defining Clause = "that clause"

, which slept in the barn,

Nonrestrictive clause modifies the entire pie. It does not restrict. It does not define.

Nondefining Clause = "which clause"

Comma is mandatory!

A matter of bovine life and death hangs in the balance and turns directly on the sentence your manager chooses. As you can see from the Cow Pie Chart (please note the correct absence of a hyphen!), if he uses the restrictive *that* clause, some of your cows did not sleep in the barn, and you might have some dead cows out there in the lower forty. But if he uses the nonrestrictive *which* clause, all your cows slept in the barn and survived.

Here's why. A restrictive clause singles out a subset from the larger universe. Thus, in our cow example, the expression—the cows that slept in the barn—singles out the alive cows in the barn from the (perhaps dead) cows *not* in the barn. From the sentence, we don't actually know whether the other cows, the ones *that did not sleep in the barn,* did *not* survive. They might be grazing over there next to the fence. But we do know, from the restrictive clause, that not all of your cows slept in the barn. Some munched clover outside when lightning struck.

A nonrestrictive clause, on the other hand, does not carve up the universe represented by the modified noun. Here, the statement—the cows, which slept in the barn,—means that all cows slept in the barn, none having to face the harsh elements of the storm.

So what governs the farm manager's choice? ***The reality of the situation.*** If all cows slept in the barn, he will use the nonrestrictive "comma *which*" clause. But if some cows did *not* sleep in the barn, he will use the restrictive *"that"* clause.

Powerful writers know these differences between restrictive and nonrestrictive clauses, also called *defining* and *nondefining* clauses. They always start the restrictive/defining clauses with *that*s and the nonrestrictive/nondefining ones with *which*es. They always set off nonrestrictive clauses with the mandatory commas.

WHO, WHOM, WHOSE

You should note that not all restrictive and nonrestrictive clauses begin with *that* and *which*. We learned in chapter 5 about the other relative pronouns: *who, whom,* and *whose.* We've already gone over the differences among these words, so I'll simply point out that any restrictive clause they introduce has no commas and any nonrestrictive clause they introduce carries the mandatory commas.

You can find a good example of how crucial it is to distinguish between restrictive and nonrestrictive clauses in a sentence at the beginning of this chapter. There I wrote, "The resulting mishmash threatens precision and diminishes credibility in the eyes of **readers who know correct usage.**" Question: Do all readers know correct usage? Of course not. Therefore, I am singling out only those readers *who know correct usage.* Thus, I use a restrictive clause and omit the comma before the word *who.* If I had included commas to set off the clause, I would have said that all readers know correct usage. That's not my meaning, because that's not true. Thus, I can express my meaning—and truth—only by knowing the differences between a restrictive clause (no comma) and a nonrestrictive clause (mandatory commas).

As you can see, meaning totally shifts with the presence or absence of a single comma. Thus, it pays off for writers, who should be able to articulate their precise meaning, to know the differences between restrictive and nonrestrictive clauses and the corresponding differences between *that* (restrictive/defining) and *which* (nonrestrictive/nondefining). (Check out the sentence you just finished reading: *All* writers should be able to show their precise meaning. Note, therefore, the mandatory commas setting off the nonrestrictive clause—**who should be able to articulate their precise meaning.**)

CLASSIC "CLAUSINESS"

Now that you're up to speed on the differences between *that* and *which,* let's learn the ins and outs of the fine art of clause cutting. Most writers use far too many clauses and ignore the leaner structure, the phrase. Again, I ask you: Ever heard of a well-claused paper? Nope. And you won't, either.

Look at this classic clausiness:

> The argument **that** the candidate makes is further countered by the fact **that**, in schools **which** deal with children **that** need teachers **who** have earned degrees in special education, once it has been determined **that** some funding should be made available, the legislature **which** is responsible for passing appropriations will not appropriate an amount **that** is large enough to pay for the teachers **that** are needed in these schools **that** educate these children **that** have needs **which** are special.

Wow. One sentence. Twelve dependent clauses. *Which*es and *that*s mixed up willy-nilly.

No Pulitzer there.

GOING ON A *WHICH* HUNT

Study this advice of *Strunk & White:*

> But it would be a convenience to all if these two pronouns [*that* and *which*] were used with precision. The careful writer, watchful for small conveniences, goes *which*-hunting, removes the defining [restrictive] *which*es, and by so doing improves his work.[1]

Truth be known, that one passage has caused a lot of problems for writers. Note the words: *removes defining whiches.* Well, that's wrong. Writers should not *remove* defining *which*es but *should change* them to *that*s.

In the late 1980s, I was commissioned to train more than 1,000 people at a federal agency. The program stretched over several years and required my review of writing samples of the participants. In one particular division, I noticed that the writers simply never used the word *which.* For nondefining clauses they would use *that* and would omit the mandatory commas. When I asked these writers why they had abolished the word *which,* one recalled an in-house training program they had attended some years back. The writing instructor followed *Strunk & White* and had told them to *remove defining whiches.* Well, they took that to mean *remove all whiches.* The instructor—and *Strunk & White*—should give the proper advice: **Change** defining *which*es to the correct word—*that.*

> As your first step in the *which* hunt, change your defining *which*es to *that*s and insert the mandatory commas before and after all nondefining *which* clauses.

I do like the *Strunk & White* advice to go on a *which* hunt, however. Most writers use *which* when they mean *that.* If you do know the differences between *that* and *which,* then you'll want to go on a *which* hunt and a *that* hunt. Your objective is to ferret out clauses that should appear as phrases.

So after writing a report, a thesis, a love letter, whatever, use your word-processing program to search for the word *which.*

As your first step in the *which* hunt, simply change your restrictive (defining) *which*es to *that*s and insert the mandatory commas before and after all nonrestrictive (nondefining) *which* clauses.

Then, after changing defining *which*es to *that*s, go back and do two word searches, one for *which* and one for *that*. You are now searching for unnecessary adjectival clauses, which should appear as phrases or some other structure.

BE CLAUSES VS. ACTION-VERB CLAUSES

As your word-processing program locates each *which* (or *that*), you'll begin to notice that all clauses fall into two major categories, those that use the verb *to be* and those that don't. Your clause-cutting technique will depend on the type of clause: You'll take one approach for *be* clauses, another for action-verb clauses.

Cutting Clauses That Use the Verb *To Be*

The *be* clauses come in five varieties, which you can effectively cut by zapping the *which is, that was, which are, that were,* and so on. Back in chapter 9, we learned all about one very important role that nouns play in our language. Remember the noun absolute? If not, go back to chapter 9 right now and reread that section. To form a noun absolute we take a noun or pronoun and add one of five different structures. Here they are:

1. adjectival phrase
2. present participial phrase (-*ing* phrase)
3. past participial phrase (-*ed* phrase)
4. prepositional phrase
5. noun appositive

Well, guess what? When you locate *be* clauses in your writing, you'll typically find the verb *to be* followed by (1) an adjectival phrase, (2) an -*ing* verb, (3) an -*ed* verb, (4) a prepositional phrase, or (5) a noun. So guess what we're going to cut the *be* clauses down to? You got it:

1. adjectival phrase
2. present participial phrase (-*ing* phrase)
3. past participial phrase (-*ed* phrase)

4. prepositional phrase
5. noun appositive

1. *which* or *that* + *be* + **adjectival phrase**
Change this structure to an adjectival phrase simply by zapping
the *which is, that is,* or *that was* or whatever:

the procedure **that is <u>free from bias</u>**

becomes

the procedure **<u>free from bias</u>**

2. *which* or *that* + *be* + *-ing* **verb**

Change this structure to an *-ing* verbal phrase by zapping the
that are, that were, or *which is* or whatever:

The newspapers **that were <u>researching the issue</u>** broke
the news first.

becomes

The newspapers **<u>researching the issue</u>** broke the news first.

3. *which* or *that* + *be* + *-ed* **verb**
These are passive-voice clauses. Cut them down to *-ed* phrases.
Please note that these *-ed* verbs are past participles and that all do
not end in *-ed,* e.g., *built, seen, made.* The trick is to cut the passive-
voice clause down to a past participial phrase or perhaps even further to a prepositional phrase or even to a possessive noun. In the
following example, assume that the reader does not already know
"which payments" the writer is referring to:

the payments **<u>which</u> were <u>made by the supplier</u>**

would first become

the payments **that were <u>made by the supplier</u>**

and then by cutting the clause you would change it to

the payments **<u>made by the supplier</u>**

Be careful, however. Many writers overuse past participial phrases when a simple prepositional phrase, single adjective, or possessive noun would do just fine. Thus:

the payments **made by the supplier**

might become

the payments **of the supplier**

or

the **supplier's** payments

4. *which* or *that* + *be* + prepositional phrase

Cut these clauses down to the prepositional phrase. Again, you'll zap the *that is, that are, that were,* and have the phrase left over:

the office **that is near the subway**

becomes

the office **near the subway**

5. *which* or *that* + *be* + noun

You can cut many of these clauses down to noun appositives:

The Great Gatsby, **which was one of the best novels by Fitzgerald,** received rave reviews.

becomes

The Great Gatsby, **one of the best novels by Fitzgerald,** received rave reviews.

Or you can start the sentence with the noun appositive, an impossible feat with the more cumbersome clause:

One of the best novels by Fitzgerald, *The Great Gatsby* received rave reviews.

Cutting Clauses That Use Action Verbs

All other clauses you encounter in your *which* (and *that*) hunt will use action verbs (or linking verbs), not the verb *to be.* The action-verb clauses fall into two categories: those having some word other than *that* or *which* as their subjects and those using *that* or *which* as their subjects. Your clause-cutting strategy changes with the type of clause:

1. **Clause with independent subject other than the word** *that*
   When an action-verb clause has its own independent subject, you can sometimes drop the *that.* Thus, instead of writing:

   > The cases **that the Supreme Court decided** ....

   you can write:

   > The cases **the Supreme Court decided** ....

   You should note that while grammatical rules allow "*that* dropping" they would not allow "*which* dropping." You simply **cannot** change:

   > The books, **which the professor recommended**, cost too much.

   to

   > The books, **the professor recommended**, cost too much

   Don't get carried away with dropping *thats* in adjectival clauses. Many style books urge you to limit *that*-dropping to short clauses. But as you become more adept, you'll develop an ear alerting you to those situations where you should, or should not, drop the *that.*

2. **Clause with no independent subject, i.e., the word** *that* **serves as the subject**
   When the word *that* serves as the subject of the clause, obviously you cannot drop it. You **cannot** take:

   > the books **that received the rave reviews** have arrived at the store

   drop the *that,* and write:

   > the books **received the rave reviews** have arrived at the store

Instead, you should consider cutting the clause down to an *-ing* phrase. Instead of writing:

the regulations **that require this procedure**

you can write:

the regulations **requiring this procedure**

Earlier in this chapter, I did not write: *clauses **that modify nouns.*** Instead I cut the subjectless clause and wrote: *clauses **modifying nouns.***

I did not write: *those **that have some word** other than* that *or* which *as their subjects* . . . . Neither did I write: *those **that use** that or* which *as their subjects.* Instead, I wrote: *those **having** and those **using.***

That's clause cutting.

WHEN YOU SHOULD REFRAIN FROM CUTTING

Under what circumstances would you decide not to cut the clause? Well, think about it.

Finished?

Good.

Your thinking undoubtedly went like this: *When I cut clauses, I'm basically turning a clause into a phrase. The sole distinguishing feature of a clause is the conjugated verb. So when I engage in the fine art of clause cutting, I'm zapping a conjugated verb. As examples, I'm turning progressive-tense clauses into present participial phrases and passive-voice clauses into past participial phrases.*

Does this sound like your thinking?

Good.

You may now continue: *Since clause cutting requires the removal of a conjugated verb, I would not cut a clause if I **needed** that conjugated verb. For example, if the conjugated verb showed a special tense or a special condition (through the use of an auxiliary verb), then if I cut the clause, I'll lose the tense or the condition.*

Excellent. See how good you're getting at grammatical analysis?

You couldn't very well cut this clause, now could you:

> the list of assets **that might have been set forth in** the com-
> pany's report

If you did, you'd get:

> the list of assets **set forth in** the company's report

All this makes sense, doesn't it? You roll out the big guns of the clause when you need to show what conjugated verbs show: tense, mood, person, number, condition, and so on. When you don't need those features of a clause, the phrase invariably does a better job of producing a tight and memorable writing style.

ONE MORE POWER STRUCTURE

There's another type of structure you should know about. It's called a *truncated clause*. Some grammarians call it an *elliptical clause*. (Actually, because the structure has no verb, it qualifies as a *phrase*.)

In this chapter, we've learned all about relative pronouns and how they start restrictive and nonrestrictive adjectival clauses. But there are other kinds of dependent clauses, which are started with other words. Remember subordinating conjunctions? We learned all about them in chapter 6. We learned that subordinating conjunctions also start dependent clauses, which might be adjectival or adverbial. Here's the partial list of subordinating conjunctions you committed to memory in chapter 6. For reasons that will become apparent, I've put some of them in **bold**:

Subordinating Conjunctions

after	how	**unless**
although	**if**	**until**
as	in order that	what
as far as	provided that	whatever
as if	**since**	**when**
as long as	so (that)	**whenever**
as though	that	**where**
because	**though**	**wherever**
before	**till**	**while**

We use these subordinating conjunctions to form dependent, or subordinate, clauses. Let's take the word *while* and form a clause:

While you are researching in the library, you might uncover the exact source you need.

Now watch what happens when I zap *you are:*

While researching in the library, you might uncover the exact source you need.

The *while researching in the library* is a truncated clause. It's also called an elliptical clause.

We form these truncated clauses in much the same way we formed noun absolutes in chapter 9. We form them in the same way we cut the *to be* clauses above. We simply watch for these five structures:

1. adjectival phrase
2. present participial phrase (*-ing* phrase)
3. past participial phrase (*-ed* phrase)
4. prepositional phrase
5. noun

We can then take some of the subordinating conjunctions and add any of these five structures to yield truncated clauses. The above subordinating conjunctions appearing in bold type will work. The others don't fit very well, if at all.

> It's profitable to look at truncated clauses and noun absolutes together, since they share the same five structures.

It's profitable to look at truncated clauses and noun absolutes together, since they share these five structures. We basically form them in the same way. For the truncated clause, we take a subordinating conjunction and add any of the five structures above. For the noun absolute, we take a noun or pronoun and add any of the same five structures. Study the chart below:

TRUNCATED CLAUSE	NOUN ABSOLUTE
Subordinating Conjunction + *5 Structures*	*Noun or Pronoun + 5 Structures*
The **<u>subordinating conjunc-</u>** **<u>tion</u>** appears in bold underline, the *addition* in bold italics.	The **<u>noun or pronoun</u>** appears in bold underline, the *addition* in bold italics.
Subordinating conjunction +	Noun or pronoun +
1. adjective	1. adjective
<u>Though</u> *old,* the Jones Study supports our conclusion.	**<u>Her research</u>** *complete,* the stu- dent began to write her thesis.
2. *-ing* phrase	2. *-ing* phrase
<u>When</u> *deciding these issues,* the personnel officer considers three factors.	The student asserts two theories, **<u>one</u>** *relying on the Jones Study,* **<u>the other</u>** *citing a variety of* *sources.* The trial was held in the Superior Court, **<u>Judge Wegner</u>** *presiding.* "**<u>A well-regulated militia</u>** *being* *necessary to the national* *defense,* the right to bear arms, shall not be infringed."[2]
3. *-ed* phrase	3. *-ed* phrase
<u>Though</u> *tortured in its reason-* *ing,* this theory does have one advantage.	The taxpayer loses on this point as well, **<u>his argument</u>** *grounded in* *theories rejected by the IRS.*

4. prepositional (or infinitive) phrase

"The other man, carrying a package, jumped aboard the car but seemed unsteady **as if about to fall.**"[3]

When *in Rome,* do as the Romans do.

5. noun

Though *a fair man,* the senator often required his staff to work far into the night.

4. prepositional phrase

"He lay flat on ... the floor of the forest, **his chin** *on his folded arms.*"[4]

5. noun

The attorney ignores precedent, **her theories** *a wish list of insupportable propositions.*

WHO WON THE WARS OF THE WORDS?

In much writing we see on the job, in institutions of higher learning, in the Pentagon, in the courtroom—indeed in way too many places—we find some huge battles going on.

Nouns vs. Verbs. In chapter 11, we saw nouns winning out over verbs. For some reason, many people want to puff up their writing and write about *the prediction of the existence.* Why not *predict?* Why not *exist?*

To Be or Not To Be. In chapter 12, we saw how people cobble their sentences around the verb *to be.* Why not the more concrete action verb? Reread the chapter. I used zero *be's* in a chapter of nearly 2,000 words.

Active vs. Passive. In chapter 13, we saw that too many writers prefer the passive voice over the active voice. But we also learned that sometimes the passive voice *is preferred.*

Clauses vs. Phrases. And now in chapter 14, we've seen that many writers put simple information in the most complex structure the language has to offer: the clause. They roll out the big cannon of the clause, light the fuse, stop up their ears, and then *Bam! Out comes a ping-pong ball!* No. Save the big guns for the complex stuff. Use the simple phrase for the simple stuff.

The wrong structures are winning these wars of the words. Use the verb form. Reduce your *be's*. Put most of your action verbs in the active voice. And favor phrases over clauses.

When *you* start winning these wars, your style will improve immensely. But you won't be entirely

The wrong structures are winning these wars of the words. Use the verb form. Reduce your *be's*. Put most of your action verbs in the active voice. Favor phrases over clauses.

ready to join The Writers Club. You must still develop a certain sophistication of style. That you achieve by learning the concepts of subordination, noun substitution, and parallel structure, which now attract our attention in part 3.

NOTES

1. *Strunk & White,* p. 59.
2. United States Constitution, Second Amendment.
3. Justice Cardozo in *Palsgraf v. Long Island Railroad,* 162 N.E. 99, 99 (N.Y. 1928).
4. Hemingway in *For Whom the Bell Tolls.*

PART **THREE**

A Theory of Style

Whenever I read good writing, I always find the same thing: a fairly high degree of subordination, a mastery of parallel structure, and a wide variety of structures used in all possible locations in the sentence. I also find that good writers typically choose the simplest structure available to express their meaning. When faced with the choice of a clause over a phrase, they always choose the simpler structure, the phrase. But if they want to punctuate what they have to say, they elevate the structure up the scale of complexity and choose the clause.

Grace, of course, comes from a practiced ear. But it must first develop from a knowledge of the structures the English language makes available to us for expressing our thoughts. For that very basic reason, this book has tried to instill in you an appreciation of those structures, indeed, a knowledge of them, so that you can now begin to try them on for size. Only by scouring your current writing style, discovering the structures you use, and trying out the ones you don't, can you increase your power as a writer.

That's what this and the next three chapters are all about: developing a theory of style so that you can then criticize your own writing and set about improving it. As you get good at it, you'll find yourself becoming a critic and mentally editing the writing (and speech) of others.

Let's begin at the beginning. All great writers start where you and I have to start—with the quintessential American sentence: John hit the ball. The great writers have a thought. They put it at the three-part structure of the sentence: (1) subject + (2) verb + (3) other stuff. What they do after that distinguishes them as great writers.

Let's see if we can figure out what they do.

John Hit the Ball:

The Basic Sentence

When we write, we all start with (1) a subject, (2) a verb, and (3) some other stuff. If we write with just those three-part sentences, we might get an *A . . .* from our third-grade grammar-school teacher:

> John hit the ball. He ran to first base. The crowd cheered loudly. They also ate lots of hot dogs.

So at our starting point, we're all the same: third graders. Then some of us break out of the pack. Some of us become good writers. Some seem born with the talent (I envied them back in Miss Hamrick's class: Mary, Phyllis, and Carolyn, always the girls). Others have to work at it.

What is it, then, that separates the good writers from the bad, the great writers from the not-so-great writers? Is there a way we can analyze their styles, come away with some principles, and then set about trying to do what they do?

BUT FIRST, WHAT'S A SENTENCE?

In Miss Hamrick's class, the second most horrible thing that could happen (after being called on to conjugate verbs in front of the class) was receiving a cryptic notation in the margin of the book report you hastily prepared on the school bus on the morning of the day it was due:

> Emily Dickinson was a good poet. Because she used vivid images. ***FRAGMENT!!!!***

I learned two lessons from this experience:

> First, I learned to write ***in complete sentences.***
> Second, I learned to write ***incomplete sentences***.

After all, what could be more effective than Miss Hamrick's one-word commentary: ***FRAGMENT!!!!***

I'm sure my second lesson was not exactly what Miss Hamrick had in mind. Instead, she insisted that we write in complete sentences. In Miss Hamrick's class, we learned that a complete sentence must have a subject and a predicate. It must express a complete thought. It cannot be a dependent clause, like because she used vivid images. It must be capable of standing on its own. Or, as defined by one authority, a sentence is:

> a group of words consisting of a finite verb and its subject as well as any complement that may be present and any modifiers that belong to the verb, to the subject, to the complement, or [to] the entire statement, the whole group of words constituting a grammatically complete statement.[1]

Now, if you're writing a paper for your English class, I'd strongly counsel you to stay away from any group of words starting with a capital letter and ending with a terminal punctuation mark (period, question mark, exclamation point) that qualifies as a sentence fragment. You'll only hurt your chances for an *A*.

But in virtually all other kinds of writing, no matter how formal, you may gain from my second lesson: *Write incomplete sentences.* I've got good authority for writing "such a portion of a composition or utterance as extends from one full stop to another."[2] (A *full stop* is simply a terminal punctuation mark.) Consider the views of Sir Ernest Gowers, the editor of *Fowler:*

The verbless sentence is a device for enlivening the written word by approximating it to the spoken. There is nothing new about it. Tacitus, for one, was much given to it. What is new is its vogue with English journalists and other writers, and it may be worthwhile to attempt some analysis of the purposes it is intended to serve.[3]

Sir Ernest then proceeded to identify six situations that might call for verbless sentences. Bryan Garner took these, expanded on them, and identified a series of circumstances where it might be appropriate for incomplete sentences to appear in expository writing. He proceeded to give examples from noted writers (citations omitted):[4]

1. Transitional: "**One other thing.** If they're not needed for a month or two, they never complain."
2. Afterthought: "It is tempting to set Cardozo and Corbin over against them as the engineers of its description. **Tempting and by no means untrue.**"
4. Emphatic: "For Mansfield this was intolerable; for Willes it was in the last resort right. **In the last resort.**"
5. Negating: "Do we say ... that comparative enquiry is merely an application of the historical method? **By no means.**"
6. Explanatory: "For the compromise theory the question of justice is a question of balance, and the balance is both impersonal and intuitive. **Impersonal because individuals become the instruments of achieving aggregate quantities—of equality as much as of utility. Intuitive because the correct balance must be a matter of inarticulate 'feel.'**" (See my comments on "length" below.)
7. Qualifying or Recanting: "The Age of Aquarius has finally dawned in presidential politics. **Sort of.**"
8. Summing up: "How different is this Treaty! It lays down general principles. It expresses its aims and purposes. **All in sentences of moderate length and commendable style.**"

Be careful, however. When you write a verbless sentence—in Miss Hamrick's words, a ***FRAGMENT!!!!***—you must make one thing crystal clear to your reader: You know what you're doing. Your reader must know that you have not made a mistake that might make Miss Hamrick level you with her one-word ***FRAGMENT!!!!*** Thus, you would not want to write:

> Emily Dickinson was a good poet. Because she used vivid images.

That looks like a sentence fragment written by a student in junior high school. But the *Sort of* fragment above was written by Maureen Dowd on the front page of the *New York Times.*[5]

One key problem to avoid is undue length. If your verbless sentence is too long, the chances that your reader will think you've blown it increase significantly. For that reason, I'd say that the ***Impersonal because . . . Intuitive because . . .*** fragments above went a bit overboard, though perhaps the writer made his technique plain by writing two in a row.

As Bryan Garner aptly put it, "Generally, incomplete or verbless sentences of the acceptable type are not classified as 'fragments,' but technically they are precisely that. Thus, it is possible, in good usage, to write fragments. ***Possible but difficult.***"[6]

The upshot of all this? Two lessons learned: Good writers write in complete sentences, and good writers occasionally write incomplete sentences.

FOUR STRUCTURES OF COMPLETE SENTENCES

Of course, most of the sentences we write are complete sentences. What separates the good writers from the bad lies in what they do to the basic sentence structure. What sort of structures do they add? Where? Do they use noun substitutes? How? Do they use parallel structure? If so, where and for what sentence structures? Let's look at the basic structure and then at the ways good writers add to it.

All complete sentences in the English language may be classified into four categories. Those four categories derive from one simple fact: We have four types of main verbs. Selecting one of them pegs the sentence type you've chosen. So take a look at the four possible sentences you can write:

1. Subject	*2. Verb*	*3. Other Stuff*

Action Verbs

1. Subject John	+	Transitive Verb (active) hit	+	Direct Object the ball.
Subject The ball	+	Transitive Verb (passive) was hit	+	Actor Phrase by John.
2. Subject The ball	+	Intransitive Verb sailed	+	Adverb or Phrase over the wall.

No-Action Verbs

3. Subject The pitch	+	*To Be* was	+	Predicate Adjective fast.
The pitch		was	+	Predicate Noun a curve ball.
The ball		is	+	Adverb or Phrase in the catcher's mitt.
4. Subject John	+	Linking Verb feels	+	Predicate Adjective nervous.
John		seems	+	Predicate Noun a natural hitter.
John		looks	+	Adverb or Phrase out of sorts.

PICKING YOUR SENTENCE TYPE

From previous chapters, you've learned to favor two sentence types: numbers 1 and 2. Now don't get me wrong. Don't think that I'm suggesting that you abolish the verb *to be* or linking verbs. I'm not. Just look at your style, figure out if you have an overwhelming urge to use *be* in every sentence, and if you do, start breaking the habit now.

FIGURING OUT YOUR MAIN MESSAGE

As a basic rule of style, try to position the main thing you have to say at the subject-verb-other-stuff location of the sentence. Then, other information will fall into place through your use of the techniques of subordination, noun substitution, and parallel structure, the topics of the next three chapters.

> **Do you have an overwhelming urge to use *be* in every sentence? If so, break the habit.**

By following this *subject-verb = main message* rule, you'll get rid of structures that rhetoricians call *throat clearing:*

> It is important to point out that . . . .
> It is clear that . . . .
> One important point to note is that . . . .

What are the three-part messages of these sentences?

> It is important
> It is clear
> One point is

Not much there.

EXPLETIVE DELETED

Those who could read in the early 1970s remember the transcripts of the Watergate tapes. Unfortunately, President Nixon had a rather vulgar tongue, so his conversations in the White House, which he was secretly taping, were laced with his own swear words, also called *expletives.* Throughout the transcripts, readers were treated to a bracketed "[expletive deleted]."

Well, there's another kind of expletive, a grammatical term. An expletive is a word that fills the syntactic role of another word. Expletives include:

> There is   It is
> There are   These are

In these expressions, the words *there, it,* and *these* fill the role of the noun following the expression. And that role is: the grammatical subject of the sentence. Thus, if we say There is a problem, the word *There* stands in for *problem* as the grammatical subject of the sentence. We could flip the sentence over and say, A problem is there.

Now listen carefully: ***There is*** *nothing wrong with these expressions.* See? I used one. And it works quite nicely.

But you can overdo it, and when you do, you should delete the expletive and make the true noun the grammatical subject of the sentence. Watch especially for an expletive followed by a *that* clause. In the vast majority of cases, these sentences beg for revision.

> **There are** several factors **that** the committee must consider.

Nope.

> The committee must consider several factors.

Bryan Garner condemns these structures:

> These phrases are enemies of a lean writing style. Rarely do they add anything but clutter to a sentence—e.g.: *"In a few jurisdictions there are* [read *A few jurisdictions have*] special statutes of limitations prohibiting the initiation of administration proceedings after a designated number of years."*[7]

As a nation, we have one gargantuan problem with *there is*. According to the latest statistics—just released—99.999 percent of the entire population butchers the use of the *there is* expression by following the *is* (singular) with a plural noun. The odds are overwhelming that you are one of the offenders. Stay tuned. In chapter 19, you'll hear a lonely voice in the wilderness plead for preserving the rule on subject-verb agreement.

> **99.999 percent of the entire population butchers the use of there is by following the is (singular) with a plural noun.**

WHAT TO DO WITH *JOHN HIT THE BALL*

So we all start with the same tool: one of four types of three-part sentences. Let's call those three parts *sentence parts,* for lack of a better term. The sentence parts include (1) the subject, (2) the verb, and (3) the other stuff. The third part—the other stuff—varies with the type of verb you choose.

If you choose sentence-type 1, which uses an action transitive verb, and you put the verb in the active voice, the other stuff is a direct object: John hit **the ball**. If you put that verb in the passive voice, the other stuff is a prepositional *by* phrase revealing the actor (if you decide to include it): The ball was hit **by John**.

If you choose sentence-type 2, which uses an action intransitive verb, the other stuff is probably some sort of adverbial phrase modifying the verb: The ball sailed **over the wall**.

If you choose sentence-type 3, which uses the verb *to be,* then the other stuff might be a predicate adjective: The pitch was **fast**. Or it might be a predicate noun: The pitch was **a curve ball**. Or it might be some sort of adverbial phrase showing *where* or *when* the grammatical subject *is:* The ball is **in the catcher's mitt**.

If you choose sentence-type 4, which uses a linking verb, then the other stuff might be a predicate adjective: John feels **nervous**. Or it might be a predicate noun: John seems a **natural hitter**. Or it might be some sort of phrase: John looks **out of sorts**.

All writers—good and bad—start out on an equal footing. They choose one of the four sentence types. So what makes good writing good and bad writing bad? Much of the quality has to do with what the writer does with John hit the ball. What does the good writer add to John hit the ball (that's subordination)? How often and how easily does the writer use phrases and clauses as nouns (that's noun substitution)? To what degree does the writer double or triple or quadruple or quintuple structures within the sentence (that's parallel structure)?

A lot has to do with word choice. A lot has to do with variety of sentences. A lot has to do with rhythm. And, of course, a great deal has to do with *substance,* that is, with *what* you say in your writing. I can't help you there. But maybe I can help with matters of style.

Before launching into the various things you can do to John hit the ball, I want to point out that *Oops, Me!* is limited to matters of grammar and style. But there's another vitally important part of writing I do not cover in this book: Let's call it *content*. By content, I do not mean *substance* or *subject matter*. The notion of content has to do with structure, organization, transition, flow, and paragraphing. You can view content as the shape of well-crafted expository writing. Into that shape you may pour your substance, your subject matter. It can be science, engineering, politics, religion, law, or any other subject. But the shape of good writing does not vary much at all. Certain features of that shape must be there before the writing is any good at all.

Now if you can get enough of your friends to race to the bookstore and scoop up gazillions of copies of *Oops, Me!*, then my publisher will insist on a sequel, which we'll doubtless have to call: *Oops, Me Too!* Perhaps there we can deal with matters of content.

Now let's start adding stuff to **John hit the ball**. Let's explore the concept of subordination.

NOTES

1. Ralph M. Albaugh, *A Dictionary of Grammar and Structure,* p. 170 (1964) (quoted in *Garner Legal,* p. 433).
2. *Fowler,* p. 674, quoting the *Oxford English Dictionary.*
3. *Fowler,* p. 674.
4. *Garner Legal,* pp. 433-34. These and other examples appear in *Garner Oxford,* pp. 186–88.
5. Maureen Dowd, "2 Baby Boomers on 1 Ticket: A First, but Will It Work?" *New York Times,* July 13, 1992, p. 1A.
6. *Garner Legal,* p. 434; *Garner Oxford,* p. 188.
7. *Garner Legal,* p. 879; *Garner Oxford,* p. 332.

16

Sentence Additions:

The Art of Subordination

As always, we start with the same beginning—one of four types of sentences, each consisting of three sentence parts: (1) subject, (2) verb, and (3) other stuff. The other stuff will be determined by the type of verb chosen.

As pointed out in the last chapter, we won't progress very far if we write with simple, three-part sentences. Consequently, to become good writers, we must learn what we can do to the basic simple sentence to turn it into streams of words deemed "good" by our teachers, bosses, colleagues, spouses, parents, and other important people.

Basically, we can do three things to *John hit the ball*. First, we can add stuff to it, and we call that *subordination*. Second, we can use certain multiword structures as noun substitutes, and, for lack of a better term, we call that *noun substitution*. Third, we can double or triple or quadruple or quintuple (1) entire sentences, (2) various parts of the sentence, (3) additions to the sentence, and (4) subparts of additions to sentences— and we call that *parallel structure*.

In this chapter, we'll deal with the art of subordination.

SENTENCE ADDITIONS: THREE TYPES
We can append three types of sentence additions to our basic sentence structure. Actually, the additions first break down into two broad cate-

gories (1) one-word additions and (2) multiword additions. The multiword additions then further break down into phrases and clauses.

Thus, the three things we can add to *John hit the ball* are:

1. One-word adjectives, noun modifiers, appositives, and adverbs
2. Multiword phrases (these contain no conjugated verb)
3. Multiword clauses (these do contain a conjugated verb)

1. One-Word Additions:
Adjectives, Noun Modifiers, Appositives, and Adverbs

By adding some one-word adjectives, we can expand the meaning of *John hit the ball:*

> **Big** John hit the **slow** ball.

We could add an appositive:

> **Big** John, the **catcher**, hit the **slow** ball.

We could add a one-word noun modifier:

> **Big** John, the **reserve** catcher, hit the **slow** ball.

We could add a one-word adverb:

> **Big** John, the **reserve catcher, powerfully** hit the **slow** ball.

These one-word additions occupy subordinate parts of the sentence and thus form part of the art of subordination. The alternative? Write like third graders:

> John hit the ball. He is the reserve catcher. John is big. The ball was slow. John hit the ball powerfully.

2. Multiword Additions: Phrases

Look at what we can do to *John hit the ball* by adding phrases:

His knees shaking with nervous energy, big John, the reserve catcher, powerfully hit the slow ball **over the fence in the bottom of the ninth to win the ALC championship game** before **50,000 screaming fans.**

Let's make an inventory:

Phrase	Type
his knees shaking	noun absolute phrase
with nervous energy	prepositional phrase
over the fence	prepositional phrase
in the bottom	prepositional phrase
of the ninth	prepositional phrase
to win the ALC championship game	verbal infinitive phrase
before 50,000 screaming fans	prepositional phrase

Notice also that our meaning expands in these multiword phrases through the further addition of noun modifiers *(ALC championship)* and adjectives *(50,000 screaming).*

3. Multiword Additions: Clauses

Now let's add a couple of dependent clauses:

His knees shaking with nervous energy, big John, the reserve catcher, powerfully hit the slow ball over the fence in the bottom of the ninth to win the ALC championship game before 50,000 screaming fans, **who drank large vats of cheap beer, which were provided by a local brewery.**

SUBORDINATION: *JOHN HIT THE BALL.*

The final sentence is not necessarily a good one. I only try to show how much information you can add to the basic sentence structure by adding the three possible types of sentence additions: (1) one-word adjectives, noun modifiers, noun appositives, and adverbs, (2) multiword phrases, and (3) multiword clauses. Using just this technique alone, you could add endless amounts of information to *John hit the ball.* You wouldn't win a Pulitzer, but you could have some terrific practice in the art of subordination:

> His knees shaking with nervous energy, big **John**, the reserve catcher, powerfully **hit the** slow **ball** over the fence in the bottom of the ninth to win the ALC championship game before 50,000 screaming fans, who drank large vats of cheap beer, which were provided by a local brewery located at 101 Main Street, the site of the city's founding in 1849, when the gold rush attracted thousands of prospectors, whose descendants would one day enjoy the uniquely American game of baseball, which actually began in ....

The entire sentence hangs on the basic sentence structure of *John hit the ball.*

You should think of the basic sentence structure as a coatrack. It has three parts: a pedestal (subject), a post (verb), and a peg (the other stuff). You can then proceed to hang all sorts of additions on the coatrack. Of course if you hang too much—as I did above—the coatrack falls over. So as you play around with the art of subordination, you must remember a very important rule of style:

Don't cram too much information into a single sentence.

As a matter of fact, you should get a sample of your writing, count the total number of words, count the total number of sentences, and divide words by sentences. The result is your "average sentence length," which should hover somewhere around the high teens to low twenties. If your average gets out of hand, you cannot consider yourself a good writer, regardless of your chosen field. We are talking about an *average.*

> We can do three things to *John hit the ball:* (1) add stuff: *subordination,* (2) add fake nouns: *noun substitutes,* and (3) double or triple or quadruple, etc., various parts of the sentence: *parallel structure.*

Good writers routinely write 60- and 70-word sentences. But they balance them out with some in the single digits.

Many writers seem afraid of short sentences. They apparently fear that a short sentence betrays a simple mind. Or, in the words of Justice Thomas Gordon of the Virginia Supreme Court: "Writers often confuse simplicity of expression with simplicity of thought." They just cannot stop a sentence and then start a new one. Instead, they want to stuff all their information into just one sentence. But countless studies show an inverse relationship between sentence length and comprehension by the reader. This relationship exists not only for readers of *Reader's Digest* but for readers of complex material on science, philosophy, law, or other disciplines. Even very smart readers find long sentences hard to follow.

Heed this advice:

> Experts in readability commonly say that, in technical writing, you want an average sentence length of 20 words or fewer. Some sentences ought to be 40 or 50 words, and some ought to be 3 or 4. There needs to be variety, but the average should be 20 or below. The writer who achieves this goal will generally achieve greater speed, clarity, and impact than the writer with longer sentences.[1]

SUBORDINATION: SENTENCE LOCATIONS

Sentences have three locations: beginning, middle, and end. As you become more adept with adding subordinate one-worders and multi-worders, you should also be aware that you can play around with *where* you add the structure.

Take a one-word adjective as an example. Ordinarily, a one-word adjective comes before the noun it modifies:

The **empty** house looked quite frightening.

But we could play around with location and get:

Empty, the house looked quite frightening.

Or:

The house, **empty,** looked quite frightening. [2]

Or take a verbal -*ing* phrase: causing injuries for which she sues.
We could start a sentence with the phrase:

> **Causing injuries for which she sues**, the scales struck the plaintiff.

Or we could put it in the middle:

> The scales, **causing injuries for which she sues**, struck the plaintiff.

Or we could put it at the end:

> The scales struck the plaintiff, **causing injuries for which she sues.**[3]

In the late 1980s, the chief counsel of a federal agency commissioned me to give a training program for all the in-house attorneys, including himself. The participants submitted writing samples, including the chief. I asked him if he wanted my honest assessment of his writing. "Absolutely," he said.

The chief counsel had a bad habit. He habitually doubled up his predicate verbs. Now, as we'll see in the next chapter, that's good use of parallel structure. But anything to excess in writing defeats the purpose of holding the reader's attention. Thus, the chief would write sentences like this:

> The court **reversed** the lower court and **ruled** that consent is not required.

To broaden his writing footprint, the chief had to learn to use the "tail-end -*ing* phrase." He just had to change the second verb to a present participle and put it at the end:

> The court **reversed** the lower court, **ruling** that consent is not required.

Or, I told him, he could play around with location and put the *-ing* phrase at the beginning:

> **Ruling** that consent is not required, the court **reversed** the lower court.

Or, if he wanted to emphasize the *consent-is-not-required* information, he could put the phrase in the middle and set it off with dashes:

> The court—**ruling** that consent is not required—reversed the lower court.

Thus, we see two major ways to improve your writing: (1) Make certain you use all structures available *(subordination)* and (2) experiment with where you put them *(sentence location)*.

WHAT DOES IT TAKE TO BE ARTICULATE?

To become an articulate writer, or an articulate speaker, you must have a long list of structures you can use when you write or speak. You must develop the ability to use this wide array of structures in all possible sentence locations. Otherwise, your writing becomes predictable and stale. To join The Writers Club, you must be able to point to the following structures in your style:

> **Do you use these 11 power structures in all possible sentence locations?**

Phrases
1. prepositional phrase (over the rainbow)
   a. as adjective
   b. as adverb
2. adjectival phrase (free from governmental control)
3. verbal *-ing* phrase (present participle) (running five miles each day)
   a. as adjective
   b. as adverb
   c. as noun

4. verbal *-ed* phrase (past participle) (written in 2001)
   a. as adjective
5. verbal *to* phrase (infinitive) (to win the game)
   a. as adjective
   b. as adverb
   c. as noun
6. truncated clause (subordinating conjunction + five structures) (when in Rome)
7. noun absolute (noun or pronoun + five structures) (his knees shaking)
8. noun appositive (the reserve catcher)

Clauses

9. dependent adjectival clause (that slept in the barn)
   a. as restrictive *that* clause
   b. as nonrestrictive *which* clause
   c. as restrictive and nonrestrictive *who/whom/whose* clauses
10. dependent adverbial clause (because he enjoyed the special effects)
11. dependent noun clause (that he would prevail)

And when you use these structures, you must be able to move them around to different locations without changing your meaning. Do you start sentences with *-ing* phrases? Do you use them inside the sentence? Do you end sentences with *-ing* phrases?

Mr. Churchill uses *-ing* phrases. Here he starts a sentence with a present participial phrase. Notice that the phrase modifies the grammatical subject of the sentence:

> **Freeing** himself from Parliamentary opposition by repeated prorogations, **King James** proceeded throughout 1686 to relieve his fellow religionists.[4]

Mr. Churchill ends sentences with *-ing* phrases. Do you?

> After Dykevelt's departure Churchill wrote to William on May 17, 1687, **giving** him assurances.[5]

Do you use *-ed* phrases? Do you start sentences with *-ed* phrases? No? Well, the time to emulate Mr. Churchill has come:

> Sincerely **attached** to the principle of legitimacy, the **English Protestants** had no other means of escape from the intolerable fact of a Papist heir.[6]

What about noun absolutes? Do you use them? Do they begin sentences? Do they come in the middle of sentences? Do they end sentences? Did you happen to notice the noun absolute Mr. Albaugh used in the quotation appearing in the last chapter? No? Well, here it is again:

> [A sentence is] a group of words consisting of a finite verb and its subject as well as any complement that may be present and any modifiers that belong to the verb, to the subject, to the complement, or [to] the entire statement, the **whole group** of words **constituting** a grammatically complete statement.[7]

Does that kind of noun absolute show up in your style?

If you answer "no" to the above questions, then you know your mission: Start using all these structures in all possible sentence locations. Play around with them. They are the tools of the trade.

In the list, you'll notice that *to* phrases (infinitive phrases), *-ing* phrases (present participial phrases), and dependent noun clauses can act as nouns in sentences. To make it into The Writers Club, you're going to have to be able to use these three types of structures as noun substitutes—the subject of the next chapter.

NOTES

1. *Garner Legal,* p. 793. See the interesting discussion in *Garner Oxford,* p. 296–97, where the author cites a study showing the average sentence lengths in 10 major newspapers and magazines. Averages range from the *Pittsburgh Press*'s 20 words per sentence to the *Wall Street Journal*'s 27 words per sentence.
2. These empty-house examples come from *Kane,* p. 707.
3. This sentence appears in a very famous court case, decided by Benjamin Cardozo. *Palsgraf v. Long Island Railroad,* 162 N.E. 99, 99 (N.Y. 1928).

4. Winston S. Churchill, *A History of the English Speaking Peoples,* p. 392 (Dodd, Mead & Co. 1960) (vol. 2).

5. Churchill, *A History,* vol. 2, p. 396.

6. Churchill, *A History,* vol. 2, p. 405.

7. Ralph M. Albaugh, *A Dictionary of Grammar and Structure,* p. 170 (1964) (quoted in *Garner Legal,* p. 433 and in *Garner Oxford,* p. 186).

17

Noun Substitutes

Here, once again, is your list of tools:

Phrases

1. prepositional phrase (over the rainbow)
   a. as adjective
   b. as adverb
2. adjectival phrase (free from governmental control)
3. verbal *-ing* phrase (present participle) (running five miles each day)
   a. as adjective
   b. as adverb
   c. **as noun**
4. verbal *-ed* phrase (past participle) (written in 2001)
   a. as adjective
5. verbal *to* phrase (infinitive) (to win the game)
   a. as adjective
   b. as adverb
   c. **as noun**

6. truncated clause (subordinating conjunction + five structures) (when in Rome)
7. noun absolute (noun or pronoun + five structures) (his knees shaking)
8. noun appositive (the reserve catcher)

Clauses
9. dependent adjectival clause (that slept in the barn)
   a. as restrictive *that* clause
   b. as nonrestrictive *which* clause
   c. as restrictive and nonrestrictive *who/whom/whose* clauses
10. dependent adverbial clause (because he enjoyed the special effects)
11. **dependent noun clause** (that he would prevail)

Note that three of the structures have the capacity to act as nouns in sentences. Perhaps some of the others could as well. After all, we could use a prepositional phrase as the subject of a sentence:

After 6:00 is a good time to call.

But the three main multiword structures that can substitute as nouns in our language include two verbal phrases, (1) the *-ing* phrase (the present participial phrase, also called the *gerund phrase*) and (2) the *to* phrase (infinitive phrase), as well as (3) the dependent noun clause (also called a *nominal clause*).

Take the following as fact: All sophisticated writers smoothly use noun substitutes in their writing. Let's put it the other way: Writing that lacks noun substitutes is not very sophisticated and not likely to win any awards.

NOUN SUBSTITUTE 1: THE GERUND PHRASE
When an *-ing* phrase acts as a noun, it's called a *gerund*. It can enter a sentence and serve many of the noun functions: subject, complement, direct object, verbal object, object of a preposition, and appositive. Look at these examples:

Subject:	**Our taking this position** should not concern you.
Subject Complement:	His main desire was **winning this race decisively.**
Direct Object:	We certainly don't like **taking this route to the beach.**
Verbal Object:	He hoped to enjoy **winning the race.**
Object of Preposition:	We worried about **his losing his money.**
Appositive:	Her goal, **winning the LPGA Open,** was finally achieved.

In the above examples, notice the *our taking* and the *his losing.* If you don't remember why I used the possessive case *our* and *his,* go back to chapter 10 and review the discussion of the fused participle. Here I wanted the *-ing* verb to serve as the noun and forced it to act that way by using the possessive case. Besides, the *Our taking* sentence is one of those where you always use the possessive case because the expression begins the sentence and the *-ing* verb serves as the subject. Again, go back to chapter 10 and review the discussion of the fused participle.

> **Do you use *-ing* phrases? Review chapter 10 to make certain you understand present participles and the problem of fused participles.**

NOUN SUBSTITUTE 2: THE INFINITIVE PHRASE

When a *to* phrase acts as a noun, it doesn't get a special name; it's still an infinitive phrase. It too can serve many noun functions: subject, complement, direct object, verbal object, and appositive.

Sometimes the infinitive phrase itself will have a subject, that is, an actor of the verbal activity. When you write such a phrase and use a pronoun as the subject, the pronoun, oddly enough, must appear in the *objective* (not the *subjective*) case. Consider this phrase, which has the subject *me:*

They wanted **me to break the bad news.**

And when you use such a phrase as a subject of a sentence, you must precede it with the word *for:*

For me to break the bad news poses some serious risks to her mental health.

Does that kind of structure show up in your style? No? Well, the time has come. To change your style, you must do just that: You must change your style. You must broaden your style. Force yourself to use *to* phrases as nouns. Try out an infinitive phrase with a subject in the objective case preceded by a preposition—all as the subject of a sentence. For you to do that will require some effort. See?

> **Do you use to phrases? Review chapter 10 to make certain you understand infinitive phrases.**

Take a look at infinitive phrases acting as nouns:

Subject:	**To become the world's best golfer** seemed impossible.
Subject Complement:	His objective was **to win at all costs.**
Direct Object:	He wanted **to improve his game each day.**
Verbal Object:	Learning **to win** became his chief objective.
Appositive:	She had just one dream, **to become a famous rock star.**

NOUN SUBSTITUTE 3: THE NOUN CLAUSE

Remember, a clause is a bunch of words with a conjugated verb in it. Independent clauses are sentences. Dependent clauses are not and must attach to a complete sentence. Dependent clauses serve as adjectives and adverbs. They also serve as nouns, and, as such, become our third noun substitute.

We use various words to start noun clauses. Igor, Amber, and Miss Hamrick called them *subordinating conjunctions* (which also start adjectival and adverbial clauses).

These words include the word *that,* which in its role as a noun clause starter is not a relative pronoun, for it serves no grammatical role in the clause; it just starts the clause. For example: **The committee stated that it would follow the agency's policy.** Here the noun clause serves the noun role of direct object of the transitive verb *stated.* But a careful look at the clause reveals that the word *that* does not serve any role within the clause, other than simply to get it going.

Other noun clause starters do serve grammatical roles within the clause. For example: **We know who caused all the trouble.** Here the noun clause starter is the relative pronoun *who.* Notice that inside the noun clause *who* serves as the grammatical subject of the verb *caused.*

Additional words serve as noun clause starters. A *relative adverb* can get one going: **How he won the election** mystified the pundits. So can a relative pronoun acting as an adjective: **We know which career she will pursue.** In these two sentences, *how* is an adverb modifying the verb *won,* and *which* is a relative-pronoun-adjective modifying the noun *career.*

Here's a partial list of noun clause starters:

Noun Clause Starter	Sample
that	**That he prevailed** did not surprise us.
the fact that	Your boss was impressed with **the fact that you read this book.**
how	She cannot understand **how he succeeded in life.**
when	She discovered **when the Native Americans began their migration.**
why	Figuring out **why the disease spreads** became the goal of the CDC.

where	I know **where she lives**.
who	Can you figure out **who is calling**?
whoever	The senator paid attention to **whoever donated the most money**.
whom	Do you know **whom he visited last night**?
whomever	The senator paid attention to **whomever he wanted**.
whose	We want to know **whose opinion shapes the policy**.

Noun clauses can serve almost all noun roles in your sentences. Study these examples, which use the rather awkward clause *the fact that you bought this book:*

Noun Function	Sample
Subject	**The fact that you bought this book** shows your interest in writing.
Complement	The reason you got a raise is **the fact that you bought this book**.
Object of Preposition	Your boss is aware of **the fact that you bought this book**.
Direct Object	Your boss applauded **the fact that you bought this book**.
Verbal Object	Stressing **the fact that you bought this book**, your boss raised your pay.
Indirect Object	Your boss gave **the fact that you bought this book** her immediate attention.
Appositive	When giving you a raise, your boss cited one important aspect of your performance, **the fact that you bought this book**.

NOUN CLAUSE CUTTING

Simply because a noun clause can act as a noun does not necessarily mean that you want it to. Often these clauses become quite awkward. *Strunk & White,* for example, labels *the fact that* as "an especially debilitating expression. It should be revised out of every sentence in which it occurs."[1] The expression is debilitating, and it should be revised out of *most* sentences in which it occurs. But how do we revise it out of our sentences? If we simply drop *the fact,* we still have a noun clause starting with *that.* And the noun clause might still be debilitating.

Do you cut out unnecessary noun clauses?

Just as you learned the art of cutting adjectival clauses in chapter 14, so too will you learn how to cut noun clauses here in chapter 17. The key typically lies in the verb of the clause.

Cutting a Noun Clause When the Verb Is an Action Verb

When the verb in the noun clause is an action verb, you can cut the clause in two ways: (1) Change the verb to a gerund so that the clause now becomes a gerund phrase or (2) find and use a true noun meaning the same thing as the verb in the clause. Let's try out this technique on our clause above: *the fact that you bought this book.*

Technique	Result
Change to gerund	**Your buying this book** shows your interest in good writing.
Change to true noun	**Your purchase of this book** shows your interest in good writing.

Cutting a Noun Clause When the Verb Is the Verb *to be*

First, let's dream up a couple of *to be* noun clauses: (1) the fact that he was drunk and (2) the fact that he was president.

Now let's use each in a sentence:

I. When imposing the sentence, the court stressed **the fact that he was drunk.**

2. When passing the bill, Congress was aware of **the fact that he was president**.

When cutting noun clauses that use the verb *to be,* focus on the word following the verb *to be.* Typically it will be an adjective *(drunk)* or a noun *(president).* When it's an adjective, you can often substitute a true noun derived from the meaning of the adjective:

I. When imposing the sentence, the court stressed **his drunkenness** (or **his inebriation**).

When the word following the verb *to be* is a noun, you can either use a gerund phrase *(being)* or you can substitute the word *status.*

2. When passing the bill, Congress was aware of **his being president** (ugh).

When passing the bill, Congress was aware of **his status as president** (better).

You can see the overall strategy in cutting awkward noun clauses: Find a true noun or a smoother noun substitute (a gerund) meaning the same thing. Take away the conjugated verb and the clause goes away.

DON'T GET ME WRONG

Please don't take this advice on noun clause cutting the wrong way. I am not suggesting that you should obliterate noun clauses from your style. Quite the opposite. Your style won't be as sophisticated as it could be if you don't ever use noun clauses in the many ways they can appear in the language. So, as step one, determine whether you even use the structure very often. Then, as step two, watch for opportunities to trim down the noun clause to a smoother phrase. All good writers try to use the simplest expression available to convey their thoughts.

Do you use the 11 power structures?

WHAT MAKES GOOD WRITING GOOD?

Now let's put in the final piece of the puzzle. What makes good writing good? The good writer uses all subordinate structures available in the language. The good writer is aware of and uses the three noun substitutes: infinitive phrases, gerund phrases, and noun clauses. And the good writer is quite good at moving all these subordinate structures around to various locations in sentences to fill all possible functions and to achieve variety, emphasis, or rhythm. Here's the list:

Phrases

1. prepositional phrase (over the rainbow)
    a. as adjective
    b. as adverb
2. adjectival phrase (free from governmental control)
3. verbal *-ing* phrase (present participle) (running five miles each day)
    a. as adjective
    b. as adverb
    c. as noun
4. verbal *-ed* phrase (past participle) (written in 2001)
    a. as adjective
5. verbal *to* phrase (infinitive) (to win the game)
    a. as adjective
    b. as adverb
    c. as noun
6. truncated clause (subordinating conjunction + five structures) (when in Rome)
7. noun absolute (noun or pronoun + five structures) (his knees shaking)
8. noun appositive (the reserve catcher)

Clauses

9. dependent adjectival clause (that slept in the barn)
    a. as restrictive *that* clause
    b. as nonrestrictive *which* clause
    c. as restrictive and nonrestrictive *who/whom/whose* clauses
10. dependent adverbial clause (because he enjoyed the special effects)
11. dependent noun clause (that he would prevail)

So what else can the good writer do? What's the final piece of the puzzle? Good writers are acutely aware of parallel structure and affirmatively use it as a strategy of writing. Did you see what I just did? Did you notice how I doubled the verb forms in the second sentence of this paragraph: writers **are** acutely aware *and* affirmatively <u>use</u>.

It's time to learn how to say not one thing but two or three or four or five . . . .

Did you see what I just did in that sentence: **not** one thing <u>but</u> **two** . . . . Remember the correlative conjunction *not . . . but*? Does it appear in your style? If not, I strongly urge you to reread chapter 6 on conjunctions before tackling the concept of parallel structure.

NOTE
1. *Strunk & White,* p. 24.

18

Sentence Shapes:

The Art of Parallel Structure

We all start at the same place: *John hit the ball.* The world's greatest writer and you use the same basic tools. You start with a three-part sentence: (1) subject, (2) verb, and (3) other stuff. The other stuff depends on the type of verb you choose. Choose an action transitive verb, and the other stuff is a direct object; choose an intransitive verb, the other stuff is some sort of adverbial phrase; choose the verb *to be,* the other stuff is either a predicate noun, a predicate adjective, or a phrase; choose a linking verb, the other stuff is either a noun, an adjective, or a phrase.

Then the good writer begins to add to the basic sentence structure. The writer adds one-word adjectives, noun modifiers, appositives, and adverbs. The writer then adds some multiword structures: clauses and phrases. The writer adds three kinds of dependent clauses: (1) adjectival clauses, (2) adverbial clauses, and, as we've just seen, (3) noun clauses. The writer adds a host of different phrases: (1) prepositional, (2) *-ing* phrases (present participial), (3) *-ed* phrases (past participial), (4) *to* phrases (infinitive), (5) truncated clauses (subordinating conjunction + five structures), (6) noun absolutes (noun or pronoun + five structures), and (7) noun appositives.

As the writing unfolds, the good writer knows all about sentence location and, seeking to achieve a pause, places an *-ing* phrase with a *to* phrase as its object smack dab in the middle of the sentence. Reread the last sentence. See how the concept of *sentence location* works?

But these are not the only tricks of the writer's trade. The good writer knows how to double or triple or quadruple or quintuple the four possible structures in the English language that can be doubled or tripled or quadrupled or quintupled or . . . .

The good writer knows all about parallel structure and uses it as a strategy of writing.

PARALLEL STRUCTURE: DEFINED

Here's the rule: Whenever you write a series of two or more things, each element of the series must appear in the same grammatical structure and perform the same grammatical function. If you get a series of adjectives going, you cannot then switch to a noun: He was **debonair, fashionably dressed**, and, alas, quite a **prude**. Once the series begins as a series of adjectives, you've got to stay with adjectives; otherwise you've written a nonparallel construction. Thus: He was **debonair, fashionably dressed**, and, alas, quite **prudish**.

Most books on writing teach parallel structure as a rule not to be broken. That is, you should avoid writing nonparallel constructions. This book will do that, too.

But I think quite a bit of magic lies in the strategy of parallelism. At least I've noticed that the writing of good writers contains the ongoing use of parallel structures as one of its prominent features. I've therefore concluded that good writers use parallel structure as a way of writing, as a way of keeping the sentence going, as a way of establishing a pattern, and as a way of beating a rhythmic drum. Indeed, as a way of repeating and thus stressing an idea.

> The rule: **Whenever you write a series of two or more things, each element of the series must appear in the same grammatical structure.**

Get my drift? . . . *way/writing . . . way/keeping . . . way/establishing . . . way/beating . . . way/repeating and stressing.*

Let's look at the array of possibilities parallel structure provides. Then we'll look at some common blunders.

PARALLEL STRUCTURE: FOUR POSSIBLE CANDIDATES

First, let me coin a term: *double up.* I'll use it to describe the act of using parallel structure. It means, of course, doubling, or tripling, or quadrupling, or quintupling (and on and on) a part of the sentence.

In the English sentence, we have four possible word types or structures that you can double up. Let's review them from the broadest to the narrowest:

Candidates for Doubling Up

Here are the four possible parts of sentences that you can double up. The best writers, of course, take advantage of all four, use parallelism all the time, and as a result gain admission to The Writers Club.

> **Candidates for Parallel Structures**
> 1. entire sentence
> 2. sentence part
> 3. subordinate addition
> 4. subpart of subordinate addition

You can double up (or triple, etc.) entire sentences by writing what's called a *compound sentence:*

> **John hit** the ball, and **he ran** to first base.

You can double up any of the three sentence parts, which I define as (1) subject, (2) verb, and (3) other stuff:

> John **hit** the ball and **ran** to first base.

It gets real fun when you play around with doubling up subordinate additions to a sentence; you might, for example, add not one prepositional phrase, but two, or three:

> John hit the ball **over the pitcher's head, above the outstretched hands of the shortstop,** but **into the waiting glove of the center fielder**.

Then the mathematical permutations blow right off the chart when you start doubling up the subparts of a sentence addition; you might, for example, add a truncated clause with an *-ing* verb but double up the *-ing* verb:

> After **stepping up** to the plate and **acknowledging** the cheers of the crowd, John hit the ball.

Some Comments

Some comments are in order. Please distinguish between writing a *compound sentence* (doubling up the entire sentence) and a *compound predicate* (doubling up just the verb). Doubling up the entire sentence requires two subject-verb pairs and a comma before the conjunction (usually *and*). Doubling up the verb requires two verbs hanging on one subject and no comma before the conjunction. (More about problems with the comma in chapter 33.)

Here's a compound sentence with a comma coming before the *and:*

> John hit the ball, and he ran to first base.

Here's a compound predicate. Notice that a comma should not appear before the *and:*

> John hit the ball and ran to first base.

Of course you can overdo it with parallel structure just as you can overdo it with subordination. In chapter 16, the chapter on subordination, we likened the sentence to a coatrack. By using the various sentence additions (one-worders and multiwords), you can add a great deal to *John hit the ball.* But at some point, the coatrack tips over. The same is true with parallel structure. If you overdo it, the sentence becomes unwieldy and hard to follow.

FOUR CANDIDATES FOR PARALLEL STRUCTURE

1. **Entire sentence**
2. **Sentence part**
3. **Subordinate addition**
4. **Subpart of subordinate addition**

So pay attention to sentence length, and shoot for an average in the high teens or low twenties. That's an average. You might write some sentences with 70 or 80 words. But you'll also write some with just two or three.

Parallel Structure in Action

Whenever I write, I realize that parallel structure is always available to me. (Now, I just finished that sentence. But, as I always do, I pause for a moment and see whether I have anything else to say. Hmmmm, yes I do. So I'll expand the sentence through the use of parallel structure.)

> Whenever I write, I realize that parallel structure **is** always available to me **and provides** a way to increase the number of things I can say in a single sentence.

I might find myself in a situation calling for a showing of multiple activities, that is, multiple verbs. So I **realize** my need for verbs; **look** around the language; **figure out** what I want to say; **find** the words *realize, look, figure out, find,* and *create;* and **create** a sentence with five conjugated verbs.

USE A WIDE VARIETY OF CONJUNCTIONS

Do great writers actually use parallel structure as a strategy, you ask? Of course they do. Good writers use a wide variety of conjunctions, and when they use conjunctions, they're creating parallel structure.

You should check your own writing by retrieving a paper you've previously written and stored on your computer. Then use the computer search program and try to locate *not only, but also, neither, either,* and *nor.* If you come up empty, your style is shallow. Search for the common conjunctions as well. Look for *and* and *or.* In this way, you'll reveal 95 percent of your parallel structures. You should look at the structures you typically join, you'll soon find a pattern, and your mission then becomes the expansion of those structures joined in a parallel series. Do you ever triple independent clauses, as I just did in the preceding sentence?

Search for *But* as a sentence starter. Search for *However* as a sentence starter and then begin using *But* as the good writers do.

Let's look at some examples, **each showing** significant *parallel* *structure* **and** the *use* of a wide variety of conjunctions. (Do you write sentences with a tail-end noun absolute, whose *-ing* verb has a series of two objects?)

Example 1

A writer might turn to subordination and introduce a sentence with a noun appositive. Then the writer turns to parallelism and modifies that noun appositive with piled-up adjectives. Then the writer turns back to the art of subordination and adds an *-ing* phrase at the end of the sentence. And finally the writer turns back to parallelism and includes within that *-ing* phrase a prepositional phrase with doubled-up objects. The parallel structures appear in **bold**, the conjunctions in **bold underline**:

> A **pulpy, spluttering, timorous, loose-lipped, dressy** country sport, he loved to loll on the corners, greeting his hundreds of acquaintances with a stale **joke and** the stock **query**, "Whaddaya know?"[1]

Example 2

In the next example, observe the predicate adjectives in parallel. Note the conjunctions *yet* and *and.* Note the additional parallel structure, the two objects of the preposition *without* joined by the conjunction *or:*

> She was, by Chaucer's . . . account, supremely **modest yet** easily **approachable, refined, temperate, light-hearted, and pious** without **sternness or coldness.**[2]

Example 3

Do you use the conjunction *for* to produce a parallel series of two independent clauses, the second one having two parallel verbs? Judge Paula Newman of the United States Court of Appeals for the Federal Circuit does just that:

> **Doubt is resolved** against the newcomer, **for** the **newcomer has** the opportunity of avoiding confusion **and is charged** with the obligation to do so.[3]

Example 4

Do you start a sentence, indeed a paragraph, with *Yet?* Pulitzer Prize winner Garry Wills does, and he doubles the independent clause:

> <u>**Yet**</u> **Lincoln drew** much of his defense of the Union from the speeches of Webster, <u>**and**</u> **few** if any **have considered** Webster a mystic.[4]

Example 5

How about starting a paragraph with *Yet* and then including the correlative conjunction *not only . . . but also* in the same sentence to join two prepositional phrases in a parallel series, the second phrase having doubled-up adjectives modifying its object. Here's Sir Winston Churchill:

> **Yet** if we look beneath the surface . . . [Cromwell] is revealed as [England's] defence <u>**not only**</u> **against the ambitions of generals,** <u>**but**</u> **from the wild** <u>**and**</u> **unimaginable forms of oppression** in which the Ironside veterans might have used their power.[5]

Example 6

Check out JFK's five consecutive verbs hanging on a *that* clause:

> Let every nation know, whether it wishes us well or ill, that we shall **pay** any price, **bear** any burden, **meet** any hardship, **support** any friend, **oppose** any foe to assure the survival and success of liberty.[6]

Note the two other parallel constructions: **well** <u>**or**</u> **ill** and **survival** <u>**and**</u> **success**.

Example 7

Witness the anger of Thomas Jefferson at the acts of George III:

> He **has plundered** our seas, **ravaged** our coasts, **burnt** our towns, <u>**and destroyed**</u> the lives of our people.[7]

If you'll look carefully at the writing you enjoy, you'll invariably find a wide variety of parallel structures. See what structures the writers double up. Notice that they don't just stick with a few pet structures. Instead, they are adept at creating varied shapes and sizes of sentences. Their trick? They combine parallel structure with the art of subordination. They can manipulate their structures by putting them at all possible sentence locations.

Example 8

Consider the flair of Mr. Churchill as he begins a sentence with four prepositional phrases, each containing an object modified by an adjective *following the noun:*

> **In manner gentle, in temper tolerant, in mood humane, in outlook broad and comprehending**, he nevertheless **possessed <u>and</u> exercised** an inflexible **will <u>and</u>** an imperturbable **daring**.[8]

Note the additional parallel structures: two verbs (**possessed, exercised**) and two direct objects of *possessed and exercised* (**will, daring**).

AVOID THE NONPARALLEL CONSTRUCTION

As you begin to practice using parallel structure, you must make sure you don't write *non*parallel constructions. Whenever you form a series, each element of the series must appear in the same grammatical structure and perform the same grammatical function. That's the rule. Breaking it marks you as a writer who needs help.

> **The rule: Whenever you write a series of two or more things, each element of the series must appear in the same grammatical structure.**

Many writers often break the rule when using the correlative conjunctions *not only . . . but (also), not . . . but, neither . . . nor, either . . . or,* and *both . . . and.* When you use these conjunctions, make sure that the structure joined with the first word grammatically matches the structure joined with the second word.

Look at these nonparallel constructions and their repairs. The **structures that are joined** appear in bold; the **<u>conjunctions</u>**, in bold underline:

Nonparallel Construction	Repair Job
Let me remind you of **not only** your **duty but** of your **promise.**	Let me remind you **not only** of your **duty but** of your **promise.**
	Let me remind you of **not only** your **duty but** your **promise.**
"Marketing quotas **not only embrace** all that may be sold without penalty **but also** what may be consumed on the premises."[9]	Marketing quotas embrace **not only** all that may be sold without penalty **but also** what may be consumed on the premises.
The trial court was correct in excluding **both** the **testimony** of [Pete Smith] **and in excluding** the defendant's exhibits.[10]	The trial court was correct in excluding **both** the **testimony** of [Pete Smith] **and the defendant's exhibits.**
You will improve your writing if you **read** this book, **study** the examples, **and if you practice** the techniques you learn.	You will improve your writing if you **read** this book, **study** the examples, **and practice** the techniques you learn.

PARTS 1, 2, AND 3: WHAT MAKES GOOD WRITING GOOD?

Here's your list. Check out your style. Check out the sentence locations where these structures appear. Do you start sentences with noun appositives? Do truncated clauses begin sentences in your style? Do you use adjective phrases? Do you double up these structures? Do you double up structures *within* these structures? Do all of them appear in your writing?

Phrases

1. prepositional phrase (over the rainbow)
   a. as adjective
   b. as adverb
2. adjectival phrase (free from governmental control)
3. verbal -*ing* phrase (present participle) (running five miles each day)
   a. as adjective

    b. as adverb

    c. as noun

 4. verbal *-ed* phrase (past participle) (written in 2001)

    a. as adjective

 5. verbal *to* phrase (infinitive) (to win the game)

    a. as adjective

    b. as adverb

    c. as noun

 6. truncated clause (subordinating conjunction + five structures) (when in Rome)

 7. noun absolute (noun or pronoun + five structures) (his knees shaking)

 8. noun appositive (the reserve catcher)

Clauses

 9. dependent adjectival clause (that slept in the barn)

    a. as restrictive *that* clause

    b. as nonrestrictive *which* clause

    c. as restrictive and nonrestrictive *who/whom/whose* clauses

10. dependent adverbial clause (because he enjoyed the special effects)

11. dependent noun clause (that he would prevail)

So here's the Top Ten List. Here's why good writing is good, and by implication, why bad writing is bad:

1. Good writers include all possible structures our language makes available to them. We studied most of these structures in part 1 (the chapters on the parts of speech) and expanded the list in part 2 (the chapters on the Wars of the Words).

2. Good writers are adept at putting these structures in all possible sentence locations: beginning, middle, and end.

3. Good writers tend to favor the verb form over noun forms. When they have a verb idea to say, they use a verb—not some derivative structure—to say it.

4. Good writers can go on for pages without using a single construction of the verb *to be*. But they realize the power of *being* and use the verb when they truly mean it.

5. Good writers favor the active voice over the passive voice, but they don't go berserk and abolish the passive from all writing. They use the passive voice strategically.

6. Good writers prefer the phrase over the clause, reserving for big, complicated thoughts the complex structure of the clause.

7. Good writers use a high degree of subordination—their clauses, phrases, and one-word additions appearing in all possible locations in the sentence.

8. Good writers also use a high degree of parallel structure. But they don't go overboard and cobble together sentences that are burdensome to read and hard to understand.

9. Despite their ability to create many shapes of sentences, good writers always use the simplest expression possible.

10. And good writers are not afraid of short sentences.

Witness the short-sentence, drum-beating style of Sir Winston. The number of words in each sentence appears parenthetically:

> In this wide and secret confederacy there were two main divisions of policy (13). The moderates, led by Halifax and Notingham, urged caution and delay (11). The Ministry, they pleaded, was breaking up (7). There had been no widespread conversions to Catholicism, as James had hoped, and he would never get a Parliament to support him (22). No case had yet arisen to warrant actual treason (9). Remember, they enjoined, how a standing army rallies to its duty once fighting has begun (15). Remember Sedgemoor (2).[11]

Do you ever write two-word sentences? If Churchill uses two-word sentences in *A History of the English Speaking Peoples,* surely they belong in your master's thesis.

Good writers do two more things. They don't make grammatical mistakes, when they write or when they talk. That takes us to part 4. And they punctuate correctly, a topic leading us to part 5 and the end of this book.

NOTES
1. Samuel Hopkins Adams, quoted in *Kane,* p. 738.
2. John Gardner, quoted in *Kane,* p. 738.

3. *In re Shell Oil Co.,* 992 F.2d 1204, 1209 (Fed. Cir. 1993).

4. Garry Wills, *Lincoln at Gettysburg: The Words That Remade America,* p. 125 (1992).

5. Winston S. Churchill, *A History of the English Speaking Peoples,* vol. 2, p. 316 (1960).

6. Quoted in *Kane,* p. 251.

7. Quoted in *Kane,* p. 251.

8. Churchill, *A History,* vol. 2, pp. 399–400

9. *Wickard v. Filburn,* 317 U.S. 111, 119 (1942), as quoted in *Garner Legal,* p. 636. See the discussion of parallelism in *Garner Oxford,* pp. 243–44.

10. A version of this error appears in *Garner Legal,* p. 637.

11. Churchill, *A History,* vol. 2, p. 401.

PART **FOUR**

Common Grammatical

Mistakes

First, a disclaimer. Part 4 cannot possibly deal with all grammatical mistakes. It would take an entire book. In fact, earlier chapters have already dealt with many mistakes. But I thought I'd devote some chapters to the biggies—those that will hurt you in your career or lower your grades in school.

After you read part 4, I hope you'll never again say or write:

There's lots of **things** we could do this weekend (chapter 19).

We could **of** gone to the beach (chapter 20).

Your going with us (chapter 21).

Me and **him** will be there soon (chapter 22).

If I **was** you, I'd use some sunscreen (chapter 23).

While **driving** to the beach, the **scenery** was beautiful (chapter 24).

There having trouble getting **their** (chapter 25).

The traffic jam will **effect** the length of the trip (chapter 26).

Its going to be a beautiful weekend (chapter 27).

Last weekend, he **lead** the way (chapter 28).

Strawberry Kool-Aid is our **principle** beach drink (chapter 29).

When we go to the beach, we must **bring** the surfboards (chapter 30).

Like, I'm like, whoa, was that **like** a big, **like**, wave ... whatEVer (chapter 31).

19

There's lots of these

subject-verb disagreements

In my career, I have reviewed thousands of writing samples of lawyers, engineers, students, government workers, and other smart people. Without any doubt, the most prevalent grammatical mistake is subject-verb disagreements in number.

One stands out and thus deserves the top spot in the chapter.

THE BIGGEST GRAMMATICAL MISTAKE
IN THE UNITED STATES

I'll go out on a limb: Sometime today, most people reading this book will make this grammatical mistake, perhaps not in writing, but certainly in speech. Listen carefully to your sentences starting with *there's,* which is to say, *there is.* You'll be surprised at the frequency of this error. Also watch out for *here's.*

Here's the rule. Here're the rules. (Are you getting my drift?)

In chapter 15, we encountered the structure called the expletive (not a curse word), which fills the syntactic duty of another word. The expressions *there is, there are, this is, these are,* and others qualify as

> **Sometime today, you will most likely make this grammatical mistake: using "there's" or "here's" followed by a plural noun.**

expletives. Though a bit different, *here is* and *here are* act in much the same way.

When you use these expressions, the number of the verb (the singular *is* or *was* vs. the plural *are* or *were*) will be determined by the noun that follows the expression. If the noun is singular, you **must** use the singular *is* or *was*. If the noun is plural, you **must** use the plural *are* or *were*. Thus, study the following mistake in a reported court opinion and burn it into your memory:

> A trial judge has an affirmative duty . . . to ascertain whether there **is** irrelevant, immaterial, or privileged **matters** contained within the records or documents.[1]

Now look at these correct constructions:

> There **are** many **cases** governing this issue.
> [Not: There**'s** many **cases** governing this issue.]
>
> Here **are** the **rules** on subject-verb agreement.
> [Not: Here**'s** the **rules** on subject-verb agreement.]

Here's one I heard on a recent Seinfeld rerun. In an exchange with George, Jerry makes two grammatical mistakes before getting it right:

> There**'s girls** over there, there**'s girls** over here. There **are** even **girls** outside on the sidewalk.

Some screenwriter had to write it down that way.

Just today, May 22, 2001, I received an e-mail from a lawyer in Texas:

> Here**'s** some **articles** you might want to review.

Say what? *Articles is . . .*?

Listen very carefully to the speech of your colleagues; listen to your family; listen to your children; listen to broadcasters; listen to politicians; listen to judges; listen to the talking heads; just listen. **Everybody** makes this mistake. Then listen to Henry Fowler, the keeper of the Queen's English:

There is a strong, not always resisted, temptation, found prominently but not only in **uneducated speech**, to introduce a plural subject with the reduced form *There's* . . . . Some informal examples from newspapers: There's *35 locations to serve you; But for every big, dumb move like this,* there's *half a dozen small, smart details.* [Bold emphasis added.][2]

Let me challenge you. This evening, turn on National Public Radio and listen to the news or to *All Things Considered.* You'd think you'd find perfect English there, now wouldn't you? I will wager any amount of money that you'll hear many mistakes with *there's* and *here's,* mistakes made both by the NPR interviewers and by the usually prominent interviewees.

Or pick up your favorite newspaper. Although this mistake appears more frequently in spoken language, it does show up in the press. Here's a humdinger from the May 8, 2001, edition of the *Washington Post:*

> On Friday, April 27, 2001, I tested my own challenge. On *All Things Considered,* a commentator from one of the "member stations" was reporting on the growing popularity of bass fishing. In his report, he said the following: "There's even bass radio programs."

> Now **there was** two **outs,** and Gibbons stepped into the batter's box.[3]

Pardon me? *There was two outs? Two outs was* . . . ?

There *are,* of course, many other **kinds** of mistakes made with subjects and verbs. Classifying the types often helps reduce the mistakes you might make.

But first, a review of the basics.

THREE RULES

Let's start with three basic and immutable rules: (1) If the grammatical subject of a sentence is singular, it takes a singular verb; (2) if the grammatical subject is plural, it takes a plural verb; and (3) the grammatical subject, not some other word, always determines the number of the verb.

The English language can lay many traps for unwary writers, who can embarrass themselves by using a plural verb with a singular subject or a singular verb with a plural subject. Once you understand the most common traps, however, you'll learn to avoid them or perhaps to recast the sentence to prevent the problem from arising.

THREE IMMUTABLE RULES

(1) A singular grammatical subject takes a singular verb; (2) a plural grammatical subject takes a plural verb; and (3) the grammatical subject, not some other word, always determines the number of the verb.

THE TRAPS

Some of the traps result from what grammarians call a *false attraction*. Unwary writers are falsely attracted to some noun other than the subject and mistakenly use its number to determine the number of the verb. Let's visit some of the more common false attractions.

False Attraction to Plural Words between a Singular Subject and Its Verb

One of the more common traps occurs when a plural noun comes between the true singular subject and the verb. Unwittingly, the writer focuses on the plural intervening word and incorrectly uses a plural verb. Now reread the first sentence of this paragraph, and you'll see an example of a potential false attraction. My subject is the singular *One*. My verb is therefore the singular *occurs*. The plural word *traps* plays no role in determining the number of the verb. Only the grammatical subject does that.

Further examples will illustrate the problem, with the correct word appearing in brackets:

> The **wording** of the reports **have** [has] changed.
> [The singular word *wording* is the subject; the verb must be the singular *has changed*.]

> A long **listing** of these problems **are** [is] simply unnecessary.
> [The singular word *listing* is the subject; the verb must be the singular *is*.]

The trap enlarges as the number of plural nouns between subject and verb increases and as the distance between subject and verb grows. Look at the blunder of this writer, with **subject** and **incorrect verb** appearing in bold type:

> This amazing transformation has not been achieved solely by a concept of "interference," for the **provision** of "works" (water, drainage, houses, transport, power, schools, hospitals and so on) and of "facilities" (such as education, health services and social security) **do** [does] not seem to be essentially interferences except to a one-track mind. [The singular word *provision* is the subject; the verb must be the singular *does.*][4]

False Attraction to Singular Words between a Plural Subject and Its Verb

The intervening-word trap usually entails a remote singular subject with plural nouns coming before the verb. But the reverse happens as well—a remote plural subject followed by singular nouns. Thus:

> The **interests** of the author, Fred Jackson, **is** [are] not the same as the interests of the publisher. [The plural word *interests* is the subject; the verb must be the plural *are.*]

False Attraction to Predicate Noun

Remember the predicate noun? If not, go back to chapters 1 and 9 and review what nouns do. The predicate noun is a noun following the verb *to be;* it restates or identifies the grammatical subject of the sentence. Thus:

> The next **topic** he addressed **was** the many **instances** of police corruption.

In the previous sentence, the word *topic* is the subject of the sentence, and the word *instances* is the predicate noun, also called the predicate nominative or subject complement. The singular subject *topic* forces the use of the singular verb *was.* The plural word *instances* plays no role in determining the number of the verb.

Remember the rule: The grammatical subject of the sentence always determines the number of the verb. Thus, the predicate noun will never determine the number of the verb. Therefore, you must watch out for a singular grammatical subject *(topic)* followed by a plural predicate noun *(instances)*. In these sentences, the verb must be singular *(was)*.

> **The subject, not the predicate noun, always governs the number of the verb.**

When you write these sentences the correct way, a singular subject with a singular verb might sound awkward to readers who don't know the rule as well as you do. If you think that your readers might lack a thorough understanding of this basic grammatical rule, you might recast the sentence to get rid of the problem. Take a look at this example, which might sound correct to many readers but is distinctly a colossal grammatical blunder by a well-regarded writer:

> The second **type** of case on which I shall spend a little time **are** [is] **cases** of negligence. [The subject is the singular word *type;* the verb must be the singular word *is* even though it is followed by the plural predicate noun *cases.*][5]

Though correct, the group of words—the second **type** of case **is cases**— might sound incorrect to many readers. Thus, to get rid of the problem, the author might have written:

> The second **type** of case I will address **is** the **case** of negligence

Now return to the beginning of this chapter. There you might have said, "Ah, gotcha! I caught you, Ed, making a grammatical mistake!" You might have thought I goofed with this sentence:

> Without any doubt, the most prevalent grammatical **mistake is** subject-verb **disagreements** in number.

But now you know I didn't. The subject is the singular *mistake.* The verb must be the singular *is.* The plural predicate noun *disagreements* plays no role in determining the number of the verb.

In works other than a grammar book—where I want to drive home a point—I would avoid writing sentences with singular subjects *(mistake)* and plural predicate nouns *(disagreements)*. The sentence, though correct, just looks wrong. So let me fix it.

> Without any doubt, the most prevalent grammatical **mistake is** *the* subject-verb **disagreement** in number.

The columnist George Will gets it right. Look at this singular subject joined to plural predicate nouns with the singular verb *is:*

> Perhaps this is pertinent to Dalton's case, but, again, it seems to suggest that the **problem is** pornographic **pictures** or other **images**.[6]

Consider the reverse situation: a plural subject with a singular predicate noun. Mr. Will's colleague, David Ignatius, has learned the rule: The grammatical subject always determines the number of the verb. In his column, directly above George Will's, he writes:

> O'Neill's **views** about international finance **are a case in point**.[7]

DETERMINING NUMBER IN A SERIES
Nouns Joined Conjunctively

A *compound subject* consists of two or more words acting as the subject of the sentence. When the series is joined conjunctively, that is, with the word *and,* in the vast majority of cases the subject is plural and requires a plural verb. Look at the following mistakes:

> But recent **research and commentary has** [have] suggested that the emphasis upon eyewitness identification may lead to questionable results. [Note that research and commentary are two different things; the verb must be plural.][8]

> At the same time, the democratic **process and** the personal **participation** of the citizen in his government **is** [are] not all we want. [Note that democratic process and personal participation are two different things; hence the plural.][9]

Sometimes two nouns joined with *and* refer to a single idea and should carry a singular verb. Study this example:

> The **confusion <u>and</u> uncertainty is** compounded by doubt regarding the question whether the complete liquidation and reorganization provisions can have concurrent application. [The words *confusion* and *uncertainty* actually describe a single mental state; the verb, therefore, is singular.][10]

Nouns Joined Disjunctively

When you have a series joined disjunctively by the word *or,* the number of the verb is determined by the number of the noun closest to the verb, that is, the last in the series.

> One apple, one orange, <u>or</u> two **bananas are** then added to the blender.

> Two bananas, one apple, <u>or</u> one **orange is** then added to the blender.

Check out this embarrassment:

> [W]henever the president <u>or</u> the **governor issue** [issues] an executive order.[11]

As we saw in chapter 6, this rule also applies to the *either . . . or* and *neither . . . nor* correlative conjunctions. Thus, number is governed by the number of the noun closer to the verb. Look at these examples:

> <u>Neither</u> the **coach <u>nor</u>** the **players <u>want</u>** to lose.
> <u>Neither</u> the **players <u>nor</u>** the **coach <u>wants</u>** to lose.

Watch out for *along with, as well as, together with,* and others. These are not conjunctions and do not form plural subjects.

Nouns Joined by Other Connectors

Writers often use other connecting words to join nouns to the subject of the sentence. If that subject—the first noun—is singular, the verb must be singular. These connectors usually are prepositional phrases. They do not perform the function of a coordinating conjunction and do not produce a plural subject.

Here's *New Fowler:*

Nouns joined by other linking words or quasi-coordinators (e.g., accompanied by, as well as, not to mention, together with, etc.) are followed by a singular verb if the first noun or noun phrase is singular.[12]

New Fowler gives this example:

> A very profitable **company** such as British Telecom, **along with** many other **companies** in the UK, **is not prepared** to pay a reasonable amount.[13]

Of course, it's difficult to absorb correct usage when all around us we find so much in error. In 1999, the *Washington Times* wrote:

> Potential Senate candidate **Hillary Clinton, along with** her **husband** Bill and **daughter** Chelsea, **are** winding up their 16-day family vacation this week in the Finger Lakes region of upstate New York.[14]

No, it should read:

> Potential Senate candidate **Hillary Clinton, along with** her **husband** Bill and **daughter** Chelsea, **is** winding up the family's 16-day family vacation this week in the Finger Lakes region of upstate New York.

If the author wanted to stress the plural nature of the grammatical subject, he should have made it truly plural by writing:

> Potential Senate candidate **Hillary Clinton, husband** Bill, **and daughter** Chelsea **are** winding up their 16-day family vacation this week in the Finger Lakes region of upstate New York.

MAJORITY DO? MAJORITY DOES?

Another problem of subject-verb disagreement arises when the subject of the sentence is a *collective noun,* that is, a word describing a bunch of people or things, such as *group, team, majority,* and many others. The question inevitably arises: Does the collective noun *group, team,* or *majority* take a singular or plural verb? The answer, no doubt, will surprise many.

And the answer is?

Sometimes singular, sometimes plural.

The collective noun takes a singular verb when you use it to refer to the group of people or things acting collectively as a whole, as a unit. Look at this group acting as a unit:

> The **team** of surgeons **has performed** this operation on many occasions.

When the group acts as a unit, you must use a singular verb. But suppose the members of the group are necessarily acting individually. Suppose, from the sense of the sentence itself, the group could not possibly act as a unit; instead, all the members of the group are individually doing something. In this case, the collective noun takes a plural verb. Thus:

> The **team** of surgeons **have gone** home.

Unless the surgeons are all bunking together, they cannot—as a group—go home. The verb, therefore, must be plural.

Let's take another example. Which of the following is correct?

> The **majority** of courts **has upheld** the right of privacy found in Roe v. Wade.

> The **majority** of courts **have upheld** the right of privacy found in Roe v. Wade.

Here the verb should definitely be the plural *have upheld,* for the courts did not get together and act as a group, as a whole, as a collective noun. Instead, they acted quite individually, incrementally over time producing a majority view.

Though it probably will come as a surprise, the collective noun takes the plural verb even without the plural-sounding prepositional phrase *(of surgeons* or *of courts)*. Thus, the following sentences from *The Oxford Guide to Writing* show proper usage:

> The **team is** leaving tomorrow.
> The **team are** dressing for the game.[15]

In the first example, the team as a unit will leave tomorrow. But in the second example, individual members of the team are individually dressing. The singular team does not wear one great big uniform.

Frankly, I would try to avoid having to say such correct things for one simple reason: The majority *think* that the plural is incorrect. I would adhere to the rule but incorporate the prepositional phrase to make it sound plural. I would write, therefore: The *majority* **of readers** *think* that the plural is incorrect.

To totally get rid of the problem, you can easily rewrite the sentence with a plural noun. Though the following is correct, you might want to redesign the sentence:

> The **orchestra have gone** home.

Instead, insert a plural noun and the appearance of a mistake goes away:

> The orchestra **members have** gone home.

So let me briefly restate the rule: When the collective noun acts as a single unit, it does so with a singular verb. But when the collective noun necessarily is acting through the individual acts of its members, it does so with a plural verb.

Here is a partial list of collective nouns: *committee, company, clergy, group, family, flock, majority, people, band,* and *team.*

And here are two more examples to flesh out the rule. Each of the following statements is correct:

> The **group** of citizens **wants** to exert its influence. (The group
> acts as a unit.)

The **group** of citizens **were** waiting to vote. (The citizens individually waited to individually vote.)

The **majority** of senators **passes** the resolution. (The majority
acts as a unit.)

The **majority** of senators **have made** similar "fact-finding" trips.
(They didn't travel as a unit; they went individually.)

The editorial page of the the *Washington Post* knows the rule. Consider
this example of using a group noun in the singular:

A large **majority of Senators**—Thursday's procedural vote went
70 to 30—**appears** to believe that NAFTA's provisions on trucking
across the Mexican border need not be implemented promptly.[16]

See the difference? When the group acts as a whole, the verb is singular. When the individual members of the group are acting individually,
the verb is plural.

Another problem merits some attention. The rule of number shows
up not only in verb forms but in later pronouns referring back to the collective noun. Make certain that you do not use both singular (verb) and
plural (pronoun) references in the same sentence. The following are distinctly ungrammatical:

Wrong: The **group** of men **wants** to exert **their** influence.
Right: The **group** of men **wants** to exert **its** influence.

Wrong: The **family wants** to go on **their** vacation.
Right: The **family wants** to go on **its** vacation.

As an interesting aside, the British always use plural verbs with collective nouns. Just last night, on May 15, 2001, I was watching a BBC-
produced documentary about a blues musician who made a comeback.
Describing the musician's band, the narrator said:

The **band are trying** to decide on the pieces for the next show.

The British delight in saying: The **jury have reached** the verdict. But what do they know? They just invented the language. We refined it! (*That will definitely get me in trouble!*)

Now let's fix the chapter title:

There are lots of these subject-verb disagreements

NOTES

1. *Peeples v. The Honorable Fourth Sup. J. Dist.*, 701 S.W.2d 635, 637 (Tex. 1985) (quoted in *Garner Legal,* p. 879).
2. *New Fowler,* p. 778.
3. "Welcome to the Bigs" *Washington Post,* May 8, 2001, p. D3, col. 2.
4. R. M. Jackson, *The Machinery of Justice in England,* p. 354 (5th ed. 1967) (quoted in *Garner Legal,* pp. 840–41).
5. H. L. A. Hart, "Intention and Punishment," in *Punishment and Responsibility: Essays in the Philosophy of Law,* p. 132 (1968) (quoted in *Garner Legal,* p. 841).
6. George F. Will, "The Puzzling Case of a Dirty Diarist," *Washington Post,* July 29, 2001, p. B7.
7. David Ignatius, "Government by Pep Talk," *Washington Post,* July 29, 2001, p. B7.
8. Charles P. Curtis Jr., *Lions under the Throne,* p. 49 (1947) (quoted in *Garner Legal,* p. 841).
9. *Garner Legal,* p. 841.
10. *Garner Legal,* p. 841.
11. Bob Dunn, *Contemplating Our Future,* Tex. B.J., May 1992, p. 448 (quoted in *Garner Legal,* p. 841).
12. *New Fowler,* p. 35.
13. *New Fowler,* p. 35.
14. *Washington Times,* September 1, 1999, p. A6, col. 4.
15. *Kane,* p. 768.
16. "NAFTA in Trouble," *Washington Post,* July 29, 2001, p. B6.

20

We could of used the right

helping verb

Discussing this problem doesn't require an entire chapter. But the problem deserves the status of a chapter because so many people make this mistake.

I did see the mistake in the *Washington Post,* but unfortunately I cannot find the citation to prove it. You will often see this mistake in informal writing, especially in e-mail:

> We could **of** made a fortune if we had sold at the right time.

Come on now: *could __of__ made*? The word *of* is a preposition. As such, it must hook a noun onto the sentence. Do you see any noun serving as the object of the preposition *of?* Of course not. Because there isn't one. The writer is trying to use the word *of* as an auxiliary verb. It simply is not an auxiliary verb.

Here the writer means to use the auxiliary verb *have:*

> We could **have** made a fortune if we had sold at the right time.

In speech, you'll hear this expression shortened to:

> We coulda made a fortune if we had sold at the right time.

Well, life is full of *coulda, woulda, shoulda.* And it's fine to adopt those terms. In speech at Bubba's. But it's not fine to butcher the language and show one's ignorance by substituting *of* for the auxiliary verb *have.*

Where did this mistake come from? Most likely it originated from the contraction *could've.* In speech, people began to shorten *could have* to *could've,* which, unfortunately, sounds like *could of.* Regardless of its origin, the mistake flags a person as one in dire need of help with the basics of grammar.

So our chapter title should read:

We could have used the right helping verb

21

Your leaving out the word "are"

This problem also deserves chapter status.

Early in 2001, I received an e-mail from a friend—college educated, very bright, used to hold a top position in government. He wrote:

> If **your** still looking for additional people, you might contact Fred.

The word *your* is the possessive form of the second-person pronoun *you.* Remember: *you/your/yours.* As in *your house, your home, your family, your job, your life, your writing ability.*

But *your still looking?* The word *looking* is a verb. It's the present participle of *look.* The writer is trying to form the present progressive tense, second person. Remember how to form the progressive tenses? Just conjugate the verb *to be* and add the present participle. Like this:

Pronoun	to be	Present Participle	Progressive Tense
you	are	looking	you **are** looking

TAKING A STAB AT CREATING A CONTRACTION

My friend, of course, was writing as people speak, and when people say *you are,* they form the contraction *you're.* But then they pronounce it differently. Carly Simon sang, **Your** so vain. The song just would not have hit the charts if she had sung, **You are** so vain. So she wrote it in the contraction form: You're So Vain. But she sang it like this: **Your** so vain.

Watch for these constructions of the verb *to be: You are* + *noun* or *adjective* or *phrase* or *-ing verb.*

Pronoun	to be	Addition	Example	Bad Result
You	are	noun	a moron	Your a moron.
You	are	adjective	crazy	Your crazy.
You	are	phrase	in trouble	Your in trouble.
You	are	-ing verb	driving	Your driving too fast.

You can get away with making this mistake in speech, for people cannot distinguish *your* from *you're* very easily. But when you commit the blunder to paper or e-mail, educated readers will spot the error and think much less of you.

So our chapter title should read:

You are leaving out the word "are"

Or perhaps:

You're leaving out the word "are"

22

You and him confuse the case

of pronouns

In chapter 5 you learned about the case of pronouns: subjective case, objective case, and possessive case.

SUBJECTIVE CASE

Subjective case appears when the pronoun acts:

1. as a grammatical subject

   You and he confuse the case of pronouns.

2. as a predicate noun

   The ones who confuse the case of pronouns are **you and he.**

OBJECTIVE CASE

Objective case appears when the pronoun acts:

1. as a direct object

   The teacher will lecture **you and him** on the case of pronouns.

2. as an indirect object

You should give **her** your attention.

3. as an object of a verbal phrase

She wants to show **him** how to win.

4. as an object of a preposition

Please write a memo for **him and me.**

POSSESSIVE CASE

Possessive case appears when the pronoun possesses some other noun or noun phrase:

Her book is better than **mine.**

MEMORIZE THE VARIOUS PERSONAL PRONOUNS

Here are the same tables you memorized in chapter 5:

SINGULAR PERSONAL PRONOUNS

Person	Subjective Case	Objective Case	Possessive Case
First person	I	me	my/mine
Second person	you	you	your/yours
Third person	he (masculine)	him (masculine)	his/his (masculine)
	she (feminine)	her (feminine)	her/hers (feminine)
	it (neuter)	it (neuter)	its/its (neuter)

PLURAL PERSONAL PRONOUNS

Person	Subjective Case	Objective Case	Possessive Case
First Person	we	us	our/ours
Second Person	you	you	your/yours
Third Person	they	them	their/theirs

THE RULE OF CASE

In formal settings, you must conform to rules governing the case of pronouns. If your sentence calls for the subjective case, you must use *I, you, he, she, it, we, you, they* (see the subjective-case columns in the two tables above). If your sentence calls for the objective case, you must use *me, you, him, her, it, us, you, them* (see the objective-case columns in the two tables above). The trick, then, in speech and in writing, is to recognize instantly the grammatical function of the noun being replaced by the pronoun and then to plug in the correct pronoun without batting an eye.

> **In formal settings, you absolutely must conform to rules governing the case of pronouns.**

Here are four pitfalls to watch for:

1. **A noun following the verb *to be* (or other linking verb) is a subject complement, which requires the subjective case of a pronoun taking the place of the noun:**

   Wrong: Knock, knock. Who's there? It is **me**.
   Right: Knock, knock. Who's there? It is **I**.

   Wrong: Who do you think did it? It could have been **her**.
   Right: Who do you think did it? It could have been **she**.

   Now that's the way you ought to write. But when you're having a cold one with friends at your favorite watering hole, you won't impress Bubba the Bartender very much by saying, It **was I** who ordered the Perrier with lime. You'll go much further in life, at least at Bubba's, by violating the rule of pronoun case and saying It **was me** who ordered the Corona. (For advancement up the social ladder at Bubba's, I'd suggest changing your drinking fare along with your pronouns. You may keep the lime.)

2. **A noun following the word *than* usually acts as the subject of an ensuing clause and therefore prompts the need for the subjective case of a pronoun taking the place of the noun.**

   Wrong: He is much taller than **me**.
   Right: He is much taller than **I**.

I know, I know, Bubba would refuse to serve you. But we're talking about writing correctly and speaking correctly when correct speech is called for (at places other than Bubba's). In the above sentence, the word *than* serves as a subordinating conjunction introducing a dependent clause. The verb in the clause is understood, so you can refer to the clause as an *elliptical clause*. The entire clause would read:

> **Right:**   He is much taller than **I (am)**.

Sometimes, however, the objective case should follow *than*. The case will be determined by the function of the pronoun in the elliptical clause. Consider these two sentences, which mean entirely different things:

> **Right:**   She gave him more sympathy than **I**.
> **Right:**   She gave him more sympathy than **me**.

Both sentences are correct, but here's what they mean:

> **Right:**   She gave him more sympathy than **I (gave him)**.
> **Right:**   She gave him more sympathy than **(she gave) me**.

Case, as you can see, determines meaning itself. Actually, to be accurate, I should say: Meaning itself determines case. To say what you mean, you must use the correct case of pronouns.

3. A noun following a transitive verb is a direct object, which requires the objective case of a pronoun taking the place of the noun.

> **Wrong:**   Join Bernie and **I** tonight at 9:00.
> **Right:**   Join Bernie and **me** tonight at 9:00.

I actually heard this blunder on CNN. The verb *join* is a transitive verb. It requires an object. If a pronoun satisfies the function of direct object, it must appear in the objective case. Thus: *me*.

Here's another doozie:

> **Wrong:**   Let **he** who is without sin cast the first stone.
> **Right:**   Let **him** who is without sin cast the first stone.

This blunder embarrassed a U.S. congressman. On December 18, 1998, Democrat Robert Menendez of New Jersey shouted in a House debate: "Let he who is without sin in this chamber cast the first vote!"[1]

Two years earlier, this same error started a brouhaha in some letters to the editor of the *Washington Post*. A letter on September 7, 1996, from Ms. "Scold" went like this:

> In your Sept. 1 newspaper, you quote Dick Morris's wife as saying, "Let him who is without sin cast the first stone." Some people may consider her grammatical sin (it's "Let he who is without sin . . . ") greater than his alleged sin.

It only took a week for a reply. On September 14, 1996, Mr. "Right" let her (not "she") have it:

> Whose is the greater sin, [Ms. Scold's] mutilation of English grammar or yours for letting her (or "letting she," as [Scold] would argue) get away with it? "Let" takes the objective personal pronoun: me, him, her, us, them. "He that is without sin among you, let him first cast a stone at her" (John 8:7) is a venerable example of the rule.

Ms. Scold needs this book. Mr. Right doesn't. He could probably write it.

The verb *let* is transitive and requires an object. Thus you might **Let Dave in the door,** or, if you prefer the pronoun, **Let him** in the door. The congressman and Ms. Scold insisted on *let he* because they were tricked by the verb *cast,* thinking that it's a verb forming a clause and thus prompting the need for a subject. But *cast* is not conjugated. Instead, it's an infinitive. After all, we often create infinitives without the accompanying *to.* Thus: **See Spot run, Help me pack, Watch him jump,** or, **Let him cast** the first stone.

One would not say **Help I pack.** Neither would one say **Let he** cast the first stone.

Pretty neat language, don't you think?

4. **A noun attached to a sentence by a preposition is the object of the preposition, which requires the objective case of a pronoun taking the place of the noun.**

> **Wrong:** A Grammar Book for You and **I** ....
> **Right:**   A Grammar Book for You and **Me** ....

Many people make this mistake. You will often hear an array of flubs:

> **Wrong:** It's a big problem for **she** and **I**.
> **Right:**   It's a big problem for **her** and **me**.

> **Wrong:** She gave a present to **you** and **I**.
> **Right:**   She gave a present to **you** and **me**.

In the above, the words *for* and *to* are prepositions, forming prepositional phrases. Each preposition has two objects. For some reason, when people add two pronouns to a preposition, they often lapse into this mistake: the correct *you and me* becomes the distinctly incorrect *you and I*. One would not say *A Grammar Book for I*, or *It's a big problem for I*, or *She gave a present to I*. So don't let the addition of a second object of the preposition lead you astray.

A NOTE TO PARENTS
You should immediately correct the mistakes your children make when they use the incorrect case of pronouns. Your children will have a hard enough time learning the basics in school and an even harder time learning the rules on the job. So you must step into the breach.

Shall we fix the chapter title?

You and **he** confuse the case of pronouns

NOTE
1. *Washington Post,* December 19, 1998, p. C1.

23

If I was you, I'd learn

the subjunctive mood

Some very smart people out there tie themselves up in what amounts to a grammatical sheepshank when they use the little word *if* and then follow it with the verb *to be*. For some reason, they think that an *if* always requires an ensuing *were*.

Check out the incorrect words penned by the author of runaway bestsellers (correct words appear in parentheses):

> Kelly regarded Tracy in an attempt to interpret her comment. Kelly couldn't quite decide **if** it **were** (was) meant to be disdainful or merely informative.[1]

> Mrs. Turner answered just as Kim opened the car door. Without any pleasantries, he asked **if** George **were** (was) available.[2]

> Now he wanted to find her with even more urgency than earlier, and **if** she **were** (was) indeed injured, he wanted to find the individual responsible.[3]

Every now and then, the author gets it right:

> He paused at the waiting-room threshold to see **if** Tracy **was** there.[4]

A MYTH: THE WORD *IF* REQUIRES THE WORD *WERE*

Let's first dispense with a myth and then recall a bit of grammar: When you use the word *if,* you do not always follow it with a *were.* You use *were* only when you need to form what's called the *subjunctive mood.* Now for a bit of grammar.

When we speak or write, we have to use verb forms in every complete sentence. Those verbs ordinarily appear in what's called the *indicative mood.* That is, we simply conjugate verbs to show tense or time, as in present, past, future, and so on. In the indicative mood, we *indicate* the way things are, the way things were, or the way things will be. Or we indicate what things do, or did, or will do. Other moods include the *imperative* (using the second-person verb form, usually without the *you,* to give a command), and the *interrogative* (putting the auxiliary verb before the subject to ask a question, e.g., *will he win?*).

> **When you use the word *if,* you do not always follow it with the word *were.***

FORMING THE SUBJUNCTIVE MOOD

The English language provides another mood, the subjunctive mood. It was used far more frequently in the olden days. In modern times, we use it mainly in these situations:

1. situations contrary to fact
2. wishes
3. suppositions
4. commands
5. suggestions
6. necessity

The first three usually show up with constructions of the verb *to be.* The last three occur with *to be* as well but also with action verbs.

We form the subjunctive mood of the verb *to be* like this:

Person	Indicative	Subjunctive
I	am/was	be/were
you	are	be/were

Person	Indicative	Subjunctive
he, she, it	is/was	be/were
we, you, they	are	be/were

We form the subjunctive for other verbs by dropping the -s ending for third-person singular verbs. Here's the verb *to complete:*

Person	Indicative	Subjunctive
I	complete	complete
you	complete	complete
he, she, it	**completes**	**complete**
we, you, they	complete	complete

As you can see, for action verbs, the subjunctive differs only for the third-person singular.

SITUATIONS REQUIRING USE OF THE SUBJUNCTIVE
Contrary to Fact
Let's look at the contrary-to-fact situation, which usually entails using the subjunctive mood of the verb *to be*. The all-time classic everyone knows is:

If I **were** you ....

Quite clearly I am not you. But if I *were* you . . . .

You do not use the subjunctive to express a lack of knowledge. You would not say, I wondered if he **were** there? Here the words *if* and *wonder* show the doubt. Thus, the indicative mood *was* would be correct:

I wondered if he **was** there.

Instead, you would use the subjunctive when you *know* that the contrary is the fact. Suppose you know that he was *not* there. Thus, you'd use the subjunctive:

He acted as if he **were** there.
If he **were** there, he would have solved the problem.

To take another example, suppose you know he was sick. Then you'd say:

> If he **was** so sick, why didn't he go to the doctor?

But suppose you know he was *not* sick. To express a situation contrary to this fact or to show a hypothetical situation, you'd say:

> If he **were** sick, he would have called the doctor.

The above examples all use *were* with a singular subject to show the subjunctive. In today's writing, we rarely see the use of the main verb *be* to show the subjunctive mood of *am, is, are*. These uses are archaic or form traditional idioms:

> **be** that as it may
> If God **be** for us, who can be against us?
> far **be** it from me

We will see correct uses of *be* to show compulsion, however.

Wishes and Suppositions
Subjunctive constructions of the verb *to be* also show wishes and suppositions: I wish I were able to help him out; If he were to stop now, he would never learn how to play golf.

Showing Compulsion
Let's take the compulsion situation. Look at this sentence:

> The parents' strict rule requires that their child **complete** her homework before watching television.

Child complete? She complete? Sound strange? Not at all if you wish to show compulsion. You simply use the subjunctive mood, which here you form by putting the base infinitive form, which is also the plural form, of *complete* with the singular noun *she*. Or, as some grammarians might say, you form the subjunctive for the third-person singular by leaving off the -*s*, –*es*, or -*ies* endings.

The use of *be* in the subjunctive does crop up in situations requiring a showing of compulsion:

> The policy requires that the paper **be** submitted to the professor personally.

Suggestions and Necessity

Consider the use of the subjunctive to show suggestions and necessity: The pro suggested that **he practice** his swing each day; This emergency requires that **they be** there.

BACK TO OUR EXAMPLES

So why are the examples at the beginning of this chapter incorrect?

Here are the examples from the best-selling *Toxin:*

> Kelly regarded Tracy in an attempt to interpret her comment. Kelly couldn't quite decide **if** it **were** (was) meant to be disdainful or merely informative.

The *couldn't quite decide* shows that Kelly doesn't know if describing the comment as *disdainful* is contrary to fact. If Kelly knew that the comment was *not* meant to be disdainful, then the sentence would read: *Kelly knew that if the comment* **were** meant to be disdainful, Tracy would have . . . .

> Mrs. Turner answered just as Kim opened the car door. Without any pleasantries, he asked **if** George **were** (was) available.

Here there's no showing of a situation that is hypothetical or contrary to fact. Kim simply wanted to know if George *was* available.

> Now he wanted to find her with even more urgency than earlier, and **if** she **were** (was) indeed injured, he wanted to find the individual responsible.

Saying *if she* **were** injured gives the impression that she was *not* injured. Thus he could not possibly find the individual responsible for her *non*injury.

Now, let's move on to another grammatical mistake some people make all the time: the problem of the dangling participle.

But first, let's fix the chapter title:

If I were you, I'd learn the subjunctive mood

NOTES
1. Robin Cook, *Toxin,* p. 16 (Berkely Books, 1999).
2. *Toxin,* p. 110.
3. *Toxin,* p. 277.
4. *Toxin,* p. 169.

24

When writing, your participle

might dangle

A t first, I wanted to name this book *Does Your Participle Dangle?* Alas, my publisher and my wife nixed that incredibly clever idea.

Why focus on the problem of the dangling participle?

Whenever I go to a cocktail party, I'll go get my soda water and lime, and then mill around, trying to engage in some conversation. After the traditional "HeyHowYew" (I'm from the South) and the inevitable games of "DoYaKnow," the conversation inexorably turns to "Say, Ed, what do you do for a living?"

I never know how to answer. If I say, "I'm a lawyer," then that'll invite all those knee-slapping jokes about skunks and lawyers and the relative lengths of skid marks. But I can't say I'm a lawyer, because I don't do traditional lawyering. Instead, I teach lawyers how to improve their writing. So when I say, "I teach lawyers how to write," that inevitably brings howls of laughter and the rejoinder, "Well, it ain't working, is it?"

And then, as surely as crabgrass takes over my lawn in summer, the conversation goes something like this: "So you teach people how to write. Well, I've always prided myself on my writing. I mean, I know all about dangling participles and all that."

For some reason, when the topic of writing comes up, people always want to say they know all about dangling participles, as if writing correctly without dangling participles forever marks someone as thoroughly knowledgeable in the art of writing. Of course, I then proceed to ask my conversationalist to give me an example or two and to distinguish between present and past participles. At that point the conversation tends to break down, and I go looking for another soda and lime.

It would be nice if everyone knew about dangling participles, for they rank as the second most frequently occurring grammatical mistake— right behind subject-verb disagreements.

INTRODUCTORY ADJECTIVAL PHRASES
Here's Rule 11 in *Strunk & White:*

> A participial phrase at the beginning of a sentence must refer to the grammatical subject.[1]

But many people seem to have trouble following this rule. The rule actually applies more broadly, goes beyond a participial phrase, and applies to any introductory adjectival phrase. Whenever you introduce a sentence with any adjectival phrase, that phrase *must* modify the grammatical subject of the sentence.

> **Whenever you introduce a sentence with any adjectival phrase, that phrase *must* modify the subject of the sentence.**

THE INTRODUCTORY PRESENT PARTICIPIAL (*-ING*) PHRASE
Many times the introductory phrase is a present participial phrase, that is, a phrase having a verb in its present participial form (*-ing*). When you use such a phrase, the grammatical subject of your sentence must be the *do-or* of that verbal activity. If the subject is not the *do-or*, then the phrase is unconnected, that is, it dangles.

Here's an example of a dangling present participial phrase:

> When **arguing** for this approach, **statistical research** must be cited.

Note that the grammatical subject, *statistical research,* is not the agent (the *do-or*) of *arguing*. A person or organization capable of human thought must do the *arguing*. Here's the revision:

> When **arguing** for this approach, the **committee** must cite statis-
> tical research.

Many dangling participles, like the one above, are caused by the passive voice:

> When **arguing** . . . research **must be cited** . . . .

I see these structures pop up all the time. They are at war with each
other. First, the *passive voice* verb boots the actor or agent out of the sentence. Then the present participial phrase pleads for the opposite. "Attach
me to the agent," it screams. "No," replies the passive voice, "I won't do it.
Actor, you're outta here!"

Readers, of course, feel uncomfortable, for they know that the following sentence would win no prizes and makes no sense:

> **Catching** a pass, the winning **touchdown** was made.

So when you're tempted to say *when arguing . . . research must be cited,*
remember the superiority of the active voice and the strong desire the
present participle has for its actor, bring the actor back into your writing,
and say:

> When **arguing** for this approach, the **committee** must cite statis-
> tical research.

After all:

> **Catching** the pass, **Herman Moore** scored the winning
> touchdown.

THE INTRODUCTORY PAST PARTICIPIAL (*-ED*) PHRASE

With past participial (i.e, *-ed* verbs) phrases, the reverse is true. When
you introduce a sentence with a past participial phrase, the grammatical
subject of the sentence must be the *recipient* of the action, i.e., the *do-ee*

of that verbal activity. If the subject is not the *do-ee,* then the phrase is similarly unconnected, that is, it dangles.

Hence the term: *dangling participle.*

Here's an example of a dangling past participial phrase:

Shown at the mall, many **people** saw *Titanic.*

Notice that the introductory past participle, *shown,* does not modify the grammatical subject of the sentence, *many people.* Instead, it modifies the direct object, *Titanic.* The participle *must* modify the grammatical subject. Otherwise, it dangles. Here's the revision:

Shown at the mall, *Titanic* attracted many people.

I should pause and point out a particular past participle that many people use at the beginning of sentences. Check this out:

Based on our research, **we** decided to adopt this policy.

As you can see, *we* are not *based on* our research. The writer is trying to modify the verb *decided to adopt.* But the introductory past participle must act as an adjective and must modify the grammatical subject. The solution is to use a true prepositional phrase, which can act as an adverb modifying the main verb in the sentence. Take a look:

As a result of our research, we **decided to adopt** this policy.

Henry Fowler urges us "to avoid using *Based on* as a kind of sentence-leading preposition: Based on this assumption, the economy is not expected to improve before the autumn. The relationship between *Based on* and *the economy* is not a direct one."[2]

Some Correct Introductory Phrases

Enacted in 1964, the **Civil Rights Act** transferred power to the federal government.

> **Hoping** to gain favorable relations with the media, the **president** called a press conference.

> **Rejected** repeatedly by the voters, the **referendum** would never see the light of day again.

> While **ascending** the stairs, the **guest speaker** tripped and destroyed the ice sculpture.

See? It's not all that hard. When you start a sentence with an *-ing* phrase, you have immediately identified your grammatical subject: the *agent* of that verbal activity. When you start a sentence with an *-ed* phrase, you have also immediately identified your grammatical subject: the *recipient* of that verbal activity.

Let's move on to another problem many people have—distinguishing *they're, their,* and *there.*

But first, the chapter title needs repair:

> When **writing, you** might produce a dangling participle

NOTES
1. *Strunk & White,* p. 13.
2. *New Fowler,* p. 94.

Their mixing up they're "theres"

After gathering wild hickory nuts one hot afternoon, Amber and Igor sat beneath a shade tree and gossiped about the tribe.

"Where did the Jones family go for vacation?" Igor asked.

"Southern France," Amber answered.

"*They're* in France? At this time of year?" Igor wondered.

"They like the beaches, I think," Amber explained.

"Why don't we ever go *there*?" Igor asked.

"I don't think our children are old enough just yet," Amber pointed out.

"But the Joneses took *their* children, didn't they?" Igor asked, scratching his hairy toes.

"Yep, *they're there with theirs*," Amber said, summing it all up succinctly.

Some very smart people make the mistake of mixing up their *theres*. They confuse these three words: *there, their*, and *they're*.

FUNCTIONS OF THERE, THEIR, THEY'RE

Word	Function	Example
there	pronoun taking the place of ensuing noun	**There** is a policy covering this matter. **There's** a policy covering this matter. **There** are policies covering this matter. **There're** policies covering this matter.
there	adverb showing a place or location	He walked **there** in just 35 minutes.
there	a noun showing a point or place	You're on your own from **there** on.
their	the possessive case of *they*	They took **their** children to France.
they're	a contraction of *they are*	**They're** in France with **their** children. **They're there** with **their** children. **They're there** with **theirs**.

So to fix this problem once and for all, just remember Amber and Igor sitting under the tree talking about the Joneses who took their children to France.

> The Joneses *(They)* ....
> The Joneses are *(They're)* ....
> The Joneses are there *(They're there)* ....
> The Joneses are there with their children *(They're there with their children)*.
> **They are there** with **their** children.

They're there with **theirs.**

Meanwhile Amber and Igor remained beneath the tree. Wishing for a vacation one day, Amber sighed:

We're here with ours, and they're there with theirs.

So the title to this chapter should be:

They're mixing up **their "theres"**

26

Bad habits will effect your writing

AFFECT VS. EFFECT

Writers often confuse these two words, usually by saying *effect* when they mean *affect:*

> These technologies can **effect** the way the company expands its business.

The correct word, of course, is *affect.*

Here's the difference: The word *affect* serves only as a verb and will never appear as a noun in almost all fields of study. The only noun meaning of *affect* occurs in psychology, where a person's *affect* is an emotion, or in psychiatry, where a person's *affect* is an observed emotional response. But in most writing, one thing *affects* (verb) another thing, but it cannot have an *"affect"* (noun) on another thing. Indeed, few, if any, writers confuse the use of *affect* by trying to make it act as a noun.

The confusion arises, instead, with the word *effect.* In the vast majority of cases, *effect* serves only as a noun, not as a verb. Thus, one thing has an *effect* on another thing or one thing produces an *effect,* a result, a consequence. Thus:

> We must analyze the **effect** of the drug on the nervous system.

One term very popular with moviegoers might help you remember that *effect* usually serves as a noun:

special effects

Unfortunately, the word *effect* does have a verb meaning: to produce, to bring into being, or *to effectuate*. Thus:

The company issued pink slips to thousands of workers in order **to effect** savings.

Or:

The company **effected** considerable savings by laying off workers.

In each example, the verb *effect* means *to produce*.

If you want to ensure that you always use these words correctly, then simply abolish the word *effect* as a verb. Plenty of other verbs mean the same thing: *produce, bring about, result in, create, originate, spawn, manufacture, make,* and the list goes on and on.

One thing will *affect* another thing. The policy *affects* the economy. That's the verb form.

One thing produces an *effect* on another thing. The policy has an *effect* on the economy. That's the noun form.

Our chapter title should read:

Bad habits will **affect** your writing

27

Should you take out it's apostrophe?

ITS VS. IT'S

In chapter 5, we learned about pronouns. We learned about third-person pronouns. We learned that the word *it* is a third-person pronoun used to refer to an inanimate noun. Of course, if the noun is alive (or at one time was alive) and can be identified as male or female, we use the personal pronouns *he, she, his, her,* and *him.* But in most forms of writing, we often use the word *it* to refer to a committee, an agency, a company, a team, or other sorts of singular nouns.

Just as the pronoun *she* has the possessive form *her* and just as *he* has the possessive form *his,* the pronoun *it* has a possessive form as well: *its.* Thus:

> The machine lost **its** power.
> The agency published **its** decision in the newspaper.

Please note the difference in forming the possessive of the pronoun *it.* We simply add *-s.* We do not add "apostrophe *-s*" like we do when forming the possessives of nouns. Thus, it is incorrect (and a gross grammatical error) to use *it's* as the possessive form of *it.*

Wrong: The machine lost **it's** power.

The agency published **it's** decision in the newspaper.

Right: The machine lost **its** power.

The agency published **its** decision in the newspaper.

The word *it's* is not the possessive form of *it*. Instead, the word *it's* serves as the contraction for the two words *it is*. Thus:

It's a shame you can't join us for dinner. (**It is** a shame ....)
It's worth the price of admission. (**It is** worth the price ....)
It's raining outside. (**It is** raining ....)

There isn't a neat trick that will help you remember to remove the apostrophe from *it's* when you mean the possessive *its*. You can try to remember that none of the personal pronouns forms its possessive with the "apostrophe -*s*":

he ... his/his
she ... her/hers
they ... their/theirs
it ... its/its

You can try to remember that some of the indefinite pronouns do form their possessives with "apostrophe -*s*":

anyone ... anyone's
anybody ... anybody's
everyone ... everyone's
everybody ... everybody's
and others

But not a single personal pronoun has an apostrophe in it. Only in contractions will the apostrophe show up at all with any of the personal pronouns:

He's coming to dinner
She's the CEO of the company.
Next week, **they're** taking some time off.
It's going to be a wonderful day.

So to fix the title of this chapter:

You should take out **its** apostrophe

_**It's**_ the right thing to do.

28

Yesterday, they lead us astray

LEAD VERSUS LED

Many writers think that the word *lead* is pronounced to rhyme with *red* and is used as the past tense or past participle of the verb *lead* (pronounced *leed*). They are wrong.

The word *lead* is not the past tense of *lead*. It is a gross mistake to say:

> Yesterday, he **lead** the parade.

Instead, the word is properly spelled *led,* and it serves both roles: past tense and past participle.

Thus, in the past tense:

> Yesterday, he **led** the parade.

Or in the perfect tenses, we use the past participle *led* to produce:

> He has **led** the parade.
> He had **led** the parade.
> He will have **led** the parade.

Or in the passive voice, we use the past participle *led* to produce:

The parade was led by John.

The mistake probably comes from the word *read* where *read* (pronounced *red*) is the past tense and past participle of *read* (pronounced *reed*).

Whatever the source of the mistake, it's time to get rid of using *lead* when you're trying to say *led*.

For other problems with past participles, please see chapter 2, "Verbs: Words That Do or Are."

Let's fix the chapter title:

Yesterday, they led us astray

29

Here's the principle reason

he flunked the course

PRINCIPLE VERSUS PRINCIPAL

Many writers confuse *principle* and *principal*. The mistake will stand out like a sore thumb in your writing, for you can rest assured that many readers out there know the difference. Let's explore the differences between these two words and straighten out the confusion.

First of all, consider this all-important fact: The two words share *no common meanings*. They are indeed as different as night and day.

Second of all, let's discard that old approach we learned in grade school, the one about your *principal* being your *pal*. That trick does describe *one* of the definitions of *principal,* but only one. It helps not at all with understanding most definitions of *principal*.

THE WORD *PRINCIPLE*

Instead, let's take a simple parts-of-speech approach to understanding the differences. The word *principle* will always appear as a noun form, never as an adjective. It is thus incorrect to say:

> This was the **principle** (meaning *main*) reason supporting the company's decision.

Also, the word *principle* essentially means just one thing (or variations of this one thing): a rule or tenet or precept or policy. The key word to remember is *rule*. If tricks help, both words end in "*-le*." Here are some examples:

> Some people have high moral **principles** (rules).
> An inventor's research must adhere to scientific **principles** (rules).
> The court followed the sound judicial **principle** (rule) of interpreting a statute in light of legislative intent.

The word *principle* will operate as an adjective only in its *noun past participial state.* In the English language, you can take a good old noun and turn it into what amounts to a past participle. Thus: the *wooded* lot, the *two-faced* politician, the *hooded* robber. (Notice how these verb-like words derive from the nouns *wood, face,* and *hood.*) In your writing, you might have the occasion to describe a decision of your boss as a *principled* decision.

But other than this *-ed* version, the word *principle* acts not as an adjective but only as a noun. It means *rule.* Remember:

> The word **ru*le*** ends in **-*le*** and so does the word ***principle***.

THE WORD *PRINCIPAL*

The word *principal*, on the other hand, has a variety of meanings and operates either as a noun or an adjective. Let's look first at its *single* adjectival meaning. As an adjective, *principal* means "chief" or "main" or "foremost in importance." Thus, the word *principal* as an adjective will likely show up in our writing like this:

> **One Adjectival Meaning**
> The **principal** argument in the company's report tried to ease the fears of investors.
> The applicant, therefore, satisfied her **principal** objective: getting a good job.
> The engineer's argument fails for one **principal** reason: a complete absence of any scientific authority supporting it.

Now let's look at the various meanings of *principal* in its noun form.

Various Noun Meanings
People:
 1. The high school *principal*. Your *pal*.
 2. The key participant in a situation. ("Let's get ready to rummmm-mmmmmble. Now, introducing the *principals*. In this corner, wearing gold and black, sporting a record of 83 and 1, from Panama, Roberto Duran! Duran!")

Legal People:
 3. A person (the *principal*) empowering another (the *agent*) to act in a legal or financial capacity.
 4. The perpetrator (the *principal*) of a crime.

Money:
 5. The balance due on your mortgage; the relatively small amount of *principal* you've paid when compared with the huge amount of interest.
 6. An account or amount of money; the *principal* of an estate.

Construction:
 7. A *principal* is also the main rafter supporting a roof.

In sum, the word *principle* is always a noun. Essentially it means "rule." It will never appear as an adjective. Its only possible adjectival form is *principled*.

The word *principal* is an adjective or a noun. As an adjective, it essentially means just one thing: "main." As a noun, it refers either to people or money (or a rafter).

With these ideas now firmly in mind, you can see how your ***main*** high-school ***principal***, who knows about finances, might refer to his ***primary money rule*** like this:

 the principal principal's principal principal principle

It is, after all:

 the main principal's primary money rule

Our chapter title should thus read:

 Here's the **principal** reason he flunked the course

30

Bring along this advice when you

go to work

BRING VERSUS TAKE

Many years ago, in my youth, I was enjoying some sake at a quaint little bar in Tokyo. A Japanese student asked if he could sit down and practice his English with me. He offered to buy me yet another sake. We introduced ourselves and began what turned out to be a most enjoyable evening. At least I'm told that I had a good time.

One of the student's main questions was this: What is the difference between *bring* and *take*? Though I had not yet declared myself an expert in writing, he must have noticed that I possessed the grammar gene and would willingly, even eagerly, enjoy an evening devoted to the discussion of language. (My affliction began at a very young age. I can blame it on my dear mother, who permitted absolutely no grammatical mistakes, and my dear Miss Hamrick, who was equally ruthless in enforcing the rules of grammar.)

So, in the Tokyo sake bar, how could I explain the difference between *bring* and *take* to my new friend? I immediately sensed the need for some examples.

"Here's the key difference," I said.

"Key? What do you mean by this 'key'?" he asked.

I then sensed a need to dramatically simplify my language. He spoke my language. I knew only a word or two of his.

"Here's the difference," I said. "A very important difference."

And I proceeded to tell him that the difference between *bring* and *take* has to do with the location of the speaker and the location of any other actors who will be *bringing* or *taking* something from some place to some other place. As I told my friend, you can break down the world into three types of people: the speaker (first person), the listener (second person), and the person being talked about (third person).

Suppose the first person and the second person are engaged in the conversation. Assume that they are engaged in a face-to-face conversation. They occupy the same location, say, in Tokyo. Their conversation might go like this:

> 1st Person (Tokyo):   "Do you plan to **take** your manuscript with you to Kyoto?"
>
> 2nd Person (Tokyo):   "Yes, it'll be **going** with me."

I explained to my friend that *take* means that an action will proceed *away from the location where the taker currently resides.* I pointed out that *take* and *go* share a similar sense: the sense of leaving the current location and *going* somewhere else. The first person and the second person are in the same location, so moving anything from their location to somewhere else necessarily requires the word *take*.

My new friend was very pleased to learn that many Americans confuse *bring* and *take*. "Yes," I said, "it's sad but true. Many Americans, even famous ones, confuse the two words."

"What sorts of mistakes do they make?" he asked.

So I explained that many people use *bring* when they mean *take*. If I had had a time machine back then, I could have flashed forward to many Seinfeld episodes, where *bring* is routinely used for *take*. Jerry will be talking to Elaine, in Jerry's apartment. He knows that Elaine will be having dinner with yet another boyfriend that night. So Jerry will advise her: "Be sure to *bring* your credit card. After all, he might not pay." If Elaine were to *bring* her credit card, she would have to be somewhere else and would then have to *come* to Jerry's apartment. But Jerry means that Elaine should *take* her credit card, because she's *going* somewhere else, that is, to dinner.

But, alas, back then Jerry Seinfeld was a mere child. So I had to devise other tricks to help my friend thoroughly understand the differences between *bring* and *take*.

"Here are a couple of trick phrases you might want to remember," I suggested.

So I explained that the concept of *take* is the concept of *take away*. The concept of *bring*, on the other hand, is the concept of *bring back*. A *taking* of something moves it away. A *bringing* moves it to the location of the speaker, or to the location of the person whose perspective is governing the conversation.

Then I got an idea. I suggested to my friend that he *take* our pile of yen over there to the bartender, who stood off to the side, apparently ignoring us, and order up a couple of more sakes. He was glad to do so.

When he returned with the sakes, I pointed out that he had **brought** them back to our position at the bar. But at the moment he left the bartender to return the sakes to our location, he was, from his own perspective, in the process of *taking* them to our position.

The grammar lesson continued:

Now, I said to my friend, let's assume that the first person and the second person are not in the same location. Let's assume that they are talking on the telephone. The first person is in Tokyo, the second person in Kyoto. This telephone conversation might go like this:

> 1st Person (Tokyo):   "Please **bring** your manuscript to me when you visit Tokyo."
>
> 2nd Person (Kyoto):   "Don't worry, I'll **bring** it along next week."

Now we have the first person correctly asking the second person to **bring** the manuscript from Kyoto to the first person's location in Tokyo. But, oddly enough, the second person says he'll **bring it along**. That seems incorrect, because, from the second person's perspective he will definitely *take* the manuscript to Tokyo. In fact, if someone else were to ask him about the manuscript, he'd say he's going to *take* it to Tokyo.

My new friend was perplexed. So I explained:

"Quite often in the English language, we will put ourselves in someone else's shoes," I observed.

"You wear someone else's shoes?" he asked. "But we don't wear shoes in a sake bar!"

I explained that it was a "figure of speech," which opened up an entirely new topic requiring even more trips of the bartender, who (from our point of view) *brought* more sake and who (from the bartender's point of view) *took* more sake to those dudes over there who seemed to be drinking far too much sake.

With the concept of "figure of speech" firmly in place, I pointed out that we often step into other people's shoes. When we do, we must choose *bring* or *take* from their perspective. If the first person in Tokyo asks the second person in Kyoto to *bring* the manuscript to Tokyo, the second person will step into the shoes of the first person, and from that perspective, *bring along* the manuscript to Tokyo.

"Here's another example. This might help," I said.

So I fashioned another conversation:

> 1st Person (Tokyo): "Hey, why don't you come for dinner Friday night."
>
> 2nd Person (Kyoto): "Great idea! Can I **bring** anything?"

Here the second person is speaking from the first person's perspective—as if he has already arrived at the party. Hence the need for *bring*. If the second person had said, "Can I **take** anything?" the implication would be that he planned to go to somebody else's house for dinner.

To illustrate the meaning of *bring*, I told my Japanese friend to get the attention of the bartender and ask him to *bring* us a couple of more sakes. I then pointed out that from the bartender's perspective he will *take* the sakes over to the Japanese student and the American traveler.

We toasted our good fortune of having met one another and continued our grammar lesson.

So far, I pointed out, we've been dealing with two speakers either in the same location, in which case either one would *take* something somewhere else, or in different locations, in which case the speaker would use *bring* to show something *coming* to the speaker. If the speaker wanted to show something moving away from his location, he would use *take* to show something *going* away from the speaker.

I then pointed out that the first person and the second person might refer to the act of moving something to some third location. Their conversation would go like this:

> 1st Person (Tokyo): "Do you plan to **take** your manuscript with you to Osaka?"
>
> 2nd Person (Kyoto): "Yes, I'll **take** it with me when I go to Osaka next week."

As you can see, from the perspective of the first person, the manuscript will move from one "somewhere else" (Kyoto) to another "somewhere else" (Osaka). It will not *come* to the first person's location (Tokyo). From the second person's perspective, the manuscript will *go* away from his current location (Kyoto) to a completely different location (Osaka). Both speakers would use *take*.

I then spotted a group of travelers at the other side of the sake bar. So I said: "Let's *take* our sake and pile of yen over to those guys and introduce ourselves." The other group, being grammatically aware, said: "We're glad you **brought** your pile of yen over here to us. Why don't you *take* some of it over to the bartender and order up a bunch of sakes for everybody."

We were only too glad to do so.

After we bought some rounds, they bought some rounds. After a while, my Japanese friend and I returned to our original position at the bar. We talked about the people we met. I pointed out that these other people were *third persons*. So I fashioned a conversation between a first person and a second person *about* a third person:

> 1st Person: "Does Fred plan to invite his mother to visit him during the holidays?"
>
> 2nd Person: "Yes, he **brought** her home last year, and I think he wants to **bring** her this year."

Here the speakers assume the perspective of the third person; they step into the third person's shoes. Thus, the mother will *come* to the third person's home. The third person will, therefore, *bring* her home for the holidays.

With this newly found grammatical wisdom, my friend caught the attention of the bartender. In perfect English he said:

| My Japanese Friend: | "See those travelers over there? They would like you to **bring** them some more sake. Here, use our pile of yen." |
| Bartender: | "I'll **take** them some right away. Doumo arigatou gozaimasu." |

Apparently, the bartender had been paying attention to our grammar lesson all along.

| Yours Truly: | "While you're at it, please **bring** us a couple more as well." |

My friend had assumed the perspective of the travelers and correctly used *bring* to describe the act of the bartender of moving some sake from the bartender's location to their own location. He was beginning to understand the in-your-shoes approach to analyzing *bring* and *take*.

So in Tokyo, at the sake bar, my friend and I stepped into each other's shoes, even though we weren't actually wearing any. It was a sake bar, after all. We learned a lot about each other's culture and language. At this quaint little bar. Where the bartender *brought* us way too much sake.

My friend learned some English. I learned that those little sake glasses are far bigger than you think.

I hope you've learned to fix the chapter title:

Take along this advice when you go to work

31

Like, I'mlike gonna like learn

how to like talk

In the late 1980s, the Drug Enforcement Administration dispatched a crack team of enforcers to a southern university. They struck pay dirt, finding drug paraphernalia in several fraternity houses. Editors of the *Washington Post* dispatched their crack team of reporters to gauge student reaction. In its story, the *Post* included one of those boxed quotations designed to attract attention to the article. Unfortunately for the university's public-relations department, the *Post* quoted a student "thinker" who summed up the reaction this way:

"We were like,'Whoa!'"

Millions of *Post* readers scratched their heads, wondering just exactly what the students thought of the DEA raid. Did they endorse it? Did they find it incredibly funny? Did they feel a sense of outrage? Relief? Fear? Shame? We know very little, of course, only that students **"were like,'Whoa.'"** We can fill in the blanks. The expression means whatever we want.

Like every generation before it (in the '60s we used *ya know* a lot), the youth of today have devised their own expression as a substitute for thought—a new verb, *tobelike*, spelled just like that, spoken just like that, as a single word, often joined permanently to its subject.

We can conjugate this new verb: *tobelike*. In the present tense, "I'm-like." In the past, "Iwaslike." And on the subway once, I heard a young professional say in the future tense, "I'llbelike."

Usually, people use *tobelike* to intro-duce quoted sources. In that form, it doesn't harm the language too much or totally prevent thought from taking place.

> **Overuse of the word *like* threatens the language— and therefore thought itself.**

We can hear entire conversations, peppered with the verb *tobelike* and gobs of *likes* thrown in for good measure, and come away at least mar-ginally informed. Thus, a law student might describe his experience in class to a friend this way:

> My professor was**like**, "Does the bill of rights apply to the states?" And I was**like**, "In most cases, yes." And she was**like**, "Well, when do these rights not apply?" So I was**like** trying to remember the case law, but she was**like** rushed for an answer so she **like** went on to **like** the next guy.

The student manages to convey some meaning. But he cannot look forward to any awards for elocution.

Sadly, the verb *tobelike* and other variations of the *like* word do more than introduce quotations. They pervade young people's speech. They threaten the language—and therefore thought itself. *Tobelike* and *like* often require the "speaker" to resort to wild gesticulations of hand and arm, accompanied by guttural grunts and groans. Thus we might hear two young professionals share the hardships of the day:

> He: "I'mlike up to here." (Hand and forearm, parallel to the ground, rise to level of eyebrow.)
>
> She: "Like yeah." (Heel of hand, with fingers curled to back of head, strikes center of forehead.)
>
> He: "Like yesterday waslike, 'Ugh!'" (The theme begins to develop.)
>
> She: "I'mlike, oh well, you know." (Gentle but rhythmic nods of total understanding.)

He: "So you'llbelike, with it." (Presumably a question denoting sympathy.)

She: "I'mlike . . . you know. What EVer." (Mutual nods of assent to newly shared precepts.)

Perhaps I exaggerate. But I do so to make a point: If people talk this way, quite likely they will find writing even more difficult. One trend I have observed: People with the *like* habit overuse the verb *to be* in their writing. They simply cannot write a sentence without saying "something *is* this" or "something *was* that."

When I teach courses in persuasive writing, as an exercise I urge the participants to write and speak at some length without using the verb *to be* and the *like* word at all. When they try it out, they often get tongue-tied or contract a case of writer's block. But after a while, they catch on to the magic of speaking without thought-stopping expressions and of writing with verb-based prose.

Overuse and misuse of the word *like* threaten your career.

Parents might try the exercise out on their children. Bribe them. Put a $10 bill on the breakfast table and challenge them to make it through a second helping of waffles without using the *tobelike* verb and without misusing the *like* word. Up it to $100. Your money's safe.

Like as a Verb

If your children ask about the correct meaning of *like,* point out that it serves as a verb, all by itself. Your children can say, "I **like** waffles" or "I would **like** another serving."

Like as a Preposition

Point out that it also serves as a preposition and in that capacity hooks nouns to sentences. Your children can say, "He runs **like** the wind." Indeed, go ahead and point out that *to be* can join *like* if they truly want to show what something or somebody *was like.* Thus the commercial "I want to be *like* Mike" has its grammar in order. So does "He was *like* a father to me." But virtually everyone addicted to the *like* word uses it to show not what something *is like* but what something actually *is*. They use it to show identity *(is)*, not similarity *(like):* He's like tall. Well, *is* he or *isn't* he?

Like as a Noun
You can also point out that *like* serves as a noun, as in *likes* and *dislikes.*

Like as an Adjective
The word spans almost all parts of speech and can serve as an adjective (she mastered lacrosse, field hockey, and like sports).

Like as an Adverb
Informally, *like* can serve as an adverb (the tree is more like 100 than 50 feet).

Like as a Conjunction
Here we stir up a hornet's nest. According to some sources, the word *like* can also act as a subordinating conjunction. Charles Darwin wrote in 1866: "Unfortunately few have observed **like you have done.**"[1] Consider the words of *Random House:*

> *Like* as a conjunction meaning "as, in the same way as" (Many shoppers study the food ads like brokers study market reports) or "as if" (It looks like it will rain) has been used for nearly 500 years and by many distinguished literary and intellectual figures. Since the mid-19th century there have been objections, often vehement, to these uses. Nevertheless, such uses are almost universal today in all but the most formal speech and writing. In extremely careful speech and in much formal writing, *as, as if,* and *as though* are more commonly used than *like:* The commanding general accepted full responsibility for the incident, as any professional soldier would. Many of the Greenwich Village bohemians lived as if (or as though) there were no tomorrow.[2]

Other sources fervently disagree with this loose approach. Mr. Fowler himself minced no words: "Every illiterate person uses this construction daily."[3] The *Oxford English Dictionary* noted that examples of the use of *like* as a conjunction do appear "in many recent writers of standing" but also pointed out that such use is "generally condemned as vulgar or slovenly."[4]

Instead, use *as, as if,* and *as though* as the proper conjunctions. Not *like.*

New Fowler examined the works of leading writers in England, America, and other countries, and identified four situations where they use *like* as a conjunction:

1. The *If you knew Susie* Exception: Repeat the Verb

In the subordinate clause, writers often repeat the verb appearing in the main clause. They introduce the subordinate clause with *like:*

> I **need** a new car like I **need** a hole in the head—E. Good, 2001.

> If you **knew** Susie like I **know** Susie.

New Fowler's Comment: "[This construction] must surely escape further censure or reproach."[5]

2. To Replace *As If* or *As Though*

> It looks like it's still a fox—*New Yorker,* 1986.

3. The *Like I said* Exception

Substitutes for *as* in "fixed, somewhat jocular, phrases of saying and telling."

> Like you say, you're a dead woman—M. Wesley, 1983.

4. To Make Comparisons

Used in the same way as "in the manner (that)" or "in the way (that)."

> How was I to know she'd turn out like she did?—C. Burns, 1985.

As a budding grammarian, you should know of this battle. At Bubba's you can easily get away with *like.* But in formal settings—the faculty lounge, scholarly writing (and talking), your master's thesis—you should use the traditional conjunctions *as, as if,* and *as though.* In the words of *New Fowler:*

It would appear that in many kinds of written and spoken English *like* as a conjunction is struggling towards acceptable standard or neutral ground. It is not there yet. But the distributional patterns suggest that the long-standing resistance to this omnipresent little word is beginning to crumble.[6]

OVERUSING *LIKE* THREATENS YOUR CAREER

Consider the views of the experts:

New Fowler:
By the mid-20c., however, [the use of *like*] as an incoherent and prevalent filler had reached the proportions of an epidemic, and it is now scorned by standard speakers as a vulgarism of the first order.[7]

Garner Oxford:
Since the 1980s, *be like* is also a juvenile colloquialism equivalent to *said* in relating a conversation—e.g.: "And I was like, 'Yes, I do.' But he was like, 'No you don't. And so I was like, 'If you're just going to contradict me, then . . . .'" In teenagers, this usage is all but ubiquitous. In adults, it shows arrested development.[8]

Urge your children to stay away from *tobelike*. Point out that saying "She was like tall" says nothing at all. And vigorously stress that grunts and groans and "like . . . ah . . . like this" and "like . . . um . . . ah . . . like that" peg the speaker as one who has some work to do before taking control of the language.

And if you write or talk for a living—as most of us do—try the exercise yourself. Listen to your own patterns of speech. I have a friend, my age, in his 50s. He has picked up the *like* habit from his teenager.

If you use *tobelike* and misuse the *like* word, just stop it. Then try writing a chapter like this one, and in 1,700 words see if you can use the verb *to be*—as I have—only once. (Can you find it? The *be*'s in the examples and quotations don't count.)

Go ahead. Try it out.

You'llbelike, "Whoa!"

Perhaps from now on you'll say:

I'm going to learn how to talk

NOTES

1. *New Fowler,* p. 458.
2. *Random House,* p. 1114.
3. *New Fowler,* p. 458.
4. Quoted in *New Fowler,* p. 458.
5. The following examples and comments appear in *New Fowler,* p. 458.
6. *New Fowler,* p. 459.
7. *New Fowler,* p. 459.
8. *Garner Oxford,* p. 212.

PART **FIVE**

Punctuation

I n this final part of *Oops, Me!* you'll find a discussion of the proper use of punctuation. As my sources, I am using *The Chicago Manual of Style* (13th ed. 1982) and *Strunk & White*. On matters not covered here, I urge you to consult these two sources. Also, unabridged dictionaries have excellent sections on punctuation.

Many people think that punctuation involves matters of taste. *I'm a comma kinda guy.* Or *I'm not a comma kinda guy.* Well, some punctuation marks are indeed discretionary. When you encounter these optional situations, you need to make certain that you punctuate consistently throughout the written piece. Don't opt for a comma in one discretionary situation and then leave it out of an identical situation.

But many rules on punctuation are inscribed in stone. Igor, Amber, and Miss Hamrick made certain of that. If you break these rules, then knowledgeable writers will look unfavorably on your work. So now that you want to join The Writers Club, it's time to learn the rules on proper punctuation. In the chapters that follow, I deal with these punctuation marks:

Confusion inevitably arises on the issue of closing quotation marks. Does the other punctuation mark come inside or outside the closing quotation marks? I deal with this issue twice, once with each mark and then all together in a concluding chapter on quotation marks.

Finally, as you read these chapters, keep your eyes wide open for new ways of writing. Look for structures you don't ordinarily use. Do you use elliptical expressions? Antithetical expressions? Complementary expressions? Parenthetical expressions? Expressions requiring a dash? Sentences with introductory phrases or clauses? Good writers do. So watch for these and many more in the chapters on punctuation.

Many of the chapters, I'm glad to report, are short.

32

Period

The period shows the end of a complete sentence, the abbreviation of words, and indented lists.

ENDING A SENTENCE

In word-processed documents, two spaces should follow a sentence-ending period. In documents destined for typesetting, however, ordinarily only one space appears after sentence-ending punctuation.

SHOWING ABBREVIATION

The period shows abbreviations such as *Co.*, *Ave.*, *Corp.*, *Bldg.*, and a host of others. If a sentence ends in an abbreviated word, the single period serves double duty to show abbreviation and to end the sentence. Thus: **We received the report of The Coca-Cola Co.** You do not need two periods at the end of the sentence. In fact, one immutable rule on punctuation states that you'll never use two sentence-ending punctuation marks at the end of a sentence.

VERTICAL, ENUMERATED LISTS

Periods also show up in an enumerated vertical list. Look at this example:

His favorite movies included:
1. *The Fight Club*
2. *To Kill a Mockingbird*
3. *Aliens*

You could also use letters to show the enumeration:

a. *The Fight Club*
b. *To Kill a Mockingbird*
c. *Aliens*

Notice that you do not include periods after the items on the list and you do not include a period after the last item on the list to show the end of the grammatical sentence. You would only include periods in the list if (1) one or more of the items is a complete sentence or (2) the items on the list are separated by commas or semicolons, in which case a period ends the final item on the list. Look at this example:

The committee found
1. that the employee had committed fraud;
2. that the supervisor had assisted in that fraud; and
3. that both would be terminated.

THE PERIOD AND ENDING QUOTATION MARKS

With only one exception, the period always comes inside closing quotation marks. This rule applies even if only one quoted word ends the sentence. Thus:

He said, "We need to tell the boss right away."
She reported that the boss was, in her words, **"miffed."**

The only exception, according to *The Chicago Manual of Style,* involves the use of single quotation marks in two situations: to show translations of foreign words and to show philosophical or theological terms.[1]

Translation
He placed the pan **'bread'** next to the mantequilla **'butter'**.

Philosophical or Theological Term
The professor discussed at length the meaning of **'being'.**

In all other situations, the period comes inside the closing quotation marks. In America, this topic is not subject to debate.[2]

THE PERIOD AND PARENTHESES OR BRACKETS
If an entire sentence or group of sentences appears in parentheses, then put the period inside the closing parenthesis. This is a parenthetical sentence. Thus:

Parenthetically Enclosed Sentence
Her mind was clouded. **(She hadn't thought of him in years.)**
But she shook it off and continued down the hill.

If parenthetically enclosed words end a sentence, then the period comes outside the closing parenthesis:

Parenthetical Words Ending the Sentence
He enjoyed all kinds of fruit **(especially apples, oranges, and bananas).**

NOTES
1. *The Chicago Manual of Style,* pp. 134, 170, 171 (13th ed. 1982).
2. See the examples in *Strunk & White,* p. 36.

33

Comma

The comma shows the smallest interruption of the structure of a sentence, the parenthesis and dash showing more severe breaks in continuity. A few rules, discussed below, have become obligatory. Otherwise, writers have considerable leeway in the use of commas.

THE SERIAL COMMA RULE:
COMMA WITH *AND, OR,* OR OTHER CONJUNCTION
Some organizations follow what's called *the serial comma rule,* and other organizations don't. The ones that do are the more enlightened, for following the rule makes the most sense and produces the most consistent writing.

Here's the rule: In a series consisting of three or more elements, separate the elements by commas. When a conjunction (usually *and, or,* or *but*) joins the last two elements in the series, put a comma before the conjunction.

As we learned in chapter 18, the chapter on parallel structure, the series may consist of *any* grammatical element. You can construct sentences with three or more subjects, verbs, direct objects, objects of prepositions, verbal objects, or any other grammatical part of a sentence. In the following examples, you'll find a variety of grammatical elements appearing in a series. Each is named parenthetically after the example.

Examples of the Serial Comma Rule

> The flag is **red, white, and blue**. (Three predicate adjectives.)
>
> In her will, the woman left **jewelry, coins, stocks, but no cash**. (Four direct objects of the transitive verb *left*.)
>
> **The director, the assistant chief, and the chairperson** held a confidential meeting. (Three subjects.)
>
> **Neither the president, the vice-president, nor the chief financial officer** may authorize this particular capital expense. (Three subjects.)
>
> The personnel committee **reconsidered this issue, found that the supervisor had exceeded her authority, and granted the relief requested by the employee**. (Three predicate verbs.)

Semicolon Examples

If the series is long and complex or any one element has a comma within it, separate each element of the series with a semicolon:

> The company has offices in Greensboro, North Carolina; Atlanta, Georgia; Los Angeles, California; London, England; and Taipei, Taiwan. (Commas within elements.)
>
> The committee reviewed the Jones Report, which was written in 1967; the Jackson Study, which came from the regional office; and the Commissioner's Report, which prompted the initial controversy. (Commas within elements.)
>
> "Since the earliest days philosophers have dreamed of a country where the mind and spirit of man would be free; where there would be no limits to inquiry; where men would be free to explore the unknown and to challenge the most deeply rooted beliefs and principles."[1] (Elements are long and complex.)

COMMAS JOINING TWO ELEMENTS

In a series consisting of just two elements, ordinarily you should not use a comma with the conjunction. This mistake usually occurs in a sentence with two verbs:

> The committee **revisited** this issue **and created** a new rule to guide the actions of supervisors.

> Not: The committee **revisited** this issue**, and created** a new rule to guide the actions of supervisors.

There is an exception to this rule. If the first of the two elements has another *and* within it, you might want to put a comma before the *and* joining the two elements, just to avoid confusion:

> The committee **revisited** this issue **and** the Jones Study**, and** created a new rule to guide the actions of supervisors.

COMMAS JOINING INDEPENDENT CLAUSES

When the conjunction joins two or more independent clauses, put a comma before the conjunction (usually *and, but,* or *or*):

> The supervisor reported the misbehavior**, but** the personnel committee ignored the evidence and refused to terminate the employee.

There is an exception (there's always an exception): If the two independent clauses are short and closely related, you may omit the comma:

> The assistants did the research **and** the manager wrote the report.

But even if the clauses are short and closely related, do not omit the comma if your readers could confuse the second subject with the object of the first verb. Look at this example and see how your brain at first interprets the words *the boy:*

> The terrorist tied up the teacher **and the boy** ran for help.

The words *the boy* could serve as the object of *tied up*. To prevent momentary ambiguity, use the comma:

> The terrorist tied up the teacher**, and the boy ran** for help.

If a sentence has three or more short, closely related independent clauses, separate them with commas and put a comma before the conjunction:

> The employees filed their complaint, the committee heard the arguments**, and** the company awaited the final decision.

COMMAS SETTING OFF
INTRODUCTORY CLAUSES OR PHRASES

You should put a comma after an introductory clause or phrase:

> **Though the agency had studied this issue before,** it went ahead with another study. (Introductory dependent clause.)

> **If I were you,** I would research the case thoroughly. (Introductory dependent clause.)

> **After researching the issue,** the committee settled the dispute before the media even noticed. (Introductory truncated clause.)

> **In determining the application of this rule,** the committee will balance the competing factors. (Introductory prepositional or present participial phrase.)

> **Exhausted by the long hearing,** the candidate took an extended vacation. (Introductory past participial phrase.)

> **Because of the sensitive nature of the controversy,** the Senate Judiciary Committee held an executive session. (Introductory prepositional phrase.)

There is, of course, an exception. You may omit the comma following a short introductory phrase:

On Thursday the committee decided the dispute.

In 1954 the Supreme Court desegregated public schools.

But if you omit this comma once, you should probably do so throughout the paper for all short introductory phrases.

COMMAS AND ADVERBIAL PHRASES
BETWEEN SUBJECT AND VERB

Put preceding and trailing commas around any adverbial phrase coming between the subject and the verb:

Ms. Smith, **after commenting on the evidence,** ruled in favor of the supervisor.

The court, **in a manner surprising to all,** excluded the press from the courtroom.

COMMAS AND ADJECTIVAL CLAUSES AND PHRASES

If the adjectival clause or phrase is nonrestrictive, put commas around it. If the clause or phrase is restrictive, do not put commas around it. See the discussion of *that* vs. *which* in chapter 14, "Word War IV: Clauses vs. Phrases." Here's a quick review:

Nonrestrictive Defined

A nonrestrictive clause or phrase does not identify or single out the noun modified. From context, the reader knows the noun modified and does not need the information in the clause or phrase to define "which one." A nonrestrictive clause is introduced by the word *which* (or *who, whom,* or *whose,* if appropriate). You must use commas to set off the nonrestrictive clause or phrase.

Restrictive Defined

A restrictive clause or phrase identifies or singles out the noun modified. From context, the reader does not know "which one" and needs the information in the clause or phrase to identify "which one." When you use a restrictive clause or phrase, there must be others (persons, places, or things named by the noun) from which you can single this one out. No commas should appear with the restrictive clause or phrase.

Perhaps examples will illustrate the distinction:

The report **that the agency submitted** was well researched (restrictive, identifies which report among all other reports, no commas).

The report**, which the agency submitted,** was well researched (nonrestrictive, from context the reader already knows which report because you've been talking about it or because necessarily there's only one report, use commas).

The judge **sitting next to the clerk** leaned over to ask a question (restrictive, identifies which judge among the other judges that necessarily exist in the context, perhaps it's a three-judge panel, no commas).

The judge**, sitting next to the clerk,** leaned over to ask a question (nonrestrictive, the reader already knows which judge, or from context there is only one judge, use commas).

COMMAS AND PARENTHETICAL PAUSES

If the information in a parenthetical pause relates closely to the sentence, enclose it in commas. Otherwise, use the dash or parentheses:

The committee's decision**, to say the least,** sparked considerable controversy.

The members of the committee were**, generally speaking,** experienced in the biological sciences.

The chairwoman—**known for her candor in contractor scandals**—submitted her report.

The report on a tax cut **(it had already been leaked to the press)** condemned the complexity of the tax code.

The report failed, **however,** to uncover the true nature of the problem.

The agency, **consequently,** needs additional funds in the next fiscal year.

Again, there's an exception. Sometimes single adverbs produce no pause and therefore require no commas. Watch for adverbs directly modifying an adjacent verb or adjective or other adverb:

The report was **indeed <u>deficient</u>.**

I **therefore <u>urge</u>** you to rewrite it.

It will **perhaps <u>influence</u>** the president himself.

Sometimes single adverbs produce no pause and **therefore <u>require</u>** no commas.

COMMAS AND THE NOUN APPOSITIVE

A word, phrase, or clause in apposition to a noun is usually set off by commas (dashes or parentheses might also be used):

The chairman of the committee, **Senator Biden,** rambled on and on.

The press surrounded the witness—**the chief accuser of the candidate**—as she exited the capital building.

Her husband, **David,** accompanied her to the hearings.

Here's the exception: If the appositive serves to identify the noun, then omit the comma:

His **brother Tom** came to dinner.

The committee defined the **term *specifically*** by referring to the dictionary.

In the first example above, the restrictive appositive *Tom,* without commas, means that he has more than one brother. If he has just one brother, then the appositive is nonrestrictive and requires commas:

> His **brother, Tom,** came to dinner.

COMMAS AND COORDINATE ADJECTIVES
When each of two adjectives modifies the same noun, put a comma between them. As a test, put the word *and* between the two adjectives. If it fits, then you've got what are called *coordinate adjectives:*

> It is going to be a **long, hot summer.**
> She was a **faithful, sincere friend.**

Here's the exception: If the first adjective modifies the idea expressed by the combination of the second adjective and the noun, do not use a comma between the two adjectives:

> He favored **traditional political institutions.**

In this example, the expression *political institutions* is a single idea. Thus, the two adjectives do not equally modify the single noun. Rather, the first adjective *traditional* modifies the single unit *political institutions.*

COMMAS AND COMPLEMENTARY OR
ANTITHETICAL EXPRESSIONS
A complementary or antithetical expression requires a comma at its beginning and end. Perhaps I should define *complementary or antithetical expressions.* These are usually groups of words complementing or contrasting a preceding word and combining with that preceding word to join it to a following word. The expression should be enclosed in commas:

> This harsh, **though at the same time logical,** conclusion provoked resentment among those affected.

> The most provocative, **if not the most important,** part of the statement piqued our curiosity.

> The committee intends to, **and no doubt will,** dispose of these
> complaints once and for all.

When you use these expressions (all good writers do), make certain
that the lead-in words and the expression enclosed in commas grammatically fit the words that follow. Many writers make terrible mistakes in
this regard. See the following example:

> Wrong: Earlier the committee **could have, and ultimately did,**
>   **avoid** the issue.

Note: You cannot grammatically join *could have* with *avoid.* The grammar breaks down. So make certain that the complementary or antithetical expression enclosed in commas or parentheses does not force the use
of a following word that will not match with the word preceding the
expression. Here you would fashion a new expression:

> Right: Earlier the committee **could have avoided, and ulti-**
>   **mately did avoid, the** issue.

COMMAS AND DATES
Month-Day-Year
When you indicate month, day, and year, put a comma after the day and
after the year (unless some other punctuation mark, like a period or
question mark, follows the year). Include these commas even if the
month-day-year expression serves as an adjective:

> On **July 1, 1991,** the committee dismissed the employee.
> We already responded to your **July 1, 1991, letter**.

A Note on Inevitable Disagreement
Many writers express their displeasure at putting a comma after the year
when the expression serves as an adjective, because "it looks funny." Perhaps so. But this seems to be the rule, and it does make sense. The year
is serving in apposition to the month and day, and thus requires commas
before and after. You can design around the problem by inserting a prep-

ositional phrase: Use "letter of January 17, 1998," instead of "January 17, 1998, letter."

Above, I said it "seems to be the rule." Actually, I cannot find any authority on this point at all. The *Random House Unabridged Dictionary* does say, "A date given in the order of month, day, and year is also followed by a comma."[2] But it does not address the issue of using the expression as an adjective. Indeed, why should the punctuation rule change as the expression serves various roles in the sentence?

In the "for what it's worth department," I have noticed that leading writers in leading newspapers put in the trailing comma even when the expression serves as an adjective.

Bryan Garner disagrees with this approach. Criticizing the use of dates as adjectives, he states:

> And it is particularly clumsy when the day as well as the month is given—e.g.: "The court reconsidered the July 12, 1994 privilege order." Stylists who use this phrasing typically omit the comma after the year—and rightly so; in the midst of an adjective phrase (i.e., the date), it impedes the flow of the writing too much.[3]

It seems to me that the year acts in apposition to the day. Commas before and after, therefore, are necessary. The same would apply if we revealed a city and state:

Greensboro, N.C., is where Miss Hamrick taught Damron and me English.

If we used that expression as an adjective, the commas would remain:

He traveled to the **Greensboro, N.C., regional office**.

Day-Month-Year

If you depict dates by day-month-year, not month-day-year, do not use commas. Make certain you use a consistent system throughout the document. Those not liking the required commas for month-day-year expressions used as adjectives (e.g., "your July 1, 1991, letter") might decide to use this form:

> On **17 January 1945** he was born in a large southern city.
> We now wish to respond to your **1 July 1991 letter**.

This technique, I should point out, is the one used in Great Britain. So if you're writing anything about to be sent over the pond, use the day-month-year approach.

Month-Year
If you omit the day and just include the month and year, do not use a comma:

> In **January 1945** he was born in a large southern city.
> We now wish to respond to your **July 1991 letter**.

COMMAS AND ELLIPTICAL EXPRESSIONS
Use a comma to show the omission of a word or words readily understood from context:

> In Illinois, there are seventeen such institutions; **in Ohio, twenty-two; in Indiana, three**.

There is an exception. When, in spite of such omissions, the construction is clear enough without the commas and semicolons, use simpler punctuation (commas only):

> One manager comes from UNC**, another from Duke, and a third from GW**.

Incidentally, superb writers use elliptical expressions all the time.

COMMAS AND ENDING QUOTATION MARKS
When the context calls for a comma at the end of material enclosed in quotation marks, the comma should be placed inside the quotation marks:

> We should study the committee's discussion of "discrimination in the **workplace**," which occurred early in its official report.

Strunk & White gives this example:

"The Fish," "Poetry," and **"The Monkeys"** are in Marianne Moore's *Selected Poems.*[4]

NOTES
1. Justice Hugo Black, *The Bill of Rights,* 35 N.Y.U.L. Rev. pp. 880–81 (1960).
2. *Random House,* p. 2461.
3. *Garner Legal,* p. 247.
4. *Strunk & White,* p. 36.

34

Semicolon

Top writers do not use the semicolon as much today as they did in the past. As a matter of style, you should try to avoid using too many sentences consisting of two independent clauses joined by a semicolon. The mark does have its uses, however, and when you do join two independent clauses without a conjunction, you must use the semicolon (or a colon).

SEMICOLON AND INDEPENDENT CLAUSES

A semicolon separates two or more independent clauses joined without a coordinating conjunction:

> The Court required police to warn suspects of their constitutional rights; in doing so, it made judicial history.

HOWEVER AND OTHER CONJUNCTIVE ADVERBS

Conjunctive adverbs include *however, therefore, thus, furthermore,* and others.

If you use a conjunctive adverb to join two independent clauses, then use a semicolon, followed by the conjunctive adverb, followed by a comma:

The committee had heard these arguments before**; therefore,** it turned its attention to other matters.

The agency trusted the report**; however,** the report proved faulty in its scientific method.

One of the most common mistakes in writing involves the use of a comma (not a semicolon) and a conjunctive adverb to join independent clauses:

Wrong: The agency trusted the report**, however** the report proved faulty in its scientific method.

Right: The agency trusted the report**; however,** the report proved faulty in its scientific method.

SEMICOLONS SEPARATING ELEMENTS IN A SERIES

We reviewed this rule when we discussed the serial comma rule in chapter 33. It bears repeating, however. When elements in a series are long and complex or involve internal punctuation, they should be separated by semicolons for the sake of clarity:

The company has offices in Greensboro, North Carolina; Atlanta, Georgia; Los Angeles, California; London, England; and Taipei, Taiwan.

The committee reviewed the Jones Report, which was written in 1967; the Jackson Study, which came from the regional office; and the Commissioner's Report, which prompted the initial controversy.

"Since the earliest days philosophers have dreamed of a country where the mind and spirit of man would be free; where there would be no limits to inquiry; where men would be free to explore the unknown and to challenge the most deeply rooted beliefs and principles."[1]

SEMICOLON AND QUOTATION MARKS

The semicolon should be placed *outside* ending quotation marks. When the quoted matter ends with a semicolon, the semicolon in the quotation is dropped:

The agency reviewed those petitions that were **"timely"**; it ignored those that were late.

The agency approved those agreements "having no significant impact on **competition"**; it refused to enforce those violating the anti-trust laws.

NOTE

1. Justice Hugo Black, *The Bill of Rights,* 35 N.Y.U. L. Rev. pp. 880–81 (1960).

35

Colon

The colon joins two independent clauses, introduces lists, and sets up quotations.

THE COLON AND INDEPENDENT CLAUSES

Many writers use the colon between two independent clauses, especially when the subject matter of the second clause expands on, or exemplifies, the subject matter of the first. Some writers start the second clause with a capital letter; others use lowercase.

In the May 17, 2001, edition of the *Washington Post,* columnist Richard Cohen uses a colon to separate two independent clauses. (In the passage, please note how Mr. Cohen uses parallel structure: He creates four present participial phrases to begin the first sentence.)

> Having been condemned to death for mass murder at Oklahoma City, having confessed to the crime, having waived all appeals, having chosen Gore Vidal to turn his death into literature, McVeigh now sees his execution delayed almost a month on account of a procedure **pimple: The FBI,** with characteristic efficiency, misplaced some 3,000 documents relating to the case.[1]

In the June 22, 2001, edition of the *Washington Post,* columnist Michael Kinsley uses a colon to separate two independent clauses and begins the second with a capital letter. (Please note that he also starts the sentence with the conjunction *But.*)

> But an equally dyspeptic conservative might say that's just the **point: For** a generation now, politicians have clamored to be called conservative without dismantling any significant aspect of big government.[2]

In *Garner Oxford,* Mr. Garner explains the use of a colon to connect two clauses or phrases:

> [The colon] may link two separate clauses or phrases by indicating a step forward from the first to the second: the step may be from an introduction to a main theme, from a cause to an effect, from a general statement to a particular instance, or from a premise to a conclusion.[3]

Note that Mr. Garner uses the lowercase to begin the complete sentence following the colon. He acknowledges that using uppercase is "the prevalent journalistic practice." He continues:

> But the other view—urging for a lowercase word following the colon—is probably sounder: the lowercase (as in this very sentence) more closely ties the two clauses together. Although the uppercase convention is a signpost to the reader that a complete clause is ahead, that signpost generally isn't needed.[4]

Strunk & White also uses a lowercase letter to begin an independent clause following a colon. Though the work doesn't expressly say so, the example shows the correctness of the lowercase letter:

> But even so, there was a directness and dispatch about animal burial: there was no stopover in the undertaker's foul parlor, no wreath or spray.[5]

In my writing, I opt for uppercase, for I think it does alert the readers to an upcoming complete sentence and in that way aids and hastens their reading. But you can't go wrong using lowercase.

The important point, of course, is this: You should recognize this use of the colon and weave it into your writing style. Good writers routinely use complete sentences to follow colons. You should, too. Pick either uppercase or lowercase. For either is correct.

THE COLON AND LISTS
Use the colon to introduce a list or a series:

> The committee's study focused on the most critical **areas: devel-opment** of software, needed **changes** in computer systems, and **recruitment** of new engineers.

If the list or series is introduced by such expressions as *namely, for instance, for example,* or *that is,* do not use a colon unless the series consists of one or more grammatically complete clauses:

> The committee's study focused on the most critical **areas, namely, development** of software, needed **changes** in computer systems, and **recruitment** of new engineers.

> We face several obstacles, **that is:** The employee must complain to the committee; the committee must review the complaint; and the commissioner must then decide the outcome of the dispute.

Do not use a colon to introduce a list that is a complement or object of an element in the introductory statement, or that grammatically completes the introductory statement:

> The agency **must** (1) **publish** the notice in the Federal Register, (2) **wait** the prescribed period of time, and (3) **consider** any comments received.

> The committee **rejected** (1) the employee's **evidence**, (2) the supervisor's **report**, and (3) both parties' **requests** for relief.

The term *as follows* or *the following* requires a colon if followed directly by the illustrating or enumerated items or if the introducing clause is incomplete without such terms:

> The factors are **as follows:** (1) reasonable expectations, (2) intent, and (3) sufficient evidence.

THE COLON AND STATEMENTS OR QUOTATIONS

Use the colon to introduce a formal statement, an extract from a passage, or a speech in a dialogue:

> **Remember the rule:** A colon may be used to introduce a statement.

> **I now quote from the committee's ruling:** "As we stated before ...."

When you introduce a multisentence quotation with a phrase, which is not a complete sentence, use the colon:

> **According to Mr. Smith:** "The government goofed again. It failed to review the matter."

If the quotation has only one sentence, use a comma after the introductory phrase:

> **According to Mr. Smith,** "The government goofed again."

Use the colon to introduce all block quotations:

> **Mr. Jackson said:**
> We must now decide the issue once and for all. Blah, blah, blah, blah, blah, blah, and so on.

Use the comma, however, to introduce quoted statements in dialogue:

> **Jane said,** "See Spot run!"

THE COLON AND QUOTATION MARKS

The colon should be placed *outside* quotation marks. When matter ending with a colon is quoted, the colon is dropped:

> The employee has two objections to the practice of **"early retirement"**: He wants to continue working, and the policy manual does not require it.

NOTES

1. Richard Cohen, "Delayed Martyrdom," *Washington Post,* May 15, 2001, p. A17.
2. Michael Kinsley, "Liberalism à la Mode," *Washington Post,* June 22, 2001, p. A25.
3. *Garner Oxford,* pp. 68–69.
4. *Garner Oxford,* p. 69.
5. *Strunk & White,* p. 8.

Dash

There are several kinds of dashes, differing from one another according to length. There are en dashes (short), em dashes (medium), and 2- and 3-em dashes (long). The term *em dash* is a printer's term meaning the dash is the width of the letter *"m"* in that type face. The *en dash* takes up a width equal to the letter *"n."*

The most commonly used dash in word-processed material is the em dash, formed in WordPerfect by typing "Ctrl W" and then typing "4,34" and then hitting the "Enter" key. In Microsoft Word, click on "Insert" and then "Symbol" and then "Special Characters." At the top, you'll find the "em dash," which you can then "Insert." Better yet, use the special assigned keys, usually the "Alt =" combination. You may also form the dash by holding down "Alt" key and typing 0 1 5 1 on your numeric pad. Release the "Alt" key, and the em dash appears.

Please note: No spaces come before and after the dash. Also note: Do not use two hyphens to form the dash; you have the correct character in WordPerfect or Word and should use it.

The dash is one of the most effective punctuation marks of all. It can halt readers in their tracks—it makes them pay attention—as they read through your words of wisdom. Basically, the dash creates the biggest of the "punctuational pauses," the smallest being the comma; next, the parentheses; and finally, the dash. Though the dash does have other uses, showing up primarily in creative writing, it can help expository writers in five situations:

1. Explanatory or Defining Phrases

Of the three punctuation marks producing a pause—**the comma, the dash, the parentheses**—the dash produces the most abrupt pause of all.

2. Parenthetical Material

The dash can halt readers in their tracks—**it makes them pay attention**—as they read through your words of wisdom.

3. Introductory Explanatory or Defining Phrase

Em dashes, parentheses, and commas—these are the major punctuation marks used to create a pause.

4. Appositives or Appositive Phrases (where commas would cause confusion)

Pauses in sentences—**explanatory phrases, defining phrases, parenthetical material, and introductory defining phrase**—prompt many writers to use the dash.

5. A Sudden Break in Thought

The committee's expansive logic—**it went far beyond any previous decision**—increased the available remedies rather dramatically.

Victory—that was her only goal.

37

Parentheses

Parentheses, like commas and dashes, may be used to set off amplifying, explanatory, or digressive elements. If such parenthetical elements bear a close logical relationship to the rest of the sentence, use commas. If the logical relationship is more remote, use dashes or parentheses.

PARENTHESES AND AMPLIFYING, EXPLANATORY, AND DIGRESSIVE ELEMENTS

Use parentheses to enclose material that amplifies, explains, or digresses from the central message in the sentence:

> The disagreement between the president and the treasurer **(they had fought over the issue a number of times)** ultimately destroyed the organization.

> The agency relied on various groups **(the ACC, the SEC, the NCAA)** to reveal the extent of the abuses.

PARENTHESES AND NUMBERS IN LISTS WITHIN TEXT

Use parentheses to enclose numerals or letters marking divisions or enumerations within the text of your writing. Remember, in indented and vertical lists, the period sets off the number or letter:

> He had discovered the various abuses in **(1)** recruiting, **(2)** scholarships, **(3)** testing, and **(4)** summer employment.

> When you create a listing in text, be sure **(a)** to enclose the number or letter in parentheses, **(b)** to separate each item with a comma, and **(c)** to precede the last item with a conjunction.

PARENTHESES AND OTHER PUNCTUATION

Before the closing parenthesis, drop almost all punctuation, such as commas, semicolons, and colons. Retain a period inside the closing parenthesis if you've written a complete parenthetical sentence. Put the period outside the closing parenthesis if the parenthetical statement comes within the larger textual sentence. Also, use a question mark or exclamation point inside the parenthetical statement if appropriate:

> His mind was clouded. **(He hadn't thought of her in years.)** But he shook it off and continued down the hill.

> He enjoyed all kinds of fruit **(especially apples, oranges, and bananas)**.

> She raised all sorts of embarrassing issues **(I could have died!)** and discussed them at length at the annual meeting.

38

Brackets

Brackets are used to enclose editorial interpolations, corrections, explanations, or comments in quoted material. Resist the temptation to use "[sic]," which in Latin means "that's your mistake, fella, not mine," to point out a mistake in a quotation. Instead, try to fix the problem in the quoted passage. The expression "[sic]" can also be used to show that something that looks strange is intentionally written that way: He used the name *e. e. cummings* (sic). (Here you would use parentheses because the strange-looking name does not appear in a quotation.)

INTRUSIONS OF THE WRITER IN QUOTATIONS

Sic 'em: "This law does not apply in our grate **[sic]** state."
Better: "This law does not apply in our **[great]** state."
Intrusion: "We refuse to consider **[the Jones Report]**."

Notice that inserting bracketed material does not prompt a need for the "ellipsis signal": three dots used to show omission.

PARENTHETICALS WITHIN PARENTHESES

If you write a parenthetical statement and need to include another parenthetical statement within it, then enclose the second one in brackets:

> While visiting Virginia, Dr. Smith and his assistant (Fred Jones, who
> would later study the state bird **[the cardinal]** for the Birdwatch-
> ers Society) discovered strange nesting habits undoubtedly caused
> by global warming.

39

Question Mark and

Exclamation Point

I n creative writing, these marks show up all the time. In expository writing, question marks do appear, but often as mistakes. The exclamation point has little, if any, role in expository writing.

THE QUESTION MARK
The question mark serves a variety of roles:

To Ask a Question
The question mark ends the sentence that is a question:

> Who will win the election?

To Express Doubt or Ignorance
These usually show up when expressing doubtful dates:

> The founder (1733?–1793) built the first house in the village.

To Show a Question within a Larger Sentence
Writers often improperly place these interrogative elements in quotations. Just use the question mark. Begin these questions with capital letters if they seem to be formal questions. If they seem informal, use lowercase:

He wondered, will I win?

As she asked herself, How will I ever pay for this? she continued to look through the medical-school brochure.

Use Italics for One-Word Questions

When you use the words *how, when, where,* or other question-asking words, put them in italics, not quotation marks, and leave out the question marks:

The question is not *if* but **when** and **how**.

She asked herself **why**.

Add a Question Mark to Turn a Declarative Sentence into an Interrogative

This is your master's thesis?

Call back tomorrow?

Omit the Question Mark for Courteous Requests

Will you please send us your answer as soon as possible.

Omit the Question Mark for Indirect Questions

How the students survived was the question the reporters wanted to ask.

Question Mark and Quotation Marks

Put the question mark inside ending quotation marks if the question belongs to the quoted source. Put it outside if the question belongs to the writer.

Question Mark Goes Inside When the Question Belongs to the Source

The committee asked, rather rhetorically, "Does this rule really apply?" (Question mark that's part of the quotation goes inside.

Notice that no additional punctuation is necessary to end the sentence.)

Question Mark Goes Outside When the Question Belongs to the Writer

Did the board really say, "We will consider the rules on charitable contributions"? (Question mark showing the writer's question goes outside.)

EXCLAMATION POINT

Use the exclamation point to shout. And don't shout much at all in expository writing. Let your prose show your emphasis:

The Supreme Court flatly ruled against us!

When 911 took the call, the operator said, "I'm on a break now"!

Exclamation Point and Quotation Marks

Put the exclamation point inside ending quotation marks if the shout belongs to the quoted source. Put it outside if the shout belongs to the writer:

Exclamation Point Goes Inside
When the Shout Belongs to the Source

The man cried out, "Fire! There's a fire! Call 911!" (An ending exclamation point that is part of the quotation goes inside the ending quotation marks. Notice that no additional punctuation is necessary to end the sentence.)

Exclamation Point Goes Outside
When the Shout Belongs to the Writer

When 911 took the call, the operator said, "I'm on a break now"! (Exclamation point showing the writer's exclamation goes outside the ending quotation marks.)

40

Hyphen

RANGES OF NUMBERS
You may use the hyphen (or the en dash) to show a range of numbers:

These statistics appear on pages 54-56.

PREFIX WORDS
As a rule, do not hyphenate words formed with prefixes like *pre-, post-, non-,* and others. Thus, pretrial, nonresident, postgraduate, etc. Hyphenate only in these four situations:

1. The root word is a date, as in pre-1960.
2. The root word is a proper noun, as in anti-Russian.
3. The last letter of the prefix and the first letter of the root word are the same (optional), as in anti-intellectual, but reexamination, reengineer.
4. You need to avoid an ambiguity, as in un-ionized, re-create, pro-verb, pro-noun.

COMPOUND WORDS
In chapter 3 on adjectives, we learned about compound adjectives, those multiword, often made-up adjectives that enliven our writing. We also

have compound nouns, where some hyphenation takes place. Most hyphenation in compounds, however, occurs with adjectives. So I will just list the major compound nouns that have hyphens and then provide more detailed coverage of compound adjectives.

Compound Nouns

Most compound nouns are not hyphenated:

> master builder
> fellow employee
> decision making
> attorney general

Others have migrated and become complete words, spelled as one word, with no hyphen:

> headache
> checkbook
> boardinghouse
> clearinghouse

For variations of these compound nouns, e.g., rest house, reference book, always check the dictionary for proper spelling.

Some compound nouns are hyphenated:

> vice-president
> scholar-poet, student-athlete
> brother-in-law
> great-granddaughter (hyphenate all great relatives)
> self-restraint (hyphenate all the *self-* compounds)
> one-half
> president-elect

Compound Adjectives

Some general observations should help you understand the principles behind the rule on hyphenating compound adjectives and therefore increase the likelihood of correct hyphenation. To begin, a compound word is simply a single expression made up of more than one word and acting as a single word. Consider the following italicized adjectives: **publicly traded** stock, **well-known** actress, **bookkeeping** system. Notice that each is spelled in a different way: (1) open (**publicly traded**), (2) hyphenated (**well-known**), and (3) closed (**bookkeeping**). And that's the issue you'll face: whether to spell the multiword expression as two or more words (open), as a hyphenated expression (hyphenated), or as a single word (closed).

THE DECISION TO HYPHENATE
1. Facilitate Reading
We hyphenate words to facilitate reading and prevent ambiguity. For example, one rule says to hyphenate adjectives formed by a noun plus an *-ing* verb when it comes before the noun. Thus:

> **thought-provoking** article
> **interest-bearing** loan

Ordinarily, you would not hyphenate these compounds when they come after the noun. Thus:

> The loan was **interest bearing**.

But what about:

> The article was **thought provoking**.

Here we have an ambiguity, for the word *thought* could act as a verb, link to the verb *was,* and leave the adjective *provoking* all by itself:

> The article **was thought** provoking.

But we mean *thought* as a noun linked to *provoking* to form a compound adjective. Thus we must hyphenate:

> The article was **thought-provoking**.

In no other way, except by rewriting the sentence, can we make our meaning clear.

2. Check the Dictionary
When in doubt, consult the dictionary. If a compound appears in the dictionary, then spell it the way it appears there. Watch carefully for the hyphen and distinguish it from a raised period dictionaries use to show word division.

3. Read the *Wall Street Journal*
As I stated in chapter 3, if you want to see usually consistent editorial work in the area of hyphenation, simply read the *Wall Street Journal.* On any given day, you will find scores of hyphenated words, all following the correct system of hyphenation. I personally like the system, for I believe it facilitates reading.

Here are just a few compound adjectives that I listed in chapter 3. These appear on the front page of the October 19, 1994, edition of the *Wall Street Journal:*

> 15-year-old reform
> bread-and-butter issues
> educational-reform efforts
> information-services industry

Now flash ahead to the present. On Tuesday, July 24, 2001, we find these correctly hyphenated compound adjectives on page C1 of the *Wall Street Journal:*

> high-quality bonds
> bond-market diversification
> inflation-indexed Treasury bonds
> second-quarter labor costs

But wait! Even the mighty can flub. On the same page, in the article about Novellus's convertible securities, we find a hyphen in the compound noun *short term.* If the expression appeared as an adjective, then the hyphen would be correct. But I can't find any rule requiring a hyphen in the noun form:

[The company] could even make some money **in the short-term**
from the transaction.

In the same column, a compound adjective is missing a necessary
hyphen:

credit rating agencies

Perhaps I'll have to retract my statement about the *Wall Street Journal's* consistency in editing.

Hyphenating Compound Adjectives
Pay special attention to those compound adjectives you make up. Most
people incorrectly leave out the hyphens:

made-up compound adjectives	**Hyphenate compound adjectives.** **product-liability** lawsuit **employment-discrimination** claim **sexual-harassment** suit **child-support** payments

Also pay special attention to compounds formed with an adverb ending in *-ly (widely)* followed by a past participle or other adjective *(used)*.
These compounds are *never* hyphenated:

adverb ending in *-ly* **+ participle or adjective**	**Always open (never hyphenated) (this is a common mistake).**
	
	publicly traded stock
	    (*-ly* adverb + past participle)
	widely used procedure
	    (*-ly* adverb + past participle)
	rapidly increasing revenues
	    (*-ly* adverb + present participle)
	privately held corporation
	    (*-ly* adverb + past participle)
	newly rich nation
	    (*-ly* adverb + adjective)

Here, for your reference, is a listing of the most frequently encountered types of compound adjectives and the rules on hyphenation. When in doubt, always check the dictionary.

Compound Adjective formed with:	Rule on Hyphenation
all	**Always hyphenate.** **all-inclusive** study
century	**Always hyphenate.** **twentieth-century** technology
cross	**Some hyphenated, some open, some closed. Check the dictionary.** **cross-referenced** section **cross-country** skis But: **crosscut** saw
fold	**Closed unless formed with numbers of 100 or more.** **tenfold** increase **100-fold** increase
full	**Hyphenated before noun, open after noun.** **full-scale** drawings The drawings are **full scale**.
half	**Most hyphenated, some closed. Check the dictionary.** **half-inch** measurement **half-baked** plan **halfway** house **halfhearted** attempt

Compound Adjective formed with:	Rule on Hyphenation
high, low; *upper, lower;* *middle, mid*	Most hyphenated before noun, open after noun. **high-volume** trading **highbrow** organization (check the dictionary!) **middle-class** voters **midlife** crisis **mid-Atlantic** region **Mideast** peace process
like	Closed unless root word ends in *l* or *ll* or has three syllables or more. **catlike** jumping ability **childlike** demeanor **cathedral-like** facade
number + *odd*	Always hyphenate compounds formed with numbers (words or numerals) plus the word *odd.* **twenty-odd** pages **360-odd** days **four-hundred-odd** socks . . . but, **four hundred odd socks**
number + percent	Always open when used to express a ratio. **ten percent** increase **100 percent** change

Compound Adjective formed with:	Rule on Hyphenation
number + unit of measure	Always hyphenate before noun; if an adjective (like *old* or *high*) follows the unit of measure, attach it with another hyphen; when compound preceded by another modifying number, keep the hyphenated compound separate (do not add yet another hyphen).

Number + Unit of Measure

> **three-mile** limit
> **two-week** vacation
> **150-yard** skid mark

Number + Unit of Measure + Adjective

> **two-year-old** daughter
> **sixty-five-year-old** man
> **two-and-a-half-year-old** child
> **twenty-five-foot-high** wall
> But: six **year-old** girls

Number + Number + Unit of Measure + Adjective

> **twenty-four six-inch-long** measurements

Number + Unit of Measure + Adjective
(coming after the noun)

> a man **sixty-five years old** (note plural *years*)
> a wall **three meters high**
> twenty-four boys **five years old**

numbers, fractional	Hyphenate spelled-out fractions used as adjectives. In mixed fractions, the whole number is not joined to the fraction by another hyphen.

> **two-thirds** majority
> **twenty-one and one-quarter** miles
> **four and one-eighth** inches

Compound Adjective formed with:	Rule on Hyphenation
numbers, whole	Hyphenate only the numbers from twenty-one through ninety-nine. All others are open.

> **twenty-four** bottles of beer on the wall
> **two hundred** rock stars

over, under	Closed unless the word *the* appears in the compound.

> **overexposed** film
> **underrated** basketball team
> **over-the-counter** stock market
> **under-the-table** deal

self	Most hyphenated. Closed if prefix *un-* is added or suffix added to *self*.

> **self-confident** applicant
> **self-conscious** speaker
> **unselfconscious** speaker
> **selfish** act
> **selfless** character trait

wide	Always closed unless cumbersome. Cumbersome compounds are hyphenated when they appear before the noun modified and open after the noun modified.

> **statewide** referendum
> **worldwide** legal services
> **university-wide** crusade
> (comes before the noun modified)
> The crusade was **university wide**.
> (comes after the noun modified)

You will also form compound adjectives by combining various parts of speech. Here's the way hyphenation works:

Combining Parts of Speech	Rule on Hyphenation
adjective + noun with -*ed* suffix	**Hyphenate before noun, open after noun.** **straight-laced** senator **coarse-grained** surface of the table (before noun) The surface of the table was **coarse grained** (after noun).
adjective or participle + noun	**Hyphenate these compounds, which always precede the noun.** **hot-water** tank **ninth-floor** office and **living-room** window
adverb ending in -*ly* + participle or adjective	**Always open (never hyphenated) (this is a common mistake).** **publicly traded** stock (-*ly* adverb + past participle) **widely used** procedure (-*ly* adverb + past participle) **rapidly increasing** revenues (-*ly* adverb + present participle) **privately held** corporation (-*ly* adverb + past participle) **newly rich** nation (-*ly* adverb + adjective)
adverb not ending in -*ly* + participle or adjective	**Open unless hyphenation needed to avoid ambiguity.** **ever faithful** friend **much loved** friend **much-loved** music (to avoid saying "much **loved** music") **less-appreciated** art (to avoid saying "less **appreciated** art")

Combining Parts of Speech	Rule on Hyphenation
adverbs *well, ill, better, best, little, lesser, least* + participle or adjective	Hyphenated before noun, open after noun, open if modified by adverb. **well-known** actress The actress is **well known.** the **supposedly well known actress** (modified by adverb *supposedly*) **least-desirable** procedure This procedure is **least desirable.**
noun + adjective	Hyphenated before noun, open after noun if ambiguity avoided. **fuel-efficient** engine **labor-intensive** business **user-friendly** computer program The computer program is **user friendly.**
noun + participle	Hyphenated before noun, open after noun if ambiguity avoided. **decision-making** process **government-controlled** economy **resource-depleted** environment The environment was **resource depleted.** **profit-making** enterprise

compound adjectives of long standing	Hyphenate phrases of long standing before and after noun.
	
	Before noun: **devil-may-care** attitude
	Before noun: **up-to-date** review
	    After noun: The review is **up-to-date.**
	Before noun: **over-the-hill** athlete
	    After noun: The athlete is **over-the-hill.**

Combining Parts of Speech	Rule on Hyphenation
phrase ending with preposition	Hyphenate before noun, open after noun if no ambiguity. **spelled-out** fraction **unheard-of** defense This defense was **unheard of**. **made-up** compound adjective The compound adjective was **made up**.
proper nouns used as adjective	Hyphenated, open, or closed depending on how the compound appears in the dictionary. **Afro-American** family **Scotch-Irish** ancestry[1] **Austronesian** heritage

NOTE

1. Please, no letters from our friends in Scotland. In America, we know that *Scotch* is the beverage, but we use *Scotch-Irish* to denote those descending from an ancestry hailing from both Scotland and Ireland.

41

Apostrophe

The apostrophe is used to show (1) possessives of nouns and some pronouns, (2) contractions, and (3) some plurals.

POSSESSIVES OF SINGULAR NOUNS, EVEN THOSE ENDING IN -S

Use an "apostrophe -s" to form the plural of a *singular* noun, even if that singular noun ends in an -s. The rule also applies to people's names. Doubters should read *Strunk & White's* rule 1, on page 1. Study these examples, and remember that we're talking about the possessives of *singular* nouns:

> This rule comes straight from the **horse's** mouth.
> He followed the **boss's** policy.
> The law displayed **Congress's** policy.
> He enjoyed **Dylan Thomas's** poetry.
> The media gathered at **Paula Jones's** press conference.
> ***Bridget Jones's*** *Diary*

POSSESSIVES OF PLURAL NOUNS

Use an apostrophe and no "-s" to form the possessive of a *plural* noun. (Some irregular plurals not ending in -s require the use of an "apostrophe -s.")

> The children watched the **puppies'** tails.
> The **children's** fathers watched, too.

TWO NOUNS POSSESSING THE SAME THING
OR SEPARATE THINGS

When two or more nouns possess the same thing, add "apostrophe -s" after the last one listed. When each separately possesses, add "apostrophe -s" to each one listed:

> My **aunt and uncle's** house always intrigued me.
> **Sam and Kay's** children played. (Sam and Kay are mom and dad.)
> **Sam's and Kay's** children played. (Sam and Kay each have their own children.)

POSSESSIVES OF SOME PRONOUNS

Some indefinite pronouns have possessive forms shown by the "apostrophe -s":

another's	neither's
anybody's	no one's
anyone's	nobody's
each one's	one's
either's	other's
everybody's	others'
everyone's	somebody's

The reciprocal pronouns also appear in possessive form. Note that these are always singular possessives, not plural possessives:

> each other's
> one another's

Not:

> each others'
> one anothers'

CONTRACTIONS

Use the apostrophe to form contractions. Though contractions rarely show up in formal writing, a well-placed one now and then can have a positive effect. I use them all the time (you've probably noticed):

> can't
> won't
> don't

"APOSTROPHE -*S*" TO FORM A NARROW CLASS OF PLURALS

Use "apostrophe -*s*" to form plurals only when absolutely necessary. Use just an -*s* (or -*es*) to form the plurals of dates, acronyms, and families:

> She longed for the **1960s**.
> The investors contributed to their **IRAs**.
> The **Elmores** came for dinner.

But:

> Be sure to dot your **i's** and cross your **t's**.
> Here are the **do's** and **don'ts**.

Quotation Marks

SPECIAL USES OF QUOTATION MARKS

Before we get to the use of quotation marks to show direct quotation, let's look briefly at some special uses of the mark.

To Show Irony or Sarcasm

In speech, you'll often see people use their hands to show that they're putting the word in quotation marks. They are showing a sense of irony:

> The police **"guarding"** the bank slept through the entire robbery.

The Use of *So-Called*

When you use the expression *so-called,* you do not need to use quotation marks or italics to set off the term referred to. The expression *so-called* handles the task quite well:

> The **so-called** right to counsel is sometimes ignored in police interrogations.

Referring to Words As Words

When you refer to a word as a word, put it in italics:

When you use the word *so-called,* you do not need to use quotation marks.

If the word referred to is usually a spoken word, then put it in quotation marks:

Southerners use **"y'all"** to refer to just about everybody.

Showing Slang
If the slang expression is unfamiliar to the reader, enclose it in quotation marks:

When cleaning out his office, the professor hauled away the whole **"kit and caboodle."**

RULES ON DIRECT QUOTATION
Many writers violate rules governing the use of quotation marks. They mix up the rules on which of the other punctuation marks go inside or outside the ending quotation marks. You'll find independent treatment of this issue in each chapter on each mark where this situation can occur. For your convenience, here are the rules collected in one place.

According to most style manuals, all periods and commas go inside the ending quotation marks. The semicolon and colon go outside. Other marks, such as question marks or the occasional exclamation mark, go inside if they form a part of the quotation or outside if they do not form a part of the quotation. Some examples:

Period Goes Inside

Ed said, "Here is a sentence with the period properly placed inside the ending quotation marks." (Period goes inside.)

Comma Goes Inside

According to the editor, writers make mistakes in "quoting from research sources," "using too many quotations," and "putting punctuation marks in the wrong places." (Commas go inside; period goes inside.)

Semicolon Goes Outside

Note: The semicolon should be placed *outside* quotation marks. When the quoted matter ends with a semicolon, the semicolon is dropped.

> According to the editor, writers do make mistakes when "quoting from research sources"; they also use "too many quotations." (Semicolon goes outside; period goes inside.)

Colon Goes Outside

Note: The colon should be placed *outside* quotation marks. When the quoted matter ends with a colon, the colon is dropped.

> The employee has two objections to the practice of "early retirement": He wants to continue working, and the policy manual does not require it.

Question Mark Goes inside When the Question Belongs to the Source

> The committee asked, rather rhetorically, "Does this rule actually apply?" (Question mark that's part of the quotation goes inside. Notice that no additional punctuation is necessary to end the sentence.)

Question Mark Goes outside When the Question Belongs to the Writer

> Did the board really say, "We will consider the rules on charitable contributions"? (Question mark showing the writer's question goes outside.)

Exclamation Point Goes inside When the Shout Belongs to the Source

> The man cried out, "Fire! There's a fire! Call 911!" (Exclamation point that's part of the quotation goes inside. Notice that no additional punctuation is necessary to end the sentence.)

Exclamation Point Goes outside When the Shout Belongs to the Writer

When 911 took the call, the operator said "I'm on a break now"! (Exclamation point showing the writer's exclamation goes outside the ending quotation marks.)

A Final Thought:

The Erosion of Grammar

DOES GRAMMAR MATTER?

It depends on what you mean by *grammar*. Some people, I'm afraid, regard grammatical rules as tired old myths. They like to cite the "rule" against ending a sentence with a preposition, the "rule" against splitting infinitives, the "rule" against starting a sentence with *hopefully,* the "rule" against starting a sentence with a conjunction, and on and on. But many of these are not grammatical rules at all. They cite these so-called rules and call them grammar.

Here's proof of my point. Here's what many people regard as grammar:

> "The Ivy League fretting about misuse of 'hopefully' has more to
> do with someone's idea of manners than with language and mean-
> ing," says . . . a retired English professor. Complaints about the
> erosion of grammar are "really tiresome," he says. "It's just snob-
> bery. It's like saying you'd rather have your appendix out in 1623.
> No, thanks. I'll live where I am."
>
> Even so, [the professor] can't suppress wonder at the fact that his
> students manage to "use 'like' [after] every third word."[1]

Why is it that many people always bring up these mostly spurious "rules" and then proceed to treat them as the entirety of the rules of grammar? They then say we don't need to worry about these rules. (And that's quite true, for most of them are myths, not rules.) They then leap to the conclusion that we don't need to worry about "the erosion of grammar." It's "really tiresome." It's just "snobbery."

Well, erosion of grammar is taking place, and many of us do not tire of worrying about it.

A dumbing-down of the language is occurring because most schools think as the professor thinks: Complaints about the erosion of grammar are tiresome. Some school board somewhere right now is concluding that we don't need to devote much class time to grammar. After all, grammar is just elitist worry about out-of-date rules or just a fretting about manners. Will that school board's decision help further erode the knowledge of grammar in this nation?

You bet.

You think I'm just making this up? Dr. Dave Williams published a wonderful book on how to write college term papers. Entitled *Sin Boldly*,[2] the book tells a true story about an English teacher at a high school in Fairfax County, just outside Washington, D.C. The teacher decided to hold voluntary after-school sessions to teach a straightforward course on the rules of grammar. When school officials learned of the course, they told the teacher to stop. He finally did when *the superintendent of schools* ordered him to stop.

Perhaps the superintendent justified the decision by pointing to worn-out rules against splitting infinitives and ending sentences with prepositions, dubbing them *grammar,* and saying we don't need to fret about grammar. We don't do it that way. The students will get it through osmosis. They will get it through reading. They will get it through "whole language."

Horse honky.

Just today, October 1, 2001, I read a brief excerpt from Elinor Burkett's book, *Another Planet: A Year in the Life of a Suburban High School.* "I was horrified to read students' papers and realize that even the best hadn't mastered basic grammar, punctuation, or spelling—or to hear scores of students blithely inform me, perhaps even boast to me, that they had never read a complete book."[3] So . . . they will get it through whole language. They will get it through reading. *If* reading takes place.

One day this nation will wake up, realize the harm we've done, and begin to insist that we get back to basics. A thorough study of grammar should head the list.

I hope you agree that the grammatical concepts you've learned in this book go far beyond a string of tired old elitist rules. The concepts go to the heart of language itself. The rules mark the logic of language. They concern meaning itself. Students won't "get it" through osmosis, not when they are immersed in a commercial, media-driven culture that often makes a virtue of ignorance. They certainly won't "get it" if they brag about never reading a complete book.

Perhaps I can draw from the retired professor's statement to illustrate the relationship among the concepts of meaning, language, and grammar. Our newly found knowledge of fused participles enables us to parse the statement to find out what it means:

> "The **Ivy League fretting** about misuse of 'hopefully' has more
> to do with someone's idea of manners than with language and
> meaning . . . ."

We might look at that "Ivy League fretting" and wonder about its meaning. Does the statement mean that the "Ivy League has more to do with manners"? Or does it mean that the "fretting has more to do with manners"? I think it's the "fretting." So perhaps the statement should have read:

> "The Ivy League**'s** fretting . . . ."

You and I know all about fused participles. We would never say, "I smelled you frying chicken." We know that ambiguity lurks. We know how we can get that word *frying*, or in this case *fretting*, to act as the noun. We just have to make the other noun possessive: the Ivy League**'s** fretting.

So just what is the meaning of the statement? To discover it, we must turn to concepts of grammar. And if the speaker says, "Oh, well, you know what I mean," then that rejoinder proves *my* point—words matter, words have meaning, grammar controls the way we ensure that our meaning comes shining through. Clearly. Without ambiguity. Without our readers' having to figure it out for themselves because they supposedly know what *we* mean.

Words do matter. Words do carry meaning. And grammatical rules do govern the way we put our words down on paper so that we can transfer knowledge to future generations. If we have no rules, then words and groups of words can mean whatever we want. Humpty Dumpty would be king:

> "When I use a word," Humpty Dumpty said, in rather a scornful tone, "it means just what I choose it to mean—neither more nor less."
>
> "The question is," said Alice, "whether you can make words mean so many different things."
>
> "The question is," said Humpty Dumpty, "which is to be master— that's all."[4]

Perhaps, therefore, our fretting about grammar has a lot to do with words and what they mean when they roll off our tongues or plop down on our paper. Perhaps our fretting has absolutely nothing to do with manners, snobbery, or elitism.

Maybe, just maybe, the erosion of grammar has a lot to do with the widely acknowledged erosion of communication skills in the United States. Perhaps the erosion of grammar would help explain why the professor's students use *like* after every third word.

Can we, and will we, relax the rules as language changes? In informal settings, of course we will. Will plagues of locusts descend upon us if a television network puts "who to foul" on its screen at the end of basketball games? No, but it would be nice if the TV execs cared enough about our language and got it right: "*whom* to foul."

But to take the entirety of grammar and boot it out of our schools' curricula makes no sense at all. And not to fret about "the erosion of grammar" is comparable to not worrying about the increasing inability of many people to communicate ideas through the spoken and written word.

I hope you agree that good writing comes directly from a broad and deep knowledge of the structures our language makes available to us. If we do not study them, if we do not learn all about them, if we do not practice using them in our discourse, then the future for our own ability to communicate is bleak indeed.

Some of us will continue to cry out that grammar and style are inextricably bound up together. We believe deeply that we cannot learn to write well without knowing grammar—not just the basics but some fairly sophisticated concepts undergirding our language.

Those, I hope, you've learned in this book.

So when you hear your local school board talk about reducing class time devoted to grammar, raise a very loud voice in protest. When you do, you might describe the regimen that Sir Winston Churchill followed. As a schoolboy, Churchill aced English. He could thank his teacher, Robert Somervell, who undoubtedly hailed from the Miss Hamrick School of Teaching English to Young People. Here's a description of Mr. Somervell's system:

> First they learned to parse sentences thoroughly. Then they practiced continuing grammatical analysis . . . breaking [sentences] up into subject, verb, object; relative clauses, conditional clauses, conjunctive and disjunctive clauses.[5]

These drills they did *daily*. The impact on Churchill? Let him tell it:

> [I completed the drills] three times as long as anyone else. I had three times as much of it. I learned it thoroughly. Thus I got into my bones the essential structure of the ordinary British sentence— which is a noble thing.[6]

A noble thing indeed. For it was the voice of Churchill—his words and phrasing—that inspired his country never ever to give in to the onslaught from Hitler's Nazi regime. These words strike a haunting chord in the days following September 11, 2001:

> Even though large tracts of Europe and many old and famous states have fallen or may fall into the grip of the Gestapo and all the odious apparatus of Nazi rule, we shall not flag or fail. We shall go on to the end. We shall fight in France, we shall fight on the seas and oceans, we shall fight with growing confidence and growing strength in the air, we shall defend our island, whatever the cost may be, we shall fight on the beaches, we shall fight on the landing grounds, we shall fight in the fields and in the streets, we shall fight in the hills. We shall never surrender.[7]

The young schoolboy had to study grammar. Every single day. Words were very important to him. On his eightieth birthday, he said:

It was the nation . . . dwelling all round the globe that had the lion's heart; I had the luck to be called upon **to give the roar**.

His biographer disagrees:

It wasn't that simple. The spirit [of the English people] lay dormant until he became prime minister and they, **kindled by his soaring prose**, came to see themselves as he saw them and emerged a people transformed, the admiration of free people everywhere.[8]

Words matter. The way they come together to convey meaning is governed by a set of rules. That set of rules is called *grammar.* Either you know it, or you don't.

It's the stuff Churchill learned at the chalkboard.

If you lose your argument to the school board—as you most likely will—then teach yourself all that grammar you never learned in high school and now need to succeed in life.

Then pass it along to your children.[9]

NOTES

1. "So I'm Like, Who Needs This Grammar Stuff?" *Newsweek,* October 20, 1997, p. 15.
2. You may visit Dr. Dave and order your own copy of *Sin Boldly* at www.sin boldly.com.
3. "Culture, et cetera," *Washington Times,* October 1, 2001, p. A2.
4. Lewis Carroll, *Alice in Wonderland,* p. 163 (Gray ed. 1971).
5. William Manchester, *The Last Lion: Visions of Glory,* vol. 1, p. 161 (1983).
6. Manchester, *The Last Lion,* vol. 1, p. 161.
7. Manchester, *The Last Lion,* vol. 1, p. 6.
8. Manchester, *The Last Lion,* vol. 1, p. 7.
9. Thank you for reading my book.

INDEX

a vs. *an,* 83–85
abstraction, 220
acronyms, noun chains and, 183–184
action verbs, 31, 46, 191–192; cutting
clauses using, 244, 246–248;
intransitive, 33–35; sentence
structure and, 261; transitive,
31–33; transitive and intransitive,
36–37, 191–192
active voice, 33; passive voice vs.,
224–225, 226–227, 252–253;
preference for, 232–233. *See also*
passive voice
"add or do something else" rule, 12
adjectival clauses, 95–96; *that*
vs.*which* and, 141–142
adjectival phrases, 94–97; introductory, 331; noun absolutes using,
187; past participial phrases and,
208
adjectives, 1; adverbs modifying,
99–100; attributive or predicative,
77; demonstrative, 134; derivative,
214, 215, 223; *different from/differ-
ent than* rule, 89–91; *fewer* vs. *less,*
86–89; identification exercise, 96–
97; linking verbs and, 42–43;
look-it-up rule, 80–81; multiword,

91–93; noun absolutes using, 187;
participle rule, 79; present participial phrases as, 201; present
participles as, 52; in sentences,
267; sounds-weird rule, 80; states
of, 77–78; summary of, 97–98;
syllable rule, 79. *See also* articles;
noun modifiers
adverbial clauses, 109, 110–111
adverbial phrases, 2, 109, 110–111;
and commas between subject and
verb, 370
adverbs, 1; comparative and superlative forms of, 106–108; conjunctive, semicolons and, 378–379;
formation of, 102–103; identification exercise, 110–111; linking
verbs and, 42–43; modifying
adjectives, 99–100; modifying sentences or clauses, 100–102; nouns
as, 185–186; positions for,
103–106; present participial
phrases as, 201; in sentences, 267;
summary of, 112
affect vs. *effect,* 338–339
afterthoughts, incomplete sentences
and, 259
all, hyphenation rule for, 400

420

ABOUT THE AUTHOR

Ed Good teaches effective writing to lawyers, scientists, engineers, business executives, tax accountants, and other smart people. He currently serves as counsel and writer-in-residence at the intellectual property law firm of Finnegan, Henderson, Farabow, Garrett & Dunner, LLP, in Washington, D.C.

Thousands of people across the country have attended Ed's writing courses, which he has presented at Caterpillar, DuPont, General Electric, Westinghouse, PPG Industries, Hershey Foods, Pratt & Whitney, Glaxo-SmithKline, Ernst & Young, and scores of law firms, federal agencies, and courts throughout the country.

Ed attended the University of North Carolina at Chapel Hill and the University of Virginia School of Law. He served as director of legal writing at the University of Virginia School of Law and as a judicial fellow at the Supreme Court of the United States.

Ed is the author of *Mightier than the Sword—Powerful Writing in the Legal Profession* and other books about legal writing and research.